WHAT THEY HEARD

WHAT THEY HEARD

How the Beatles, Beach Boys and
Bob Dylan Listened to Each Other
and Changed Music Forever

Luke Meddings

WEATHERGLASS BOOKS

For Zaki, Marina and Lea,
in the order I met them,
with love.

CONTENTS

INTRODUCTION

It was said of a boy at my primary school that he could only spell one word: T. Rex. They were then the most famous group in the country, but although I could spell the names of all the dinosaurs, I had no idea what a pop group was. A certain kind of professional home woke up to Radio 3 or Radio 4, read Pelican books with blue spines on childcare and philosophy, and ignored the pop charts altogether. Save for some new classical recordings, there was little that might not have been in our house a decade earlier. There was no television until 1975, which now seems as eccentric as refusing an electric toaster.

There is a hint of the true path about a classical household. There must be, to keep the world at bay. I loved the music I knew at home, but I also went to primary school, and the contemporary world crept in. My parents at length bought a TV, and on Boxing Day morning 1975 my cousin shouted that *Let it Be* was on. It was the first time I'd seen the Beatles, but we only caught the end of it, office workers craning their necks to the sound of the group up on their windswept rooftop. That evening, by contrast, the whole family gathered to watch Ingmar Bergman's television adaptation of *The Magic Flute*.

One day I found an actual Beatles record in the cupboard under the stairs. It was the *Twist and Shout* EP, the group pictured leaping on an unimproved bomb site, but it turned out to have been a joke leaving present from my father's work. Progress was slow, until unexpectedly that quiet life yielded a source too respectable to be spurned. My future headmaster was a family friend, and his daughter had all the Beatles' records. Better still, she was prepared to lend them to me.

The Beatles rearranged my emotional geometry, representing as they had for countless others a kind of freedom in the heart. At first I didn't want to consider that any music might be as good as theirs, any more than John Lennon twenty years earlier had wanted to believe that Little Richard could rival Elvis; for a while I didn't find any that was.

But one day a French exchange student bought a copy of the Beach Boys' *20 Golden Greats*. Here was music that rivalled the Beatles' in its immediacy, richness and variety; I could hear in the trajectory across two sides from 1963's 'Surfin' USA' to 1969's 'Break Away' something like the Beatles' own – even the dates matched. I knew nothing about the group, and the songs didn't make me *feel* things the way the Beatles did, but the sound was delicious, their voices soaring as the music purred. My father even liked 'Heroes and Villains'.

I had played the violin from the age of four, and I still took it out for weekly lessons. But the world of recorders and madrigal singing was now decisively breached, and I yearned for an electric guitar. I was told to prove myself, and learned on my sister's classical, forcing the high nylon strings into chord shapes from *The Beatles Complete* with its mystic tears, rainbow waterfalls and painted flesh. It qualified me for a cheap electric; I can still smell the strings. I was thirteen, and a little more like the world outside.

Rock and roll's jubilee came in 1980, a quarter of a century after 'Rock Around the Clock' hit the charts. I heard Bob Dylan for the first time on Radio 1's *25 Years of Rock*, the archive audio from JFK's assassination segueing into 'Blowin' in the Wind'. Although I imagined myself living in the 1960s, there was no natural order to the records I bought. I was piecing together my own version of the decade, picking up the Byrds' first LP in a village here (there were record stores in such places then), and Dylan's *Greatest Hits* in a second-hand store there. I barely enjoyed Dylan's music, but it felt elemental, raw, a piece of the world's pattern you needed to absorb. The cover photo caught him in contemplation, holding a book of Old Masters that might have come from the shelves of home.

The vinyl on these records was flimsy, and the covers sometimes knock-offs; CD reissues with their booklets and essays were years away. I knew the release dates of the albums, as I had known the reigns of the kings and queens not long before. But I didn't think too hard about the connections between the artists, even when the Byrds covered four Dylan songs on *Mr. Tambourine Man* – they sounded so different. I knew Lennon had sported a 'Dylan cap' for *A Hard Day's Night*, but I couldn't imagine Dylan liking the Beatles. The records felt sufficient unto themselves.

Except they weren't. Their encounters with one another's music fundamentally changed them. Without hearing, meeting and reacting to each other the Beatles might have remained a glorious pop group and Dylan a spartan solo performer of Beat-influenced poetry; the Beach Boys might never have escaped the beach and the race track to which Brian Wilson's early songs were confined. The great records of the mid-1960s were provoked by each other's creative genius. The music that has influenced us for half a century did not arrive by magic but was itself influenced. This book explores how that came to be.

Influence at a basic level is a kind of imitation, and there are many examples of this in the mid-1960s, from copying sounds like the sitar or twelve-string guitar, to aping form in the style or structure of a song. This kind of influence is adoptive, and one can usually see through it. I'm more interested in what we might call adaptive influence, when gifted artists take impetus rather than specific ideas from one another. This can be harder to hear. Surface similarity can be minimal even when the deeper connection is vital, as is the case with *Pet Sounds* and *Rubber Soul*. The creative mind is a prism to influence; the brilliant source is diverted and changed. As a rule, the more our artists were influenced by each other, the more they sounded like themselves.

This book is an invitation to hear these familiar records anew. To do this myself I listened chronologically, season by thrilling season, responding as freely as I could. There is no detailed lyrical analysis; I have heard some of these songs a thousand times and still don't know the words when I sit down to play them. What interests me is the sound, and the feel, which for the purposes of this book sometimes means exploring the musical structure. This isn't theory-heavy: the Beatles' intervention in childhood meant that I didn't pursue classical music, and my own songwriting and listening remain more instinctive than technical. The occasional notes on keys and chord changes are one more way to say: look how marvellous this is – like the B minor chord under the word 'home' in 'A Hard Day's Night', which undercuts the lyric about everything being right and makes a joyous song feel suddenly poignant and unresolved.

Listen to this book with a device and online music player to hand: all the remastered albums on vinyl and in the original mono would be nice (and hideously expensive), but this music was largely mixed for transistor radio and sounds perfectly good through a modest Bluetooth speaker. Stop and play the songs when you reach them in real time – records you thought you knew will sound different. There may be ones you skipped over before, or familiar ones which you misremembered. 'Like A Rolling Stone', for instance, all grit and snarl by reputation, is creamy and expansive in the flesh.

In these years Dylan would write through the night while the studio musicians slept around him; they awoke to freshly minted songs. *What They Heard* wants you to hear the music like this, as the Beatles, Beach Boys and Bob Dylan did at the time: new sounds that seduced, inspired and transformed them.

THE SINGULARITY

They were all born near water: distance, passage, trade.

Bob Dylan's grandparents arrived in Minnesota from Ukraine and Lithuania in the early years of the twentieth century, his paternal grandfather fleeing the last of the Odessa pogroms in 1905. Duluth was a land rush town shacked up on iron ore; the Ojibwa lands had been taken only fifty years earlier. It was America's polar opposite to California: 'a dark place, even in the light of day'.[1] His parents married in the grey heart of the Great Depression and moved to Hibbing, where by the 1950s the iron was depleting and jobs were scarce.

Five-year-old Murry Wilson arrived in California from Kansas in 1922, the family camping in a tent on the beach for want of money. By 1950 there was a house in Hawthorne, five miles from the ocean. But his three sons still shared a room, and beatings from their father. Hawthorne was a step back from the beaches of Santa Monica Bay, but not from the broad violence of America: half a century younger than Duluth, it was a 'sundown town', off limits to Black Americans after dark.[2]

Liverpool was by a distance Europe's busiest slave trading port, the traffic peaking at the turn of the nineteenth century as abolition approached. Half of the three million Africans taken by British slavers across the Atlantic came that way. Packet steamers carrying refugees from the famine in Ireland followed, doubling the population of the city in the first half of 1847 alone; all the Beatles had Irish roots.[3] The Beatles' parents laboured as ship's stewards, merchant seamen, midwives, nurses. Two of their fathers were away at birth — at sea or on wartime fire duty; two left home before the war ended. Rationing in the UK wore on until 1954. 'You couldn't even get a cup of sugar,' George Harrison recalled, 'let alone a rock and roll record.'[4]

The roots of the music that emerged blinking into the light and colour of the mid-1960s led back through war and depression to plantations, pine woods and black hills. It was a product not of unbroken community or formal tradition but of flight, encounter and exchange. It wasn't from the sunny side of the street, sometimes not even the sunny side of the house.

○

It was lately the time of dance bands and swing, warm saxophones contending with blaring brass. Gershwin was on the family gramophone in California, Bing Crosby and Glenn Miller in Liverpool. Country music also crept in. George Harrison heard Jimmie Rodgers, the 'Singing Brakeman'; Rodgers' style is stark compared to the crooning of the swing singers, embellished only by his trademark yodel. Bob Zimmerman was unsettled by a country gospel record he found in the gramophone, 'Drifting Too Far from the Shore'.* It made him think he had been born to the wrong parents.

There was music in the home beyond records and the radio. Pianos were widespread by 1900, and people sang together where now they listen apart. A copy of the brown-bound *News Chronicle Song Book*, for example, lingered between the *Lieder* in my father's piano stool.[5] It was full of sea shanties, spirituals and morbid folk songs like 'The Ash Grove', which made me feel ill to sing. Brian

---

* John Lennon was a lifelong Bing Crosby fan, drawing on the wordplay in Crosby's 1932 hit 'Please' when writing 'Please Please Me'; Brian Wilson reinterpreted Gershwin in the 2010s (*Brian Wilson Reimagines Gershwin*, 2010) as Dylan turned to Sinatra (starting with *Shadows in the Night*, 2015).

Wilson's father Murry was a would-be songwriter who scored a modest hit with 'Two-Step Side-Step', and his sister Glee Love sang in a professional choir; the Love family had struck it rich in sheet metal, and Brian's cousin Mike lived in a house with fourteen rooms.[6] Paul McCartney's father Jim was an amateur musician who led his own jazz band, and his grandfather had played tuba for the tobacco works brass band.[7] There was encouragement – Brian had accordion lessons, John's mother taught him to play the banjo, Bob took a lesson from his cousin on the new spinet piano[8] – and there were cheap guitars when the money could be found: Silvertone Stellas, Supro Ozarks, Zeniths and Rosettis.

Of all our leads Wilson was the most analytical, the most driven to unpick the elements of sound, and so in time the best able to put them together. Tall and athletic, he was also shy and deaf in one ear. He spent hours listening to the Four Freshmen, moving between the record player and the piano, figuring out the different vocal parts.

○

It was rock and roll that brought everything into focus as they hit their teens. It had tumbled out of gospel, swing, jump blues and country, but the genesis was lengthy and the world didn't change overnight. Apart from Bill Haley's 'Rock Around the Clock', the best-selling Billboard singles of 1955 were a soothing mix of orchestra cocktail, anodyne doo-wop and nursery country.* Everything was genre-lite, including Pat Boone's cover of Fats Domino's 'Ain't That A Shame' (it was). If anyone wonders why

---

* Orchestra cocktail (Perez Prado's 'Cherry Pink and Apple Blossom White', Mitch Miller's 'Yellow Rose of Texas'), anodyne doo-wop ('Love Is a Many Splendored Thing' by the Four Aces), and nursery country (Bill Hayes' 'The Ballad Of Davy Crockett)'. Tennessee Ernie Ford's 'Sixteen Tons' strikes a solitary note of dissent.

Bill Haley, all moon face and kiss curl, was a sensation, listening to the competition will help explain: a gauzy sky over white America.

'Rock Around the Clock' was not the first rock and roll record, although for many listeners at the time it must have seemed that way: it was the first, in 1955, to make number one on the Billboard Pop chart. Haley had been attempting since the late 1940s to do what Elvis managed overnight in 1954 – to blend rhythm and blues with country.* His band were Saddlemen before they were Comets, mixing styles to the dismay of club owners.[9] Mixing styles implied mixing races, the lunatic fear of white supremacists, and – while salty hokum records were made by country artists, including Jimmie Rodgers – the more explicit lyrics in rhythm and blues were bound to stir this.†

Big Joe Turner's 'Shake, Rattle and Roll' had reached number one on the Billboard R&B chart a year earlier, and Haley immediately covered it, bowdlerizing it to a point where the lyrics make little sense (he declined to mention getting over the hill and way down underneath).‡ But the risqué language of the jump blues was now hiding in plain sight. Turner's 1940s sides 'Ooo-Ouch-Stop' and 'My Gal's a Jockey' might have been off limits, but a different kind of jelly was shaking in Betty Crocker's kitchen.

Its roots lay in the African American music of the forties and before. 'Hoooold back the dawn,' Wynonie Harris hollered on 'All She Wants to Do Is Rock' in 1949, 'stop all the clocks.'

---

* When 'Rock Around the Clock' hit, propelled by its use in the movie *Blackboard Jungle*, Haley bought the band Cadillacs. But a tour of the UK didn't go well. Elvis happened. He drank, and died a country singer's death in 1981, alone in the pool house of the family home.

† 'The White Citizens Council of North Alabama issued a denunciation of rock 'n' roll because it brought "people of both races together".' Tim Weiner, 'Little Richard, Flamboyant Wild Man of Rock 'n' Roll, Dies at 87', *New York Times* (9 May 2020), https://www.nytimes.com/2020/05/09/arts/music/little-richard-dead.html.

‡ The original is about getting out of bed to make some food, not coming randomly out of the kitchen.

Rocking meant dancing, it meant sex, but it was also an attitude, an imperative. In Jimmy Preston's 'Rock the Joint' there's an involuntary scream of the kind the Beatles would build into their records via Larry Williams and Little Richard; these are thrilling recordings, the saxophone solo in Preston's 'Hucklebuck Daddy' breaking down into twenty-eight honks on the same note, on and on, too much fun to stop.

'Rock Around the Clock' was a Sunday-clothed cousin to 'Around the Clock', which in Big Joe Turner's version takes in a comfort break and a broken bed. The marathon sex session rhymed against the hours goes back at least as far as 1922, and Trixie Smith's recording of 'My Man Rocks Me (With One Steady Roll)'. The Jazz Masters blow mournfully as Smith's clock strikes one for fun, six for lots of tricks and ten for 'glory, amen!'

In 1934 the Boswell Sisters performed 'Rock and Roll' in a rowing boat, accompanied by a line of seasick dancers.* Singing both bluesy and sweet, anticipating the close harmony sound of the Andrews Sisters and via them the Four Freshmen, they popularized blues styles for white audiences. 'Why don't you choke those Boswell Sisters?' asked one radio listener; they were called 'savage chanters'.[10] But influence itself wasn't bothered. Having been entranced by the blues singer Mamie Smith, who she saw live in New Orleans, Connee Boswell in turn inspired Ella Fitzgerald.[†]

These songs came out in the years my parents were born, my father at the dawn of recorded blues and country music.[‡] This was

---

* In the film *Transatlantic Merry-Go-Round*; the boat also served to conceal the fact that Connee Boswell used a wheelchair, sitting to perform.

† Fitzgerald said: 'I listened to records by all the singers, white and black, and I know that Connee Boswell was doing things that no one else was doing at the time.' Tom Reney, 'Connee Boswell', *New England Public Radio* (3 Dec. 2014), https://digital.nepr.net/music/2014/12/03/connee-boswell/.

‡ Mamie Smith's 'Crazy Blues' was cut for Okeh in 1920, and Fiddlin' John Carson's 'The Little Old Log Cabin in the Lane' for the same label in 1923.

not his field: although he had attic 78s of Meade Lux Lewis and Jelly Roll Morton, that thread led to bebop. He showed no interest in rock and roll. It's not that he didn't like music with swing: he had several Patti Page albums. It's not that he didn't like clever pop: we sang from the Cole Porter and Gershwin songbooks. He didn't wholly reject the music his own family had enjoyed; he would listen to a military band. But classical music and jazz had helped pave a road away from that milieu, and perhaps next to them rock and roll sounded inauthentic, amateurish and thin.* It was a gap between us that couldn't be bridged, although I never stopped trying. Like an obstacle on a fell walk, we had to go around it.

My father's old 78s were wrapped in plain brown paper like something from the ironmonger's, and among them I found 'Up Above My Head' by Sister Rosetta Tharpe and her lover Marie Knight. Tharpe's gospel records were driven by her bluesy guitar, and she repurposed a Thomas Dorsey song, 'Hide Me in Thy Bosom', as the sassier 'Rock Me'. Performing it at the first of John Hammond's two *From Spirituals to Swing* concerts in December 1938, she shared a stunning Carnegie Hall bill with jazz, boogie-woogie and blues artists including Count Basie, Meade Lux Lewis and Big Joe Turner. Turner was long enough in the business to have been discovered and championed first by John Hammond in 1938, and then by Ahmet and Nesuhi Ertegun in 1951. Seen across the canyon of World War Two, 1938 feels far from the dawn of the Cadillac 1950s. But it was only a dozen years in people's lives.

Tharpe maintained that rock and roll was faster rhythm and blues – 'I've been doing that forever' – and she influenced all the mid-1950s rockers, including Elvis.[11] When he lit on Arthur 'Big

---

* Writing in 1956, Anthony Samson noted that while rock and roll was mysterious and new to London teenagers, jazz experts considered it unrespectable and dull: 'A naked, aggressive kind of jazz which most jazz pundits despise.' Anthony Samson, 'Dig That Crazy Jive, Man!', *The Observer* (16 Sep. 1956), via https://www.theguardian.com/music/2018/sep/15/observer-archive-rock-around-the-clock-16-september-1956.

Boy' Crudup's 'That's Alright Mama' in July 1954, Sam Phillips had been waiting for him to do something at Sun Studio that was beyond pretty, to 'make some noise that satisfied the soul'.[12] Elvis had grown up on gospel , and – as with Sam Cooke, born only a hundred miles away in Mississippi – the sound of the church was always there.

'That's Alright Mama' was already eight years old, and was itself derived from one of Blind Lemon Jefferson's first recordings, 1926's 'Black Snake Moan'. Crudup had been told that the best route to writing your own material was to lift the third or fourth verse from an older record: 'Mama that's all right, mama that's all right for you,' sings Jefferson in his high and keening voice.[13] Circles and stairs, leading back to the blues and forward to rock and roll, up and down and round the different musics of the first half of the century.*

Rock and roll channelled the fervour and energy of gospel and the jump blues, but a significant portion of its melodic and rhythmic directness came from country music – a streetcar named regret. Hank Williams had already recorded some of his greatest songs by the turn of the 1950s, and a decisive backbeat is evident on 1947's 'Move It on Over' – another candidate for the first rock and roll record until you realize that there isn't one, rather precursors in different styles.

The rock and roll that emerged from 1955 can be seen as a singularity because it drew together all these root sources in an unanticipated way and changed what followed. Paul McCartney later said: 'You can't imagine a time when rock and roll was only

---

* Crudup was given this advice by Tampa Red, whose 1928 hit 'It's Tight Like That' also featured Georgia Tom - better known as Thomas A. Dorsey, the 'Father of Gospel Music'. For reasons of practicality or conviction, or both, singers and writers cycled between gospel and secular styles, sometimes using pseudonyms. Hank Williams released largely spoken word narrations as Luke the Drifter. Tharpe herself sang both gospel and secular songs as a young woman, to the consternation of the congregation: she was contracted to Lucky Millinder, and the 'tall skinny papa' she sang about with his Jazz Orchestra wasn't John the Baptist.

one of the musics." But if its novelty was to make the musics feel like one – not just jump blues, gospel and country but also swing and boogie-woogie – its strength was to include them all. Rock and roll as a genre is elusive and various, and it was less the homogeneity of the music and more the nature of the experience that made it feel like a coherent event.

Little Richard's is the music that superficially most resembles its immediate roots, retaining elements of swing from the jump blues but juicing it up. The white crooner Pat Boone covered his first hit 'Tutti Frutti' and sold more records, so Richard, reacting like the beboppers before him, sang his next single 'Long Tall Sally' even harder.[†] He won out this time, although Boone still tried, sounding like a car running out of gas.[‡] No one was wilder than Little Richard. Born poor in Georgia, set uneven on his feet, voyeuristic and exhibitionist, he joined medicine shows and carnivals to get out of Macon and circled his way up to fame via dishwashing, cross-dressing and encounters with performers like Esquerita (at the bus station) and Sister Rosetta Tharpe (at Macon City Auditorium, where she invited him to perform as a fourteen-year-old in 1947).

Where Elvis Presley revisited Arthur Crudup's blues, Chuck Berry based 'Maybellene' on Bob Wills and the Texas Playboys'

---

[*] Wonfor and Smeaton, 'Episode One', *The Beatles Anthology* (1995). Complexity theory, specifically the idea that 'processes having a large number of seemingly independent agents can spontaneously order themselves into a coherent system', can also be applied (definition via https://www.dictionary.com/browse/complexity-theory).

[†] 'Anyway, [Thelonius] Monk said … "We're going to create something that they can't steal, because they can't play it."' 'In her own words … Mary Lou Williams interview', *Melody Maker* (April–June 1954), via rat haus reality press, https://ratical.org/MaryLouWilliams/MMiview1954.html.

[‡] There is considerable irony in the wholesome Boone covering these songs: 'Tutti Frutti' had to be cleaned up before it was even recorded. Richard's producer Bumps Blackwell engaged the songwriter Dorothy LaBostrie to repurpose Little Richard's lyrics about anal sex – 'blues that would make your hair curl', as she put it – as he sang them to her with his face to the wall. 'Rock and Roll; Renegades; Interview with Dorothy LaBostrie,' *GBH Archives*, http://openvault.wgbh.org/catalog/V_CF6582AFE3E0492587D87B54983733F7.

1938 hit 'Ida Red': later he would model 'Promised Land' on a folk song, 'Wabash Cannonball'. Buddy Holly had grown up on country music in Texas, but tuned into far-off stations late at night to catch rhythm and blues.[14] The music was picking up freight from the different traditions of America's Black and white communities, and as it crossed and recrossed those lines it became something twice other.

There's a spring and release in the new music that distinguishes it from its sources: not just from the pull of the blues but from the sheen of croon. Echo becomes an instrument, and the sound of the record takes on its own life. On Gene Vincent's 'Be-Bop-A-Lula' and Buddy Holly's 'Peggy Sue' there is almost nothing on the surface and everything in the deeps; the latter is recorded quietly enough to hear Holly's pick on the strings, but the reverb on the drums fills out the sound. Elvis's 'Mystery Train' sounds more immediate and strange than Junior Parker's original, recorded in the same studio two years before. Presley's is a subjective evocation, not a descriptive one – Parker's beautiful vocal carries a weariness that is truer to the lyric, and long saxophone notes evoke the locomotive whistle – but Elvis, playing with the echo and picking up speed, takes us closer to the mystery.

This emphasis on sonic effect can also be found in rock and roll lyrics. These could be minimal and almost meaningless provided they were percussive and the overall sound thrilling. From 'Tutti Frutti' to 'Be-Bop-A-Lula' these are not scats in the middle of a narrative but the thing itself: this is taken to extremes in the music of Bo Diddley, whose signature sound was its own stuttering rhythm. It can also be heard at the height of the next decade's experiment, in the 'oom bop bop' chorus to 'Good Vibrations'.

A metanarrative about music and the teenage experience emerged in the songs of Chuck Berry. From 'Roll Over Beethoven' in 1956 to 'Sweet Little Sixteen' two years later, the songs were not simply exciting, they were *about* the excitement. Drawing T-Bone Walker's electric blues guitar style into rock and roll, Berry's songs leap with the thrill of escape: in cars and canteens and on continental journeys, rock and roll becomes its own reason for living, a new hormone indistinguishable from desire. This would feed into the more literal songs of the early Beach Boys, whose first hit, 'Surfin' USA', repurposed 'Sweet Little Sixteen'. The Beatles covered nine of his songs, more than anyone else's. And the rollocking narrative of 'Bob Dylan's 115th Dream' is closer to Chuck Berry in feel than it is to any blues archetypes.

In 'School Day (Ring! Ring! Goes the Bell)', recorded in January 1957, Berry writes as if school were a single, shared experience in the America he gathered so infectiously in song. But desegregation was resisted in the South, and that September nine Black American students were denied entry to high school in Little Rock by National Guardsmen.[*] It took three weeks for President Eisenhower to intervene, sending five hundred troops to ensure that nine children could attend high school without being murdered.[†] Photographs of the Little Rock Nine being menaced and screeched at added to the momentum of the civil rights movement, and this wrenching juxtaposition is a constant through our narrative: joyous music accompanied resistance and hope, but also reaction and rage.[‡]

---

[*] School desegregation was mandated by the Supreme Court in the same week that 'Rock Around the Clock' was first released, in May 1954.

[†] 'I was glad he did, the only thing was I wondered what took him so long,' recalled Carlotta Walls LaNier, 'because here we were three weeks out of school.' It wasn't over. A year later Orval Faubus closed all the high schools in Little Rock, and in 1960 LaNier's home was bombed. Lina Mai, '"I Had a Right to Be at Central": Remembering Little Rock's Integration Battle', *Time* (22 Sep. 2017), https://time.com/4948704/little-rock-nine-anniversary/. The quote is from the embedded video.

[‡] Eulogizing rock and roll in 'School Day', Berry hoped it would deliver him and his audience from the days of old. But while the music reflected and in some ways embodied the times, it couldn't fix them. The degree of integration in schools attended by Black children in the US remains modest and is now slipping back.

There was something else in the musical moment that tran-scended its component styles, which Dylan, looking back in 2017, identified as danger.[15] 'Rhythm and blues, country and western, bluegrass and gospel were always there,' he said, 'but it was com-partmentalized – it was great but it wasn't dangerous.' The sense of transgression was present in the records, some of which (like Jerry Lee Lewis's 'Great Balls of Fire') challenged the instincts of their own singers, and it was there in the reaction to the music. Even on the Isle of Man, a young Ringo Starr was thrilled to see people ripping up the cinema during a screening of *Rock Around the Clock*.* It helps to explain the visceral reaction of Dylan, who knew when he heard Elvis that no one was going to be his boss. At Liverpool College of Art the new music was banned: 'We had to con them into letting us play rock and roll there on the record player,' Lennon recalled, 'by calling it blues.'†

As they thrilled to the sounds they heard, they began to make their own. Paul McCartney encountered John Lennon per-forming with his skiffle group the Quarrymen at a church fete in Woolton, Liverpool, and impressed the older boy by playing through some rock and roll songs backstage. It was July 1957; by October McCartney was in the group. Bob Dylan formed high school bands called the Cashmeres and the Golden Chords, singing Elvis and Little Richard songs so wildly at the Jacket Jamboree Talent Festival that Principal Pedersen cut the sound.[16]

In 1958 they made their first amateur recordings. Dylan sang Little Richard's 'Jenny Jenny' into a friend's recorder, sitting at the piano to hammer out his own one-chord tribute to the singer.‡ In June Brian Wilson was given a Wollensak tape recorder for his

---

* 'It was just sensational.' Wonfor and Smeaton, 'Episode One', *The Beatles Anthology* (1995).

† Ibid.

‡ Gray, *Bob Dylan Encyclopedia* (Continuum, 2006), p. 202. The thirty-second recording is cited as 'Hey Little Richard'.

sixteenth birthday, and began using the four tracks to layer vocals. Modest recording operations from Memphis to Merseyside meant that making your own shellac record was just within means: Elvis Presley had recorded an acetate at Sun Studio in the summer of 1953 before anyone asked him to, and the Quarrymen, now joined by George Harrison, did the same at Percy Phillips's Sound Recording Services in July.* They already wrote their own songs: McCartney's 'In Spite of All the Danger' is plaintive and already assured, those familiar voices blending as they would four years later, the shellac hissing like an old Victrola. Where Dylan favoured Little Richard, and Brian Wilson idolized the Four Freshmen, the future Beatles – now joined by George Harrison – loved Buddy Holly; they also recorded 'That'll Be the Day'.

●

A mythology quickly grew around these years, according to which rock and roll fast faded and burned, and nothing interesting happened until the Beatles.

The first part of this is essentially true – certainly the Beatles and Dylan saw it that way at the time – but the second is not. The years around the turn of the new decade saw the emergence of soul in Detroit, of modern pop songwriting from the Brill Building, and of the folk revival that sent singers to the back roads and back catalogues. Our protagonists' souls had been fired by rock and roll, but it was these new developments that shaped their musical intelligence and stylistic range.

Rock and roll was now mainstream, parodied by the British comic actor Peter Sellers on his 1958 album *The Best of Sellers*. The enterprising Earl of Prong in 'We Need the Money' has his

---

*The group circulated the single aluminium and acetate copy in weekly shifts, according to https://www.percyphillips.com.

own record to plug: 'I say a-doodle-up-a-dong-ding ... they call me Earl Creole'. The record was produced by George Martin for Parlophone, which gave him kudos when he signed the Beatles to the same label four years later; they were huge fans of Sellers via *The Goon Show*.*

By the end of 1958 Elvis was a soldier, Jerry Lee Lewis in disgrace after marrying his thirteen year-old cousin, and perhaps most unexpectedly of all (especially to anyone familiar with his invigorating account of a backstage threesome with Buddy Holly), Little Richard a preacher in the Seventh Day Adventist Church.[17] Holly himself would perish in a plane crash the following February – just after Dylan had seen him live in Duluth, experiencing a mysterious psychic transfer from six feet away – and Eddie Cochran in a road accident in the spring of 1960. The day the music died was a long, sad season.

The Beatles' early press conferences are full of references to its demise. 'Rock's supposed to have gone out about five years ago,' said Harrison in early 1964.[18] Rejecting the 'Liverpool Sound' tag, they portrayed themselves as revivalists *avant la lettre*: 'It's just us playing rock and roll,' Lennon insisted.[19] His question to Elvis when they met for the only time in 1965 was why he didn't record the good old stuff any more.

Dylan also felt the change in the weather, attributing his own move into folk to the dousing of rock and roll's holy fire. 'At a certain time,' he told Swedish radio in 1966, 'the whole field got taken over into, into some milk.'[20] The dairy takeover was not absolute, but it is presaged in the difference between, say, Dale Hawkins's ominous 'Suzie Q' from May 1957, and Ricky Nelson's 'Poor Little Fool', number one in the first Billboard Hot 100 the following August. In the UK Cliff Richard's 'Move It' showed signs of life in Hank Marvin's echoing guitar, but it was followed

---

* The actor would go on to appear on *The Music of Lennon & McCartney* for Granada TV in 1965.

in 1959 by the inaptly named 'Living Doll', as moribund a side as ever was made. Richard's voice is feeble and unreliable, and the comparison with Elvis at his tamest – 'Teddy Bear' is the obvious reference point – shows the gulf in talent.* Frankie Avalon ('Venus') and Fabian ('Tiger') now represented what Dylan called the athletic, superclean vibe.[21] So it was that he stopped playing piano in rock and roll groups, discovered artists like Odetta, Lead Belly and Josh White, and became a folk singer.

But the sources that rock and roll had drawn into the cultural moment continued to flow and carve new ground. Gospel and rhythm and blues were distilled into the poppier sound of Sam Cooke, who hit number one with 'You Send Me' in November 1957, never losing the aqueous gospel catch in his voice. James Brown emerged from a two-year slump with 'Try Me', inspired in part by 'For Your Precious Love', a hit for Jerry Butler and The Impressions. The contrast is instructive: while Butler's vocal is ceremonious and the pace stately, Brown's record draws momentum from the piano triplets, his singing strikingly unmannered and direct.

In Detroit a lighter, less self-conscious style also began to emerge from the familiar doo-wop changes. Tamla's second ever single, in early 1959, was Eddie Holland's 'Merry-Go-Round', anchored in a fruity tenor, but later that year the Miracles' 'Bad Girl' floated in on flute and Smokey Robinson's falsetto. The Miracles' 'Shop Around', which blends Robinson's ballad grace with the kind of irresistible groove Ray Charles had introduced a year earlier on 'What I'd Say', was the first Motown song to sell a million records, in 1960.

The Beatles, while retaining the rock and roll they loved, began

---

* One of the benefits of being young during such a time is that it forces you to look for the stronger stuff. Punk and post-punk had fizzled out by the time I was eighteen, while pop curdled in posture and synthesizer stabs. But there were radio series on genres that were remote and even ridiculed at the time, and I found myself transcribing gospel and country songs, trying to hit Claude Jeter's high notes, playing Clara Ward's 'Canaan' on the piano, and earnestly singing Ernest Tubb songs at my first gigs.

to absorb what was thrilling in the new rhythm and blues as it became soul music. They pushed the vocals harder than in some of the originals and performed the male–female call and response within the group: this sounded both visceral and irreverent, paving the way for their early sound.

A companion style to Motown began to emerge, also driven by young writers blending urban sophistication with teen appeal, many of them working out of the Brill Building in New York. An early example was Phil Spector's 'To Know Him Is to Love Him', released in September 1958 by his own group the Teddy Bears. The sound is decorous, but the writing is complex: the classic 50s progression turnaround used in The Everly Brothers' 'All I Have to Do Is Dream' is reshuffled, and the middle eight is full of surprising changes.* It is not the 'dead fish' of Greil Marcus's estimation; to know it is to marvel at it.[22]

The Beatles quickly picked up on the song, and set to work on the harmonies: McCartney remembered it as 'the first three-part we ever did'.[23] They had a good ear for covers, based mainly on the feel of the records. But songwriters also learn structure from other people's songs, where questions are posed and resolved. These songs were more overtly melodic than rock and roll, and the sophisticated new pop writing would animate Brian Wilson's early style for the Beach Boys.

Another component in the Beach Boys' sound was a subgenre that both pre-dated and survived rock and roll. Doo-wop was music you could make at home, rooted in a cappella arrangements sung on street corners, at church and in high school stairwells. Its

---

* See Appendix 1 for detail on the turnaround and musical notation. The middle eight sits in an unsettled D minor, modulating briefly to G minor, before resolving to the home key of D major. I am indebted to the pianist and composer Alexander Metcalfe (you can view his website at https://www.alexmetcalfe.com) for this analysis: he notes that 'It's a powerful effect, changing to a colourfully related key without ever settling on the new tonic. It's the sort of thing Schubert would do if he wanted to suggest a sense of searching or "ungroundedness" in the lyric.' From a conversation with the author on Facebook Messenger, 8 April 2020.

first stars, the Mills Brothers, sang the vocal parts and impersonated the accompanying bass and brass instruments, a pre-war beatbox. On Christmas Eve 1938, the night after Rosetta Tharpe had sung at the first *From Spirituals to Swing*, the Golden Gate Quartet opened the second: 'Golden Gate Gospel Train' features its own sound effects, while 'I'm on My Way' and 'Noah' hum to the internal motor of the gospel quartet, urgent and modern-sounding (Elvis loved them, and his vocal debt to the baritone Willie Johnson is startlingly clear). The following month, the Ink Spots recorded 'If I Didn't Care', still one of the top-selling singles ever: tinkling with tasteful piano, the sound looks back to the precise diction and high tenor parts of 1930s movie interludes, but it leans forward in its chordal backing vocals and velvety spoken passage to the 1950s.

Frankie Lymon & the Teenagers hit big with 'Why Do Fools Fall in Love' in 1956, by which time Frankie Laine, introducing them on his TV show, could call rock and roll the most popular musical style in the country. The Teenagers were cute, but also raw and streetwise; a young Ronnie Spector fell in love with Lymon's voice, and there is a rush to the music which isn't there in the work of groups like the preppy Hi-Lo's, somewhere between big band jazz and easy listening, or the actual Four Preps.[24] There was a goofy side to doo-wop in its pop expression, too, even before Frankie Valli and the Four Seasons took it into screeching self-parody, and this found its way into the Beach Boys sound via Mike Love's bass parts and Brian Wilson's high harmony: the Rivingtons' 'Papa-Oom-Mow-Mow' was a hit as late as autumn 1962.*

The Everly Brothers managed to bridge rock and roll and the early 1960s. Their records were infused with country but blended

---

* Lymon, who had gone solo, was not there to compete: the limits of rock and roll's ability to challenge racism were exposed when he danced briefly with a white girl on Alan Freed's TV show *The Big Beat* in 1957. The show was cancelled in the furore that followed, and Lymon's career faded into heroin use and an early death.

with rock and roll, sounding lighter and more sweetly melodic than either. Mike Love remembers walking home from youth nights at church with his sister Maureen and Brian Wilson, who broke the two-part harmonies into three for them to sing; the Everlys' tight twin vocals are a key reference point for early Beatles music.[25]

So the years when rock and roll turned to milk yielded vibrant new sounds in Motown soul and Brill Building pop, modes of expression that spoke directly to the dreams and love lives of teenagers. Gerry Goffin and Carole King's 'Will You Still Love Me Tomorrow', sung by the Shirelles at the end of 1960, is a moment of nervous anticipation caught in time. Ten years later Carole King recorded it again for *Tapestry*, bookmarking a decade when young people took steps into love, sex and drugs which, for better or worse, could not be retraced.

○

Our protagonists were not yet ready to influence that journey. The turn of the new decade found Bob Dylan – now calling himself by that name – halfway through his solitary year at the University of Minnesota. He hung out with other folk enthusiasts at the Ten O'Clock Scholar cafe in Dinkytown; he played there and at the Purple Onion in St Paul.

Brian Wilson began studying psychology at El Camino Community College in September 1960, taking additional music classes. Mike Love, working at his father's now faltering sheet metal business by day and a gas station by night, would soon be pitched into a shotgun marriage. They began the decade like countless teenagers then and now, pursuing studies they weren't convinced by, or doing jobs they had never wanted in the first place, or fixing things that had happened too soon. Music was what made them come to life, but making it their lives was unrealistic for now.

The Beatles were only a little further down the road, but not for want of trying. In autumn 1959 they had taken part in three rounds of the talent show *TV Star Search*, drummerless and calling themselves Johnny and the Moondogs. In May 1960, as the Silver Beetles, they secured a tour of the Scottish Highlands supporting a Liverpool singer named Johnny Gentle, who belonged to the impresario Larry Parnes's stable of singers.* In June they were billed for the first time as the Beatles, but they were still shedding drummers, and they spent the early summer playing roughhouse venues on the Wirral. One afternoon in Liverpool they provided the backing music for a stripper from Manchester named Janice.[26]

That was nothing compared to the milieu they encountered in Hamburg that August, where they performed to gangsters, prostitutes and brawling sailors for forty-eight nights in a row at the Indra Club, and then for fifty-six nights at the Kaiserkeller club, on the corner of Schmuckstrasse, just off the Reeperbahn. It was a blend of barracks and burlesque: they were accommodated by the toilets and woke to the sound of people pissing, but they now dated strippers. They had come from a world where girls still wore figurative corsets to the 'naughtiest city in the world', to borrow Harrison's phrase; his bandmates were physically close enough to hear him losing his virginity in one of the bunk beds, and applauded him.[27]

If there was something universal in this coming of age – McCartney would later characterize them as army buddies who grew apart, although they were the first cohort in the UK not to

---

* Gentle's name stood in muted contrast to Parnes singers like Billy Fury and Marty Wilde. Parnes was reputed to name his protegés after their sexual characteristics, which adds piquancy to monikers like Vince Eager and Dickie Pride. Mick Brown, 'The mystery of David Jacobs, the Liberace lawyer' (3 Jun. 2013), *The Telegraph*, https://www.telegraph.co.uk/news/uknews/law-and-order/10094665/The-mystery-of-David-Jacobs-the-Liberace-lawyer.html.

do military service* – it was also a specific introduction to a low-rent showbiz world where musicians dropped pills to play through the night. Somehow, sophistication found its way to them. Art school influences from home were reinforced when the group was befriended by Klaus Voormann and his friends Jürgen Vollmer and Astrid Kirchherr, a black-clad trio Lennon called the Exis (after 'existentialists' – only fifteen years after Hitler's defeat, they inclined more to French than German style and culture).[28] The group were photographed in moody black-and-white, and persuaded to comb their hair forward.

At length George was deported for being underage, followed by Paul and new drummer Pete Best for alleged arson. Stuart Sutcliffe, until that point the group's bass player, chose to stay in Hamburg with Kirchherr and study art.† So it was an exhausted and disenchanted John Lennon who made his solitary way back to Liverpool in December, where he found that McCartney had taken a job sweeping the yard at Massey and Coggins' coil-winding factory.

Just before New Year, the reconvened group played at Litherland Town Hall and caused a sensation. Toughened and tightened by their stay in Hamburg, where they had played up to five hours a night in shifts, they were a revelation to themselves as much as the audience. 'It was only back in Liverpool that we realized the difference and saw what had happened to us,' Lennon recalled.[29]

There must be agency for things to happen to you, and the Beatles had put themselves on the line. Dylan, who had taken what he could from Minnesota, was about to do the same. By the end of 1960 he had travelled west to Denver and back again like Kerouac, encountered Woody Guthrie via his autobiography

---

* Introduced in 1939 on the outbreak of World War Two, National Service was phased out from 1957, the oldest Beatle – Lennon – missing the age cut by a year.

† Beautiful but musically unreliable, his chosen nickname on the tour of Scotland (Stuart de Staël) reflected his true vocation.

Bound for Glory, and been told by the folk blues singer Odetta that he might have a shot at making it as a musician. It was time to leave Minneapolis, and his parents – with considerable good grace – agreed to give him a year. 'We couldn't see it,' said his father, 'but we felt he was entitled to the chance.'[30]

1961–62: RECORDING ARTISTS

		Bob Dylan	Beatles	Beach Boys
1961	Nov			[27] 'Surfin'
	Dec			
1962	Jan			
	Feb			
	Mar	[19] BOB DYLAN		
	Apr			
	May			
	Jun			[4] 'Surfin' Safari'
	Jul			
	Aug			
	Sep			
	Oct		[5] 'Love Me Do'	[1] SURFIN' SAFARI
	Nov			
	Dec	[14] 'Mixed-Up Confusion'		

NOTE: Release dates throughout are the initial US (Bob Dylan and Beach Boys) or UK (Beatles) release dates. Singles are listed via the A-side, which would have got the radio play, unless released as a double A-side.

The nascent Beatles played anywhere they could, from the Stanley Abattoir Social Club in November 1957 to Knotty Ash Village Hall a full four years later. The venues are a map of the age as well as of the north-west: halls, ballrooms, jazz societies and service clubs. In many respects 1961 looked much like 1960, with only a three-month stint at the Top Ten Club in Hamburg to break up the routine of almost daily gigs in and around Liverpool. This Hamburg trip led to a recording session backing the singer Tony Sheridan on *My Bonnie*, but they were only credited as the Beat Brothers, and the two tracks they recorded on their own went unreleased.* When in December they secured their first appearance in the south, they played to a largely deserted Palais Ballroom in Aldershot.[31]

But things were about to change. They were now holding meetings with a local businessman called Brian Epstein, who had come to see the group one lunchtime at the Cavern Club. In his own way he was as much a misfit as they were, his thwarted artistic ambitions cushioned by prosperity but complicated by sexuality. He had told his family at sixteen that he wanted to be a dress designer, and had spent a year at RADA in the mid-1950s before dropping out after an arrest for importuning; set up by the police, he believed himself ruined. He kept getting drawn back to the family business in Liverpool, which now included a music store, and was sufficiently well known to be announced from the stage when he arrived at the Cavern. Even before a deal was agreed, and despite having no experience in artist management, he began to make things happen. Soon the group had their first photo session, and, on the first day of 1962, an audition with Decca Records in London.

Bob Dylan had by this point recorded his first album, his trajectory by comparison an overnight success. He travelled to New York in January 1961, and soon marched up to the door of the Guthrie household in Queens – meeting his ailing idol, who

---

* 'My Bonnie Lies Over the Ocean' sounds like a lame choice for a cover, and it is, pretty much; it shows how widely and even randomly the net was cast when singers who didn't write needed material. But one thing old folk songs and early century standards share is melody.

now resided in hospital, the following weekend. He had learned how to zone in on who mattered on any city folk scene, and this now served him well on the biggest of them all. By April he was supporting, and befriending, John Lee Hooker. In September he upstaged the Greenbriar Boys at Gerde's Folk City, and was interviewed by Robert Shelton for the *New York Times*. Shelton glossed over Dylan's invented backstory about travelling with a carnival, working as a farmhand and learning bottleneck guitar from an old New Mexican named Wigglefoot: even then the singer wouldn't be pinned down. But he bought into Dylan's romantic relationship with the music: 'He is consciously trying to recapture the rude beauty of a Southern field hand, musing in melody on his porch', wrote Shelton.'[32]

The rude beauty was about to be harnessed, as noise around Dylan reached John Hammond – the producer we last encountered in 1938, promoting Big Joe Turner and Sister Rosetta Tharpe. Hammond had discovered two of the greatest voices of the twentieth century in Billie Holiday and Aretha Franklin, but he did not consider Dylan's voice, or his guitar playing, or even his harmonica playing, remarkable. It was rather Dylan's originality, his 'extraordinary personality', which he signed to Columbia Records in October 1962. Dylan's reinvention, or his self-invention from raw material he considered too mundane, had succeeded.

Another larger-than-life personality circled Dylan himself in the ursine shape of Albert Grossman, who wished to manage him. He was more experienced than Epstein; he already managed Odetta, and would soon assemble the folk group Peter, Paul and Mary to his specification. He was certainly more urbane and educated than Elvis's manager Colonel Tom Parker, to whom Dylan, many lawsuits later, later compared him. He had a degree in economics from the University of Chicago, which he applied with enthusiasm to his own eye-watering percentages. But he was also passionate about artistic integrity, which he saw in stark terms: 'A non-authentic piece of creativity to him was not just to be ignored or discarded,' said Peter Yarrow (the Peter in his group), 'it was *bullshit*'. He protected his artists with the same rigour.[33]

Brian Wilson had been making music in various combinations with family and friends: his brother Carl, his cousins Mike and Maureen, and their friend Al Jardine. Sometimes when they played at parties they were Carl and the Passions, sometimes Kenny and the Cadets. But the line-up didn't coalesce until the second half of 1961, when, galvanized by Dennis's enthusiasm for surfing, they called themselves the Pendletones, after the Pendleton shirt favoured by local surfers. They neither travelled beyond their own home town, nor hustled especially hard, but they were the first to release a record. In his own way, it was the Wilson brothers' belligerent father Murry who had put in the hard yards, trying for years to write a hit record and associating with music publishers and record producers in the process. It turned out that he had made enough connections to set the younger generation on their way. He did so, and soon resented it.

27 November 1961 'Surfin' , 1 October 1962 SURFIN' SAFARI

The Beatles had struck out for Hamburg in an Austin van, and Dylan for New York in an Impala sedan; the Pendletones didn't need to leave the house. With their parents away on a Labor Day trip to Mexico City, they used the food money they'd been left to buy instruments, a kind of reverse intervention. Murry was naturally livid when he got back, but was sufficiently impressed by the tape they had made to contact friends who ran a music publishing company. By Christmas the group had their first publishing deal, their first single, and a new name. They were surprised to find their record credited to the Beach Boys, a name chosen by a PR man to align them even more closely with surf rock, a Californian craze that broke that autumn with Dick Dale's 'Let's Go Trippin''. For their first gig proper, they played in the break between Dick Dale sets at the Rendezvous Ballroom in Newport Beach, at the heart of the surf scene.

'Surfin'' bears roughly the same relation to their first Capitol single, 'Surfin' Safari', as the Beatles' 'Love Me Do' does to 'Please Please Me' – a little clunky and gauche, a trace of the famous sound rather than the actual thing. And while the *Surfin' Safari* album contains many influences and tonal notes the Beach Boys would retain – rock and roll, whimsy, soda perving, cars and a cleaned-up take on surf rock – it lacks the more extravagant flavours of the Four Freshmen, or the thicker production that Brian Wilson would adopt after hearing the Ronettes' 'Be My Baby' the following summer. But we learn by doing: Wilson wrote nine out of the twelve songs on the album with Mike Love. The only song that hints at discoveries to come is 'Heads You Win – Tails I Lose', whose compact chorus accents the minor {vi} chord, momentarily plaintive, like someone else's cigarette smoke on the street.

19 March **BOB DYLAN**

Dylan didn't start with a single: he recorded his first album in November 1961. It was hastily assembled, and only two of the songs were his own. Never the easiest to engineer, he was almost unproduceable at first, and couldn't see the point in second takes. The album was erratic, but it was not diluted. Neither was it a commercial success; the Columbia salespeople called him Hammond's Folly.[34]

The spirit of rock and roll is palpable in the first song, Jesse Fuller's 'You're No Good', which Dylan leaps into with abandon like a child into a laundry basket. The singer pokes fun at his own energy on 'Talkin' New York', where he arrives in Greenwich Village and tries his luck at a coffee house and is told he sounds like a hillbilly: 'We want folk singers here.' It does get more folky, but never comfortable. It's always at the hard edge, Dylan trying it on, sounding at times as if he's picking a fight – raging through a skinful at the biggest guy in the bar.

The most accomplished arrangements, on 'Baby, Let Me Follow You Down' and 'House of the Risin' Sun', aren't his own. As detailed in Scorsese's *No Direction Home*, it was a time of sharing, borrowing and stealing: flats, licks, records.* The mood quietens, and Dylan's voice starts to come into focus on 'Song to Woody'. Here he sketches a 'funny ol' world' in the making, and gently acknowledges his debt to Guthrie, Cisco Houston, Sonny Terry and Lead Belly.

14 December 1962 **'Mixed-Up Confusion'**

He quickly started work on his next album. Sessions began on 24 April and spanned an entire year in which his development, and the country's preoccupations, can be traced in seasonal leaps. 'Blowin' in the Wind' was recorded in July, 'A Hard Rain's a-Gonna Fall' in December, a month after the Cuban Missile Crisis, and 'Girl from the North Country' the following April.

One of the enduring myths of 1960s music is that Dylan 'went electric' in 1965, but he recorded with a backing band as early as 1962 – releasing a single, 'Mixed-Up Confusion', that December.

---

* Dylan asked Dave Van Ronk if he could use his arrangement of 'House of the Risin' Sun' (which Van Ronk aimed to record), but only after he had already done so. Van Ronk was forced to give up singing it after Dylan made it his own, a fate which befell Dylan himself once the Animals took it into the pop charts. Scorsese (dir.), *No Direction Home* (2005).

It's a rattling song with a jug band feel, bar room piano and subtle electric guitar, lingering much longer than expected on the {V} chord in what would become a Dylan motif: he does the same thing in 'Like a Rolling Stone', drawing out the chord as he sings 'didn't you?'. It's a jalopy headed for Highway 61, guitarist Bruce Langhorne already in back.

5 October 1962 **'Love Me Do'**

Decca had passed on the Beatles in January 1962, opting instead to sign Brian Poole and the Tremeloes. It was the flunk of the century, but recordings from the audition give it some context. Despite their miles on the clock the group sound callow, with McCartney's vocals especially ingratiating. The set was full of curious covers, which with their shifts in mood and rhythm helped prime the group to be inventive songwriters and responsive musicians. But it must have sounded very odd that day. Alongside a handful of their own songs and some obscure rock and roll were hoary standards like 'Bésame Mucho', written in 1940, 'September in the Rain', from 1937, and 'The Sheik of Araby', which dates back to 1921.* The group audibly make fun of their own selections ('not half!' interjects Lennon during 'The Sheik of Araby'), which must have made them even harder to categorize.

Epstein now secured a meeting with George Martin, who ran EMI's subsidiary label Parlophone. It was June before the group recorded for him, and then – as with Dylan and John Hammond – it was not their music that compelled but their personalities. When after a largely disappointing session he outlined everything he didn't like, it was their sense of humour that won the day.

---

* Even the oldest of these songs was more recent to the Beatles then than any of their albums to us now: one measure of the cultural shift they helped to shape is that it should feel otherwise.

Asked by Martin if there was anything *they* weren't happy with, Harrison replied: 'Well, for a start, I don't like your tie.'[35] Martin had produced hit albums for Peter Sellers and *Beyond the Fringe*, and he knew his comedy. They hit it off immediately.

On the face of it the pairing seems an unlikely one, but, like Epstein, George Martin was more of an outlier than his urbane exterior suggested. He sounded posh, but was the son of a carpenter and had emulated the speech of the officers he encountered when serving in the Fleet Air Arm. His background and grammar school education would have been a calling card in the 1960s; born fifteen years before the Beatles, however, he chose to obscure them. Like Dylan, who traded his respectable upbringing for a picaresque persona, Martin, who was moving in the other social direction, found a way of being the person he wanted to be. There was still misalignment: Martin was until 1962 leading a double life, with a girlfriend in London and his wife and children out of town.

Where one senses that Dylan might have made it irrespective of who he encountered (he secured a recording deal with Columbia on the back of a few appearances in Greenwich Village), it took two men who fell in love with the Beatles to make sense of them. As it was they recorded last, but picked up speed the quickest. 'Love Me Do' came out as a single in October, its awkwardness quickly followed that frozen winter by the more worldly and accomplished 'Please Please Me'.

'Love Me Do' sounds transitional, and it was: the leap from the audition tapes in the first half of 1962 to 'Please Please Me' would be miraculous without it. George Martin had been unconvinced by Pete Best's work at their first EMI session in June, and had said he would need to use a professional drummer for recording. Although he told Epstein they might retain Best for live work, the Beatles – to the consternation of their local fan base, and without telling Best that they had at last secured a record deal –

chose to replace him with Ringo Starr.* Starr was concluding a summer season with Rory Storm and the Hurricanes at Butlin's, Skegness. He knew the Beatles well, and had sometimes subbed for Best in Hamburg and Liverpool; called to the phone over the holiday camp PA, he left for Liverpool to join the group the same week. Today there would have been a Twitter storm; back then, Harrison was given a black eye in the Cavern. Even so, Starr was confined to tambourine for the single.

By the end of 1962 Dylan, the Beatles and the Beach Boys had the line-ups, managers and record labels that would make them famous. But hardly anyone knew about them now. And, based on their first records, it was by no means inevitable that anyone would. In contrast, the records they released in 1963 will never be forgotten. This is due both to the songs themselves and to the impact they made on the wider culture and on other musicians. As it turned out, this would soon include each other.

---

* The dismissal was inelegantly handled, but it chimed with the views of Tony Sheridan ('a crap drummer') and George Martin's assistant at EMI, Ron Richards: 'he's useless,' he had concluded in June. Mark Lewisohn, *The Beatles – All These Years: Volume One* (Little, Brown and Company, 2013), pp. 448, 668 [Kindle edition].

1963: MILLION SELLERS

		Bob Dylan	Beatles	Beach Boys
1963	Jan		" 'Please Please Me'	
	Feb			
	Mar		²² PLEASE PLEASE ME	⁴ 'Surfin' USA'
				²⁵ SURFIN' USA
	Apr		" 'From Me to You'	
	May	²⁷ THE FREEWHEELIN' BOB DYLAN		
	Jun			
	Jul			²² 'Surfer Girl'
	Aug		²³ 'She Loves You'	
	Sep			¹⁶ SURFER GIRL
	Oct			⁷ LITTLE DEUCE COUPE
				²⁸ 'Be True to Your School'
	Nov		²² WITH THE BEATLES	
			²⁹ 'I Want to Hold Your Hand'	
	Dec			⁹ 'Little Saint Nick'

This was the year our three leads, one way and another, first sold a million. We tend to map this era by its albums, but in 1963 people encountered and related to artists via singles. This was true even for Dylan: 'Blowin' in the Wind' led off his second album in May, but it was Peter, Paul and Mary who sold a million with it in August. Like 'Surfin' USA' and 'She Loves You', it transformed its author's fortunes; he was astonished to receive a royalty cheque.

Each of these hits represents a door to the young decade – 'Surfin' USA' by focusing Chuck Berry's broad map of America on a single idealized location, California, that would soon become central to the culture; 'Blowin' in the Wind' by universalizing a yearning for change that young people could relate to not only in America but around the world; and 'She Loves You' because – well, because it was so joyous and unapologetic.

11 January 'Please Please Me' , 22 March PLEASE PLEASE ME

'Love Me Do' was disarming, unadorned and largely acoustic, bearing traces of the skiffle band Lennon's Quarrymen had once been. But 'Please Please Me' crashes and rolls to electric guitars, pounding drums and the throaty vocal attack they had developed live. The descending 'last night I' vocal line (suspended by a high drone E) is followed by an ascending set of no less than eight *come on*s climbing to an airy chorus, reached inside half a minute.* The B-side, 'Ask Me Why', was a skipping mid-tempo ballad, comparable in songwriting quality, with its confident use of major sevenths and augmented chords, to the work by writers like Goffin and King and Bacharach and David that would feature on the album.

The album *Please Please Me* was completed in January with Dylanesque dispatch, but navigating the greater variables presented by recording four musicians live. It featured complex harmonies,

---

* Here George Martin made his mark as producer, urging the group to up the tempo and work in some harmonies: dreary by Martin's estimation in September, it was irresistible by November. Martin announced from the control booth that it would be their first number one, and it topped most UK charts: when sales were later amalgamated into a single chart, 'Please Please Me' was demoted to a number two, which is why the *1* compilation (2000) fussily omits it.

and at least one lead vocal by each: ten songs in ten hours, enough to give anyone who has recorded in a studio the heebie-jeebies. All those hours in Rialtos, Majestics and the Smethwick Baths Ballroom poured into the music. Best heard in mono, the voices sound more alike than they ever would, partly because Lennon's heavy January cold leaves him sounding like George Harrison, especially on 'Baby It's You', and partly because all break with weariness and exertion. The assurance of the group's live playing allows for considerable subtlety in the arrangements given the sparse instrumentation – on the swinging repeated bridge in the show tune 'A Taste of Honey', for example – although even here McCartney sings hard enough to crack and the '*hunny*' harmonies are determinedly Scouse.

The last song, their faster arrangement of the Isley Brothers' 'Twist and Shout', became their calling card. But they almost didn't make it. The session at Abbey Road came on the back of thirteen shows in eleven days and Lennon's voice was shot. He took throat lozenges, gargled with milk and took his shirt off for good measure: it was all or nothing, and it shows. Lennon's voice was in rags, and a second take was abandoned, but the first was enough to change British music.

Two days later the BBC broadcast a play called *Madhouse on Castle Street*, featuring the then-unknown folk singer Bob Dylan. He had been flown to England for shooting, although the plan to feature him in a speaking role was quickly abandoned. The songs Dylan performed in the play represented a pivot of sorts: from versions of 'Hang Me, O Hang Me' and 'The Cuckoo Is a Pretty Bird' to the still unreleased 'Blowin' in the Wind'. That week's *Radio Times* introduced him as a 'skilled guitarist', noting that 'his special kind of haunting music forms an integral part of tonight's strange play.'[36]

The Beatles and Dylan had been moved by the same records in the mid to late 1950s, but they sounded different now. The extent to which their paths of influence had diverged is apparent in their choice of non-original songs for their debut LPs: while the oldest of the Beatles' covers, 'Boys', was only two years old, all of Dylan's originated from the first half of the century and before.* This doesn't tell the whole story – the Beatles had persisted with the wartime bolero 'Bésame Mucho' until a few months before, while Dylan was drawing on contemporary arrangements by fellow musicians – but it reflects their modus operandi at the time. To sound more similar, Dylan would need to be less studied and the Beatles more poetic: this, in no small part, they learned from each other.

25 March **SURFIN' USA**

Crammed with exotic Spanish and Hawaiian beach names, based on a daft but infinitely tempting notion ('if everybody had an ocean'), especially to anyone growing up on an island surrounded by cold seas crowded with haddock, 'Surfin' USA' is one of the first great summer pop records. Mike Love's decisive lead was key to the Beach Boys' uptempo songs: it speaks of fun and brooks no doubt. The track is self-evidently a version of

---

* The Beatles wrote eight out of the fourteen songs on *Please Please Me*. Arthur Alexander's 'Anna' was released in September 1962; 'Chains', recorded by the Cookies and written by Gerry Goffin and Carole King, was released in November 1962; 'Boys' was written by Luther Dixon and Wes Farrell, and released by the Shirelles in November 1960, as the B-side to the more famous 'Will You Love Me Tomorrow'; 'Baby It's You', also by the Shirelles, written by Burt Bacharach with Dixon and Mack David (elder brother of Hal) and released in 1961; even 'A Taste of Honey', which sounds older, wasn't (they were familiar with Lenny Welch's vocal version from 1962). By contrast, the songs on *Bob Dylan* reach back not just to the blues of the 1940s (Bukka White's 'Fixin'' to Die Blues'), 1930s (Blind Boy Fuller's 'Mama Let Me Lay It On You', adapted by Eric Von Schmidt as 'Baby, Let Me Follow You Down') and 1920s (Blind Lemon Jefferson's 'See That My Grave Is Kept Clean'); but to American folk songs first published in the 1910s ('Man of Constant Sorrow'), African American spirituals ('Gospel Plow'), and the mists of the Scottish folk tradition ('Pretty Peggy-O'). He would have discovered many of these songs from recent and contemporary versions by singers he heard and encountered: for example, 'Gospel Plow' via Odetta's 'Hold On' from *Odetta at Carnegie Hall*. Only two songs on the album are attributed to Bob Dylan alone.

Chuck Berry's 'Sweet Little Sixteen' with new lyrics, and as such a direct tribute, although this was obscured in the credits until three years later.

Capitol's appetite for short and scrappy Beach Boys albums only accelerated Brian Wilson's development. They released three in 1963, the subject matter so restricted as to resemble a creative exercise in which the student is told: 'Write about your feelings, but only in reference to cars and surfing.' But Wilson can be heard straining at the brief as early as *Surfin' USA*, where 'Lonely Sea' is sandwiched between an instrumental called 'Stoked' ('stoked!', the group shouts at intervals) and 'Shut Down' ('jack it up, jack it up!'). Recorded at the exact pace of the Platter's' 1960 hit 'Ebb Tide', it takes rock and roll ballad form and twists it strangely out of shape: the surprising change from major to minor on the dominant chord {V to v} at 0:43 changes the feel entirely.[37]

The duality of surf, cars and girls signalling fun on the one hand, and a kind of sun-drenched anguish on the other – a tension embodied in the differing personalities and ambitions of Mike Love and Brian Wilson – was set. The lonely sea was a proxy for Wilson himself.

27 May THE FREEWHEELIN' BOB DYLAN

The folk singer is a figure of fun today, reduced to a cartoon somewhere between *Friends'* Phoebe Buffay and *The Simpsons'* Lurleen Lumpkin. But that figure once did matter, and it was part of a scene that took itself very seriously. This scene flourished in the States and in Belgium and France, where beloved artists like Jacques Brel and Léo Ferré performed modern 'chanson'. Even now some acoustic venues shush the restive crowd as a folk singer relates the story of some long-forgotten train wreck.

This earnestness must be borne in mind when we go back to

Dylan's early records, because it shapes the way the songs are sung and the way they were originally heard in New York cafes. It also illuminates Dylan's use of humour, which persists at least as far as *Highway 61 Revisited*; partly because it helped retain the attention of small audiences as a solo singer, but also because it was his way of rejecting the oppressive reverence that readily attaches itself to folk song.

The Freewheelin' Bob Dylan contains some of his most direct and affecting music. 'Blowin' in the Wind', 'Girl from the North Country' and 'Don't Think Twice, It's All Right' speak heart-to-heart, the singing private, grainy and true. Elsewhere there are tonal lurches, from goofy humour that one can imagine going down a storm in coffee houses at the time, to apocalyptic rambles that test the listener's endurance.

Hope and fear went hand in hand: the world teetered on the brink of nuclear war in October 1962, and the new impetus for civil rights was marked by violence and murder. 'A Hard Rain's a-Gonna Fall' has a strong hook but works better excerpted, as it so often is, over documentary footage. 'Masters of War' survives on its wits, but the grim minor chord chug legitimized countless trying imitations. Dylan's diction would soon become extravagant under the influence of Beat poetry and Rimbaud, but for now his best poetry was stark: the bathetic 'pale afternoon' in the final lines of 'Masters of War', for example, brings abstraction suddenly down to earth – you can *see* the singer following the casket.

'Blowin' in the Wind' sits in open D, the specificity of the civil rights movement legible but generalized as an appeal to sensory as well as political alertness. Dylan's singing is at its least affected, and the timing falls over itself – the first verse speeds up at 'how many seas', the second at 'how many years'. It's a little song with a big heart and an indestructible melody, and although it draws on folk archetypes, it also owes something to the directness of

Buddy Holly's 'Everyday': the development of the melody in 'the answer, my friend' is as much pop as folk.

The immediate source for the melody is the African American spiritual 'No More Auction Block', recorded by Paul Robeson and familiar to Dylan from the 1960 album *Odetta Live* at *Carnegie Hall*. Hear a momentary passage in a context which suggests it, and the similarity can be striking: 'Blowin' in the Wind' does set off on the same path.[38] But one needs the whole song to get the whole picture, or we are colour-matching the sky in a Rubens to the sky in a Titian; the same shade of blue does not make them one. Dylan, who sang 'No More Auction Block' live and has released a recording in his *Bootleg Series*, never claimed or aspired to received notions of originality: 'There's always some precedent,' he said in 2017, 'most everything is a knockoff of something else.'[39] Brahms would have agreed. Nagged about the similarity between the concluding theme in his First Symphony and the 'Ode to Joy' in Beethoven's Ninth, he replied that 'any ass' could hear it.[40]

Besides, ownership is of no interest to the ears. We enjoy what we enjoy, and the contemporary edge in 'Don't Think Twice, It's All Right' compared to Paul Clayton's stately 'Who's Gonna Buy You Ribbons (When I'm Gone)' is what gives us pleasure, just as the variation in 'I Feel Fine' is what distinguishes it from the sponsor riff in Bobby Parker's 'Watch Your Step'. If Dylan is right and almost everything is a knock-off, the (artistic, not legal or moral) question to ask here is: does the use justify the theft? The role of influence here is more subtle than the idea that great artists steal where others borrow.* It's more about the use to which the existing idea is put, and the distance in that use from

---

* T. S. Eliot put it this way in 1920 in *The Sacred Wood*, saying: 'Immature poets imitate; mature poets steal,' reversing the way it had been used by W. H. Davenport Adams a generation earlier: 'That great poets imitate and improve, whereas small ones steal and spoil.' https://quoteinvestigator.com/2013/03/06/artists-steal/.

the original. As Goethe put it in *Faust*, more or less, you have to earn influence to own it.*

Peter, Paul and Mary's million-selling version of Blowin' in the Wind was followed by the Staple Singers, and by Sam Cooke, who recorded it for *Live at the Copa* and was impelled to write 'A Change Is Gonna Come'. The questions in Dylan's song are still unanswered, even in their original context: neither roads, streets nor beds were safe for Black Americans in 2020.

Freewheelin' is a classic album for the best of its songs, for what it did for Bob Dylan and the people who heard it, and for a cover which suggested how cute wised-up hipster love could be. But it's also a period piece in some respects. Dylan's reaction to what that love was like – 'Don't Think Twice' was written when his girlfriend Suze Rotolo was in Italy and threatening to stay – is musically resigned but lyrically barbed, more cruel than cool.

Dylan acquired a new producer in the course of the *Freewheelin'* sessions, with the veteran John Hammond replaced by Tom Wilson. Wilson was a Black Harvard-via-Fisk graduate from Texas who had recorded Sun Ra, Donald Byrd and Cecil Taylor for his own label, Transition Records. 'I thought folk music was for the dumb guys,' he recalled. 'This guy played like the dumb guys.' But he was won over by the lyrics, telling Albert Grossman: 'If you put some background to this you might have a white Ray Charles with a message.'[41] Wilson's dream was delayed, as Dylan's next two albums were entirely acoustic, but he would see it brought to fruition (with a more ambiguous message) when he produced Dylan with a band on *Bringing it All Back Home* and 'Like a Rolling Stone'.

In any case, Dylan was already experimenting with accompa-

---

* 'Was du ererbt von deinen Vätern hast | Erwirb es, um es zu besitzen': 'That which you inherit from your fathers | You must earn in order to possess.' *Goethe's Faust*, trans. Randall Jarrell (Farrar, Straus & Giroux, 1976), p. 35.

niment. There are numerous outtakes from the *Freewheelin'* sessions, including a startling déjà vu in 'That's All Right'. The song choice harks back to Dylan's teenage love of Presley, but Bruce Langhorne's guitar licks and the whole raucous shuffle shoot us forward to 'Maggie's Farm', recorded in the same key over two years later. Plugging in didn't signify much to Dylan, who later pointed out that country music was electric anyway.*

●

The Beatles had written just over half the songs on their first album, and Dylan the bulk of his second; *Surfin' Safari* and *Little Deuce Coupe* were chiefly written by Brian Wilson.† All were approaching self-sufficiency in a world where this remained the exception, not the rule. It helped that they were by design or default sufficiently self-absorbed to achieve it.

Having kicked the Minnesota traces, Dylan moved through other people's lives like a thief, rifling through their artistic possessions: friends who had lent him a room would find their records gone. Liam Clancy of the Clancy Brothers judged that it wasn't even necessary for Dylan to be a definitive person. 'He was a receiver,' concluded Clancy, 'he was possessed.'42

Brian Wilson, the greatest autodidact of them all, had his own otherness to live, a bruised interiority that mixed badly with the drugs that entered his life from 1964 onwards. But for now he kept stepping up: by May 1963 he was producing the Beach Boys' recording sessions. He brought tenacity, attention to detail and a competitive streak fuelled by his desire to master what others did well – and by his father's continued presence as manager.

---

* 'That's All Right' was also in the Beatles' repertoire at this point, and they recorded a lukewarm version for the BBC in July 1963.

† Working with Mike Love, or with early collaborators Gary Usher and Roger Christian.

By committing to Hamburg as a team, the Beatles had sheared away from their own peers, becoming both more worldly and more sophisticated. The shared experience soldered them into a single unit, absorbing life and music influence as one: Mick Jagger called them 'the four-headed monster'.[43] Lennon, depicted in the press as a contended house husband in the late 1970s, ventured in his final interview that 'so-called artists are completely selfish,' confessing that he still found it easier to write a song about his young son than to play with him. Putting anyone else first remained a challenge.[44]

23 August **'She Loves You'**

Dylan had employed a bare three chords on 'Blowin' in the Wind' (arrangements of the song, starting with Peter, Paul and Mary's, often add a minor {vi} chord on the first 'wind'). 'Surfin' USA' also used three chords, but 'She Loves You', which sounds just as carefree, uses three times as many. The writing shows the influence of contemporary soul in its use of minor chords, and the changes are lavish – slow it right down and it could be a pensive ballad. The trick lies in using those minor chords to create a rush, the descending 'yeah yeah yeah' motif teased on the electric guitar before the chorus, a delirious chant over thunderous toms.

Written in a Newcastle hotel room and recorded within a week, the third-person narrative feels thrilling – a bit of *really good news*, and one expression of a change in manners that swelled that summer as the Profumo affair broke in the UK. 'Life was never better,' wrote Philip Larkin of 1963 in his poem 'Annus Mirabilis', although Mandy Rice-Davies, whose celebrated response to Lord Astor's denial of an affair ('he would, wouldn't he') had helped to expose the Establishment's hypocrisy, later said she wished the year had not existed.[45] Life for the Astors of this world continued undisturbed: British prime minister David Cameron would later marry his granddaughter.

'She Loves You' tipped the scales from excitement to delirium. It was released in August during the group's six-day stint at the Bournemouth Gaumont, during which the music could still be heard; by November at the Winter Gardens, it was inaudible above the screams. Beatlemania was named in the press that autumn, and when at the Ardwick Apollo in Manchester Gerry and the Pacemakers dared to sing 'Twist and Shout' on the same bill, they were booed continually.[46]

●

Another song was recorded in the first week of July 1963: the Ronettes' 'Be My Baby'. The song was only kept from number one in the US by Jimmy Gilmer and the Fireballs' 'Sugar Shack', and the contrast is instructive. 'Sugar Shack' is a sunny, well-crafted piece of pop, like the theme tune to a kids' TV show, and has been forgotten. The narrative is wrapped up in conventional terms, as the 'cute little girly' working at the coffee shop becomes the singer's wife, and their life is pretty much over by 1:30: 'we just sit around and dream of those old memories.'

'Be My Baby' is like dark wine next to soda pop, the singer zeroing in on the object of her desire. The only clear things in the Phil Spector production are his future wife Ronnie's wiry voice, the high-mixed claves and Hal Blaine's drums. All else – pianos, guitars, saxophones, strings – is muffled, the colour of cloud about to break. Drums thunder through the fade, and for all the determined romance of the lyric there is something heartbreaking about it.

Brian Wilson had to stop his car when he first heard it on the radio – 'I really did flip out, balls-out totally freaked out when I heard it' – and set about trying to work out what was *in* that sound.[47] An all-star cast might have asked the same question: session musicians like Carol Kaye and Leon Russell, and studio guests including Sonny and Cher and Darlene Love, can barely have distinguished their own parts in the final mix.

The song became an obsession for Wilson, played over and over as the years went by, a two-and-a-half-minute madeleine for his kids to remember childhood by. It's unlikely, though, that this was the first time he had heard a Phil Spector production. 'He's A Rebel' was a number one for the Crystals in November 1962, and it has a striking depth of field in the production, saxophones gurgling far below the tinkling piano. It was broadly, fondly, in the doo-wop tradition, and it was carried by the strength of Gene Pitney's songwriting: the song sets off in F but modulates beautifully to F♯ for the first chorus, an effect that is both striking and subtle – the obvious temptation to move up another semitone into G at the next chorus is resisted. Once was enough to make the record strange, to make you want to hear it again.

'Be My Baby' is also a skilful piece of writing, moving tentatively from the tonic E {I} to F♯m {ii} on 'needed you' before drawing confidence from the gospel-infused major chords in the bridge. But it's made by the arrangement and production – the heartbeat drum pattern, hopeful backing vocals and sheer impulse in the music carrying Ronnie's aching voice into the chorus.*

The early rock and rollers had been forces of nature: Elvis wild-eyed and swivelling, dry-humping Eisenhower's post-war America; Little Richard stood at the keyboard loose as a push puppet and hanging a foot up on the piano; Jerry Lee Lewis summoning little scraps of nothing into hellfire, hollering, transported. But the

---

* Not orchestrated but accidental – Hal Blaine dropped a stick. Chuck Parker, 'Classic drum sounds: Be My Baby', *MusicRadar* (18 Jan. 2014), https://www.musicradar.com/news/drums/classic-drum-sounds-be-my-baby-590941.

recorded sound itself was comparatively spindly.*

Oddballs and innovators started to push at the limits of the thin recorded sound: Joe Meek in the UK, Phil Spector in the US. 'I've tried,' said Meek of 1959's galactically themed *I Hear A New World*, 'I mean I've had to do it rather carefully, to create the impression of space, of things moving in front of you.'[48] 'Telstar', his 1962 hit with the Tornadoes, starts with whirring tape, as if to conjure the depths of the universe: in truth its soaring melody is more suggestive of a Kenwood Chef than a rocket being launched into space. Anyone who has worked on home recordings will recognize it as the sound one tries to mix away, maddeningly thin and muddy at the same time.

While Meek was operating from a flat in the Holloway Road, Spector worked out of Gold Star Studios in LA, with access to the all-round smarts of the local session musicians later known as the Wrecking Crew.[49] By concealing his means in the reverberant mix, Spector created a mask within a mask: the finished track was no longer a straightforward record of the musicians' parts, designed to show what they sounded like, but a transformation that effectively disguised what the original performances had been. Even the Ronettes, Ronnie aside, were absent from proceedings for 'Be My Baby'.

Its impact on Wilson's work can be read clearly in the girl group songs he produced for the Honeys, featuring Wilson's girlfriend, Marilyn: from 1963's 'The One You Can't Have', which channels the Crystals' 'Da Doo Ron Ron', to February 1964's 'He's a Doll', full of Spector-style flourishes and a nostalgic sax solo. Brian

---

* When Dylan calls it 'skeleton music [that] came out of the darkness', he captures the menace but also a stripped-down vibe that can be heard in the shimmering late 1950s gospel of the Staple Singers: a teenage Dylan was magnetized by 'Uncloudy Day', rightly figuring that Mavis Staples, whose contralto carries it, must have been around the same age. (The scene is set for a romantic ending, but she later declined his proposal of marriage.) Skeleton music: 'Q&A with Bill Flanagan', *bobdylan.com* (22 Mar. 2017), http://www.bobdylan.com/news/qa-with-bill-flanagan/.

Wilson never bettered 'Be My Baby' on its own terms, but by blending its richer sound with the Beach Boys' voices and his own songwriting he was able to break new ground, extending the scope of Spector's work to a point where it sounded wholly original.

16 September **SURFER GIRL**, 7 October **LITTLE DEUCE COUPE**

Brian's apprenticeship ended with *Surfer Girl*, released that September, which he produced in full. A string section appears on 'The Surfer Moon', and the clicky, sticky, pizzicato sounds delight – 'Catch a Wave' even features a harp, played by Mike Love's sister Maureen. A dreamy triplet acoustic guitar part opens 'Your Summer Dream', although inevitably we're in a car; it's as if Sinatra had sung 'In the Wee Small Hours of the Morning' to an Oldsmobile.

The ascending melody to 'Surfer Girl' is derived from the Disney song 'When You Wish Upon A Star' – warbled to within an inch of its life on the *Pinocchio* soundtrack, and revived by Dion and the Belmonts in 1960. Like Dylan, Wilson was prepared to borrow and steal at this point, and 'South Bay Surfer' reaches back even further – it repurposes Stephen Foster's 'Old Folks at Home' and swings delightfully, at least until one looks up the lyrics of the minstrel song original.*

---

* An American standard, and the state song of Florida, Ray Charles had made it over as 'Swanee River Rock (Talkin' 'Bout That River)' in 1959. Oddly enough, the Beatles had recorded a variant in 1961 in their brief incarnation as Tony Sheridan's backing group. Within a year or two all any club band needed to do was cover Lennon-McCartney songs; even the Supremes, their only commercial rival in the US, would do so. But to begin with, the Beatles – partly curious, partly crowd-pleasing – mixed contemporary covers with numbers by Cole Porter, Hoagy Carmichael and Consuelo Velázquez. In covering a Stephen Foster song from the 1850s, the Beach Boys referenced an even older tradition; the Byrds, having concluded their *Mr. Tambourine Man* LP with Vera Lynn's wartime hit 'We'll Meet Again', revisited Foster's 'Oh! Susanna' on *Turn! Turn! Turn!* These temporal and stylistic shifts are largely lost to today's music, often so intent on recapturing the sounds of the 1960s that it ignores the older styles that contributed to its range of expression.

Little Deuce Coupe was devoted almost exclusively to cars and released only a month later, but invention still escapes constraint. 'No-Go Showboat' is about a prize-winning car that's 'just for looks, man, not for drags', and opens with an almost maniacally high C♯.* But the song features another lovely shift from major to minor, emphasized by a change in the drum pattern; insouciant and clever, it brings to mind the resourcefulness of Rossini. The composer worked at a similar pace at the same age, and even when the writing was under pressure of time he couldn't help doing something interesting.[†]

22 November **WITH THE BEATLES**

The Beatles' second album, *With the Beatles*, was released on 22 November, the Friday President Kennedy was shot in Dallas. The cover is in stark contrast to the clunky colour and garish fonts of *Please Please Me*. There the album title had echoed the hit single, subtitled 'with Love Me Do and 12 other songs'. *With the Beatles* confines itself to the title, set above an austere black-and-white photo where their faces float like moons. Other photos from the same session – held at noon on a summer's day in a Bournemouth hotel – reveal the band's roll-neck sweaters, and in one they are grinning. But the photograph chosen for the cover shows them as Garbo appeared in the final shot of *Queen Christina* (1933), directed by Rouben Mamoulian to 'think of nothing'. The band who were actively changing the showbiz world are presented as the calm at the eye of the storm, alert but impassive. The singles that

---

* Falsetto, but still a semitone higher than the famous high C's in 'Ah! Mes Amis' from Donizetti's *La Fille du Régiment* (1840).

† Bel canto opera provides an interesting parallel to these early Beach Boys records. Sonically gorgeous, thematically flimsy, prompted as much by the immediate demands of the market as by artistic intention, musical feeling escapes almost despite the form – but escape it does, repeatedly. Rossini completed four operas in the year he was twenty-one, the age Brian Wilson reached in June 1963.

made the storm, 'She Loves You' and 'I Want to Hold Your Hand', and whose recording bookended sessions for the LP, don't even appear on the album – this time the 'other songs' stand alone.

'It Won't Be Long' sets the tone. It reprises the triple *yeah*s from 'She Loves You' in the call and response, but the lead guitar is richer in the mix and the ride cymbal – a constant on this LP – crashes ceaselessly. 'It Won't Be Long' not only sounds better than 'She Loves You', but has a beautiful bridge where the pressure drops before we are propelled back into the verse by Ringo's toms. The canard that he wasn't even the best drummer in the Beatles (not a quip from Lennon, but someone else's joke in a 1981 radio comedy*) is a damaging one. In truth Starr was versatile, inventive and superbly responsive to the music: a listening bandmate is better than a virtuoso one.

The different personalities in the lead voices and writing start to emerge here, echoing their stage stances: McCartney winning, bobbing, bounding up and down musical stairs; Lennon planted, implacable, exploring the emotional potential in less extensive melodic space. Each gets straight to the point: the confidence in Lennon's plaintive 'All I've Got to Do' and in McCartney's exuberant 'All My Loving' is equivalent. Harrison's 'Don't Bother Me', his first song for the group, has its own distinct flavour: full of minor chords and heavy with reverb, it anticipates Gene Clark's ballads with the Byrds. Harrison was a superb and characterful singer in his own right, and few singers have featured on more great records – he can be heard on nearly every Beatles song, never mind his own. The youngest member, he wouldn't have survived without a certain flintiness, and he later recalled the band's certainty that they were going to make it: 'We were

---

* The programme was 'Radio Active', written by Geoffrey Perkins and broadcast in October 1981. 'Did John Lennon Say Ringo "Wasn't Even the Best Drummer in The Beatles"?', *Radio X*, 7 July 2020, https://www.radiox.co.uk/artists/beatles/did-john-lennon-say-ringo-wasnt-even-best-drummer/.

just cocky. There was no justification for it – I don't know, just an inner feeling.'[50]

The Beatles were now, by virtue of their success, broadcasting not only their own music but the music they loved. Where the sleeve notes to *Please Please Me* had denied that the group sounded transatlantic, asserting that the Beatles' only real influence was 'the unique brand of Rhythm and Blues folk music which abounds on Merseyside', *With the Beatles* acknowledged the source material more clearly: from their 'immense admiration' for the Miracles, to 'professional respect' for the unfancied Donays.

The Beatles covered these rhythm and blues songs straight, neither hiding their sources nor mimicking them: their Liverpool accents subtly reshape 'Please Mister Postman' and 'Roll Over Beethoven'. The best of the covers are '...Postman' and Smokey Robinson's 'You Really Got a Hold on Me', played heavier than the originals, steamy as a bus window on a rainy day. It's easy to see what the Beatles and especially Lennon heard in the girl group recordings, with their frayed, open-throated vocals; the Beatles' sound, lacking horns, is filled out by the ubiquitous ride cymbal and the vocal oddness of men singing female harmony parts.

Stung by a revisionist *New York Times* article by Craig McGregor in June 1970 which said the Beatles had first exploited the 'hot' tradition of Black American music and then betrayed that tradition by cooling it,[51] Lennon wrote to its author to stress that they had loved the music and 'wanted to spread it in <u>any way we could</u>'. We can read Lennon's reply in the light of white privilege, but it says something about how the process felt at the time, to the Beatles at least: 'It wasn't a rip off,' Lennon insists, 'it was a love in.'[52]

The Beatles had mixed their rock and roll with ballads and standards from the start. Paul McCartney came upon the 1950 show tune 'Till There Was You' via Peggy Lee, and it proved a useful calling card, opening their Royal Variety Performance that November and sweetening their first Ed Sullivan appearance in February 1964. In that context it reads like a ploy, one for the aunties, but it had been in their repertoire for some time – at least as far back as their audition sets in 1962. It was part of the idiosyncrasy that had made them so hard to sign, but their familiarity with the style would inform the ballad-writing on *A Hard Day's Night*.

●

The success of 'She Loves You' and 'Blowin' in the Wind' in the summer of 1963 propelled their authors into rarefied, if contrasting, social and political space. While the Beatles' ascent was crowned by their televised appearance at the Royal Variety Performance in November, Dylan's association with the civil rights movement peaked in August at the March on Washington, enshrined in memory by Martin Luther King's 'I Have A Dream' speech. Its partly improvised climax was prompted by the gospel singer Mahalia Jackson, who urged him to 'tell them about the dream' – a theme he had used in Detroit two months earlier but which was not in the script that day.

James Baldwin was considered too radical to be trusted on the podium in Washington, and women like Lena Horne and Rosa Parks were sidelined. Yet twenty-one-year-old Dylan was asked to sing. 'Blowin' in the Wind' was taken by Peter, Paul and Mary, so he performed 'Pawn in Their Game', a topical but nuanced choice. The song, about the assassination of Medgar Evers, can be read as a deconstruction of systemic racism. But it evinces a degree of sociological empathy for the killer that could have jarred: Evers had only been killed in June.

Perhaps the song choice hinted at Dylan's thorny relationship with party lines. As it was, his close association with the movement didn't survive the year. He had initially stood out on the folk scene for his lack of political engagement, and now Kennedy's death shook his faith in progress: 'Don't even hope to change things,' was his immediate takeout.[53] He stumbled into trouble in New York when receiving the Tom Paine award from the Emergency Civil Liberties Committee (ECLC) in December. Laughter and applause at the Americana Hotel turned to boos and hisses as he extemporized a speech in which he wished the attendees were younger, criticized how Black Americans had dressed for the march on Washington, and at length empathized with – of all the people in America in December 1963 – Lee Harvey Oswald. 'I got to stand up and say I saw things that he felt, in me,' said Dylan. 'Not to go that far and shoot,' he clarified hastily, but it was too late. 'It is true that he is not as respectable as Lord Russell, the winner of last year's award,' admitted Corliss Lamont of the ECLC in a follow-up letter to attendees, 'but neither was Tom Paine.'[54]

Lamont appended to his own supportive letter a response by Dylan himself. It took the form of a lengthy message in free verse in which he revisited his speech, evinced pride in his roots, and asserted his right to make art free of claims to truth: it was 'a fierce heavy feeling', he said, to be burdened with unnamed expectation. It's a reminder of how close Dylan was to the storm and spirit of the times in 1963, and also of how young he was – still only twenty-one, and a little drunk, when he made the speech.

The stakes were different at London's Prince of Wales Theatre in November. The Royal Variety Performance was the show business event of the year, bringing to the surface the snobbery of a small and class-bound island. The Beatles were part of a vanguard of actors and photographers who were working or lower-middle class in origin, and – with the score of British life still marked *common*, *posh*, *U* and *non-U*, and all points in between – their Scouse accents were a talking point. Asked if they would tone them down for the occasion, McCartney replied that not everyone spoke like the BBC.[55] Lennon was at this stage wild and unpredictable, on occasion greeting cheering crowds on balcony appearances with a Hitler salute, and had threatened to tell the audience to rattle their fucking jewellery.* In the event he dropped the profanity and made the line cute, acknowledging the cheek with an apologetic smile and drawing a gracious wave from the Queen Mother and assorted stiffs in the Royal Box. 'Most intriguing,' she is reported to have concluded, which in upper-class English can mean practically anything.[56] Both shared the bill with a different kind of royalty that night, Marlene Dietrich posing gamely for pictures with the group at rehearsal, a sparrow in a house coat.

29 November 'I Want to Hold Your Hand'

If there's one event that sets the train of mid-1960s musical influence in motion, it's the release of 'I Want to Hold Your Hand' on the last Friday of November 1963. The song is marvellously abrupt, all handclaps and twangs, quickly reaching a manic peak on 'haaand': it dusts off and dismisses the old rock and roll turnaround in a supremely concise six-second chorus. The repeated bridge, dropping to the {v} minor, is breathing space, but not for long: Dylan can't have been the only one to mishear the already suggestive 'I can't hide' line as 'I get high'. And a whole generation, straining at the bonds of the previous century's morality and their parents' wartime sacrifice, did just that. 'She Loves You' had been released in the US to no acclaim at all on

---

* He had beaten someone up at Paul McCartney's twenty-first birthday party in June for pressing him on a rumour that he and Brian Epstein had had an affair. 'John Lennon beats up Cavern DJ Bob Wooler at Paul McCartney's 21st birthday party', https://www.beatlesbible.com/1963/06/18/paul-mccartneys-21st-birthday-party/.

Swan Records, as Brian Epstein struggled to land a meaningful record deal. But 'I Want to Hold Your Hand', the last release of their breakthrough year, was taken up by Capitol – and by the public, who bought 10,000 copies an hour in New York City alone when it was rush-released at Christmas.

Despite its ubiquity since then, we can still taste the surprise in 'I Want to Hold Your Hand', a song which with its abrupt twists and turns was as crooked as the Beatles' teeth. Without that single, Dylan wouldn't have had to sit up and listen. Without the Beatles' first US tour (in truth a whistle stop with two live shows sandwiched between appearances on the *Ed Sullivan Show*), the Beach Boys could have rested on their laurels. Without the British Invasion, the future members of the Byrds might have tarried on the folk circuit with its Ramblers, Minstrels and Balladeers.* The Beatles had already seen off manufactured UK pop, but now the folk revival lay exposed. They were about to return the singular gift of rock and roll to the soil of its origin.

---

* David Crosby played with Les Baxter's Balladeers, and Gene Clark with the New Christy Minstrels.

1964: LISTENING IN

My encounter with the Beatles was a falling in love: a steady pull on my internal organs, the terminus of thought. But it was not my first time. I had already fallen hard for the landscape of the Lake District on family holidays, and in their music I experienced something of the same variety: placid lakes and rainy crags, lonely tarns and melodious fells. Just as nothing felt the same as the Lake District, the pretty milkmaid lanes of Sussex rendered flat as Sunday by comparison, nothing sounded as interesting as the Beatles. A memory blends the two loves: sitting in the back of the Cortina estate with my sister singing songs from the *White Album* over and over, as the brown bracken of August peeled by. There was no Walkman, no cassette, no way to take it with you save by heart.

I was thrilled to see Paul McCartney on *Top of the Pops* when I was twelve, but I knew 'Mull of Kintyre' wasn't the real thing. The Beatles were already gone. So while their music entered me as straightforwardly as sunshine, loving it was also an imaginative engagement, a reaching for a world abstracted from me by time and upbringing. I was experiencing in microcosm what the country had experienced fifteen years before, a release from stricture, the hand on the shoulder of the old culture.

There is a sensory, experiential quality to the Beatles' music which recommends itself to childhood. Their songs are never as urbane as the music on *Pet Sounds*, and their lyrics are neither as penetrating nor as expansive as Dylan's. Even at its most outré their music does not demand subtle attention but claims the heart, takes it up in its sphere. I have adult friends with broad tastes who revere the Beach Boys or Dylan or both, but who don't care for the Beatles: perhaps it's a love that has to be acquired like a second language, before adolescence. After all, some of our artistic passions are time-bound. Daniel Mendelsohn has written about Rimbaud only fully making sense to readers in adolescence, and records his disappointment on first reading him seriously in his mid-forties: 'Although I found much that dazzled and impressed me,' he concludes, 'I couldn't get swept away.'[57] This fading can be poignant, signalling a part of one's perception that is gone, changed with the cells on their seven-year passage. I experience it often with poetry – even with poetry itself, which I once loved as much as music. But where Lorca now speaks to me like a memory, Chopin and the Beatles still speak to my living ear. And what was inside me, what had me drawing their faces over and over as I listened to the records I had borrowed and took so long to return, was the music they began to make in 1964.

January to June 1964

		Bob Dylan	Beatles	Beach Boys
1964	Jan	[13] THE TIMES THEY ARE A-CHANGIN'		
		Dylan and the Beatles hear each other's music		
	Feb		[7] *The Beatles hit the States*	[3] 'Fun, Fun, Fun'
	Mar		[20] 'Can't Buy Me Love'	[2] SHUT DOWN VOLUME 2
	Apr	[26] *Dylan first takes LSD*		
	May			[11] 'I Get Around'
	Jun		[19] Long Tall Sally (EP)	

The Beatles, Beach Boys and (as a songwriter) Bob Dylan had

enjoyed wild success in 1963. They were by nature enquiring and self-critical, working in an industry that was inherently competitive, measured in sales and chart placings. But that impetus was now turbocharged by each other's music, which they heard for the first time at the turn of the year. Dylan first had an impact on the Beatles in January, when they discovered his music in Paris while working on the songs for *A Hard Day's Night*; as this was also when Dylan and the Beach Boys started to pay attention to the Beatles, it's fair to say that this winter changed everything.

January Dylan and the Beatles hear each other's music

Beatles records were already distinctive enough to have attracted the attention of classical music critics. *The Times*' William Mann famously identified pandiatonic clusters in 'This Boy' as early as Christmas 1963, and the Aeolian cadence he spotted in 'Not a Second Time' has been ridiculed ever since. (Lennon wondered if it was an exotic bird, and Mann's comparison of the song's ending to Mahler's 'Das Lied von der Erde' ('Song of the Earth') is perhaps a stretch.) But he was trying to convey in the old language what in the new music was so arresting. 'This Boy' was the B-side to 'I Want to Hold Your Hand', and the harmonies do feel strange in ways that songs like – for example – the Miracles' 'I've Been Good to You' do not. Mann's article is perceptive and prescient.* 'One gets the impression,' he writes, 'that they think simultaneously of harmony and melody, so firmly are the major tonic sevenths and ninths built into their tunes'; he can see that they are streets ahead of the immediate competition.[58]

A famous example of this is the unexpected fourth chord in 'I Want to Hold Your Hand', the B major {III} which we hear

---

* Lennon thought he was writing in the style of the Miracles, but the Beatles' use of three-part harmony as a lead instrument is quite different.

first on 'under*stand*' and then in the octave leap of 'I want to hold your *hand*'. This has musicologists using the old language tied up in knots, identifying an aborted modulation or deceptive cadence when really it's a rush, a lucky find, the chord that – as Lennon and McCartney, writing at the piano, immediately realized – made the song.

Dylan encountered this strangeness at the same time as other Americans, at the turn of the year. By April 1964, the Beatles were occupying all five top spots on the Billboard Hot 100,* and Dylan was driving through Colorado reeling from that fact, and from their music: 'They were doing things nobody was doing,' he told Anthony Scaduto in 1971. 'I started thinking it was so far out that I couldn't deal with it.'[59] He also picked up on the 'outrageous, just outrageous' chord changes, and on the harmonies which made sense of it all.

Something else struck Bob Dylan: he saw that 'you could only do that with other musicians.' As we have seen, he had tried this during late autumn sessions in 1962, but this was more in the way of accompaniment than organic ensemble playing. Hearing the Beatles was the seed for a real band sound, even if he didn't let on how much he dug the group for now.[60]

As it turned out, as Dylan was discovering *them*, the Beatles were discovering *him*. Their Christmas Show concluded, the Beatles spent most of January in Paris, accommodated in style at the George V hotel just off the Champs-Élysées. They earned this by playing two or three sets a day at the Olympia Theatre, learning after the first night that 'I Want to Hold Your Hand' had gone to number one in the States. The group were pictured celebrating the news, Brian Epstein wearing a chamber pot on his head, George Martin sitting by his side, hair combed tightly

---

* In order: 'Can't Buy Me Love', 'Twist and Shout', 'She Loves You', 'I Want to Hold Your Hand', and 'Please Please Me'; in fact, they had eight tracks in the Top 10 at this time.

against his head, as if visiting from another time and place. High jinks were accompanied by high stakes, as Epstein immediately received a telephone offer of $100,000 for a single show in Detroit.

On a visit to American Forces Network radio they noticed some Dylan records and emerged with *The Freewheelin' Bob Dylan* and *Bob Dylan*, although probably not with *The Times They Are 'a-Changin'*, which had only just been released ('With God On Our Side' would have been an interesting addition to the Forces playlist).[61] 'Paul got them off whoever they belonged to,' Lennon told *Melody Maker* a year later, 'and for the rest of our three weeks in Paris we didn't stop playing them.'[62]

Lennon and McCartney had been installed in a suite with a piano so they could work on songs for *A Hard Day's Night*, and it's telling that Dylan entered the picture as writing for the movie and album began; there is a photo of them with the *Freewheelin'* LP.[63] 'We all went potty on Dylan,' Lennon said.[64] He and Harrison went a little potty over the Ronettes, too, encountering them and Phil Spector at a London party on a night off: Harrison went on to date Estelle Bennett, while Lennon, trying his luck, was turned down by Ronnie.[65]

Based purely on the music they were making at the time, it's hard to see what the Beatles and Dylan saw in each other. But their musical intelligence meant they recognized quality; and their openness to influence, their ability to absorb and transform, was what had brought them this far. They also recognized in each other's work music they knew. A page from George Harrison's school exercise books lists faithfully Lonnie Donegan records from the mid-1950s (at 78, 45 and 33 rpm), and the songs are a snapshot of the musical landscape Dylan and indeed Johnny Cash would soon travel, including 'John Henry', 'Stockalee' [*sic*], 'Wabash Cannonball' and 'I Shall Not be Moved': ragtime, folk, spiritual, country and blues.[66]

Paths of influence aren't always obvious, even when artists think they are – John Lennon never sounded like Smokey Robinson, although he fancied it so. Even when they aimed to replicate their own work, it didn't follow: 'We say, we'll do one like 'The Word' – make it like that,' said Lennon, but 'it never does turn out like that.'[67] Epiphanies can take time to bear fruit: Lennon's most overtly Dylanesque song, 'You've Got to Hide Your Love Away', was a year off, while Dylan, hiding his own love for the Beatles, gives no hint of it on *Another Side*. But starting with the acoustic thrum of *A Hard Day's Night*, and moving through the more introspective songs that open *Beatles for Sale*, Lennon in particular began to absorb the raw, confessional feel of Dylan's music.

_{13 January} **THE TIMES THEY ARE A-CHANGIN'**

Dylan's early artistic voice reaches its fullest expression on *The Times They Are a-Changin'*. He sounds awful weary, and the material is as sombre as his expression on the front cover suggests. But it's tonally coherent, as much sad as angry; the Marine Band harmonica is reined in, to advantage. The album gutters like a candle around a last hand of protest songs, including his finest, 'The Lonesome Death of Hattie Carroll'.

'Boots of Spanish Leather' is the only straight-up love song, un-sentimental but not unkind. He sounds even more beat on 'One Too Many Mornings', which would roar in the face of exhaustion when played live two years later, but which here sounds as pallid as the dawn. It's a song about a state of mind rather than the state of the nation, and it points forward. 'I'm one too many mornings, and a thousand miles behind,' he sings, sounding as if the world is asleep by his side and he doesn't want to wake it.

Even the lengthy free verse sleeve note sounds like a surrender of sorts: after all the bluff about living in Gallup, Cheyenne and

Sioux Falls, here was a biography of his own town, neither rich nor poor but – and here he identifies most with the abandoned North Hibbing – deserted and dying: 'The town I grew up in,' he wrote, 'is the one that has left me with my legacy visions.'

By the time the record was released, Dylan had already outgrown it. The topical focus of his first albums was strongly influenced by his relationships with Suze Rotolo, the artistic daughter of Communist parents, and Joan Baez, raised pacifist in a Quaker household. That focus now changed. On Boxing Day 1963 he was introduced to Allen Ginsberg, reviving his earlier love of the Beats, and by early February he was telling his entourage all about the French symbolist poet Rimbaud. 'That's the kind of stuff means something,' he told them. 'That's the kind of writing I'm gonna do.' Later he recalled the impact of Rimbaud's famous 'je est un autre' ('I is another'), deadpanning: 'I wished someone would have mentioned that to me earlier.'[68]

3 February **'Fun, Fun, Fun'**, 2 March **SHUT DOWN VOLUME 2**, 11 May **'I Get Around'**

There's no evidence that the Beatles and the Beach Boys were especially conscious of one other at the turn of 1964. Only 'Surfin' USA' had charted in the UK, peaking at number 34; Mike Love says he knew about the Beatles,[69] but 'She Loves You' hadn't yet hit in the US. The competition in Wilson's mind at this point was Phil Spector, and the sound of Beach Boys records had been getting progressively richer since he had heard 'Be My Baby'. Autumn's 'Be True to Your School' features the Honeys on cheerleader backing vocals alongside horns and pipes, and they were never more broish – jacked up on the football game, true to their school and girl.

But the subject matter was starting to expand, almost imperceptibly at first. 'Fun, Fun, Fun', recorded on the first day of 1964, reflects this. A narrative song about modest teenage rebellion in the Chuck Berry tradition – announced with the guitar riff from 'Johnny B. Goode' – it rocks with the help of the Wrecking Crew, saxophones and a six-string bass. The hook is irresistible, enhanced by genuinely enjoyable lyrics (comparing the Indy 500 to a Roman chariot race) and the song is only marred by a cheesy organ solo.

In a song recorded a few days later, 'Don't Worry Baby', the sound and feel coalesce deliciously. The rhythm explicitly references 'Be My Baby', and with Brian Wilson singing up high, the song, ostensibly about a car race, signals a deeper anxiety, like someone mouthing 'help me' in a video. There's no solo over the middle eight: it's an invitation to listen to how delightful the backing is.

The Beach Boys were on tour in Australia and New Zealand in January 1964, and would recall coming back to find that the game had changed with the Beatles' arrival.[70] In reality it was probably worse. The New Zealand leg ended on 1 February, so they would have arrived home in time to see the Beatles take the country by storm on the *Ed Sullivan Show*: 73 million people tuned in for their first appearance on 9 February, well over a third of the US population.

Part of Wilson's complex make-up was a strong competitive streak, and Hal Blaine remembers him being spooked by the British Invasion: 'That's it, we're out of business.'[71] It didn't help that the Beach Boys' record company, Capitol, was now the Beatles' label in the US: promotional resources were diverted, with Capitol sales employees instructed to wear Beatle wigs at work 'until further notice'.[72] On the market that winter were merchandise items ranging from hats and T-shirts to cookies, egg cups and ice cream; branded motor scooters for kids and even a 'Beatlemobile for adults' were in the offing. 'Anytime you spell "beetle" with an "a" in it,' Ringo was quoted as saying, 'we get the money.' [73]

The only option for Wilson was to work harder, a resolve evident in the crunchy hum of 'I Get Around', their most tightly constructed single to date. Like 'She Loves You' it kicks off with the hook, and the whole song is in the pocket before twenty seconds are up, the chorus circling ever higher like smoke from a contented burger stand: that the lyrics are literally about driving up and down is immaterial. The stacked vocal intro, daring hand-clapped stops and purring instrumental engine made the song their first US number one, and it was the song they led with when they did make it onto the *Ed Sullivan Show* in September.

Mandatory Beatle wigs aside, Capitol retained their enthusiasm for releasing Beach Boys albums, and their fifth duly appeared in March (the Beatles had only made two at this point). Thuddingly titled *Shut Down Volume 2*, it wasn't even a second volume of their own work: the original *Shut Down* was a 1963 hot rod compilation featuring two Beach Boys songs alongside offerings such as 'Brontosaurus Stomp' by the Piltdown Men and Robert Mitchum singing 'The Ballad of Thunder Road'. The road to art pop was full of potholes.

July and August 1964

1964		Bob Dylan	Beatles	Beach Boys
	Jul		[10] A HARD DAY'S NIGHT	[13] ALL SUMMER LONG
	Aug	[8] ANOTHER SIDE OF BOB DYLAN		[24] 'When I Grow Up (To Be a Man)'
		[28] The Beatles and Dylan meet for the first time, in NYC		

Midsummer 1964 saw the release inside a month of three albums wholly written (and in Brian Wilson's case, produced) by our three leads. *A Hard Day's Night* was the Beatles' third LP, *All Summer Long* the Beach Boys' sixth, and *Another Side of Bob Dylan* his fourth – at fifty minutes, it was twice the length of *All Summer Long*.

They were self-sufficient, and they were ahead of the game – the Rolling Stones had just released their first LP. Now fully aware of one another, the stirrings of mutual exchange would be hastened by the first in-person meeting at the end of August, when Bob Dylan drove down to Manhattan to meet the Beatles.

Their work was still distinct, but the sounds now began to coalesce until briefly, in 1965, it would sound as if they were working on the same broad project. Collectively they were about to give birth to the Byrds, a group whose success depended on all three of them.

[10] July A HARD DAY'S NIGHT

The Beatles were recording between shows all through 1964: they appeared live on the first day of the year and the last, and on Christmas Day, and on 123 other days. You can hear that breathless rush all through *A Hard Day's Night*, the Beatles' most tonally and thematically consistent album. The songwriting, performances and production are by turns raucous and restrained, insouciant and sophisticated. The photos on the album cover, like the movie, are in black-and-white, but it all *feels* like colour: the invention in the music never dips, and listening to the LP is about the happiest thing a human being can do with half an hour.

The title track retains that early strangeness, the ride cymbal that so dominated *With the Beatles* still ringing. But there's a new ease and warmth to the sound, tumbling along to bongos and cowbell. This time the magic chord is the B minor {iii} 'When I'm *home*', where McCartney's voice takes over for the middle eight. It's another example of a minor Beatle chord that isn't sad, which is part of the bizarrerie in these early records.[74] There's a lovely moment at 1:52 where Lennon takes over after the second middle eight with a casual 'Mmm,' as if in passionate conversation.

The song's opening chord has been fretted over more than the *Mary Celeste*, and not only by guitarists. It's been excavated with audio software and decomposed by mathematics: Dr Jason I. Brown of Dalhousie University, Nova Scotia, used the Fourier transform to detect the presence of 29,375 frequencies, including harmonics and ambient noise captured in the recording, and at length unearthed a hidden piano.[75] The conclusion to his paper carries the excitement of Sherlock Holmes building up to a proof: 'But what about the three left over D3's? If all belonged to a single piano note, then where would the single D4 come from?' *The Case of the Stray D4*, the 'perfect reasoning and observing machine' of Holmes's mind made flesh in a formula.[76]

You can get close to the Beatles' Tristan chord on any old guitar by playing a first-position F with a G on top, as George Harrison confirmed.[77] But there's more to it: McCartney plays a surprising

D on the bass.* Add to that the compression of the mono mix – which is how most people heard it in 1964 – and you have a moment which, bashed out in a hurry by brilliant people, will always resonate in hopeful ambiguity.†

A comparison with Wagner's Tristan chord does lead somewhere: Robert Erickson described that as 'an identifiable sound, an entity beyond its functional qualities in a tonal 'organization'.[78] This is pretty much what musicologists are dealing with when they try and unravel certain chords or changes in songs by the Beatles, who knew what they were doing artistically but were unbound – and unsupported, when it came to it – by theory. The parallel ends there: the *Hard Day's Night* chord is a momentary sensation rather than part of an extended thought structure, and unlike the Tristan chord, you know what's coming next is going to be a blast.

'I'm A Loser', from *Beatles for Sale*, is often cited as the first fruit of Lennon's engagement with Dylan. But the *A Hard Day's Night* album already bears traces: driven by his acoustic guitar, the songwriting is direct and forthright as well as musically inventive. Lennon later described assimilating the music around him by using other people's tunes for the words he had in his head, and it's not impossible to imagine him trying out 'I should have known with a girl like you' to the tune of 'Blowin' in the Wind' before alighting on 'I Should Have Known Better'.[79] The title track certainly started out in Dylanesque mode, Lennon admitting as much a year later: 'We Beatle-fied it before we recorded it.'[80]

There are a number of intriguing and satisfying song pairs on

---

* Play the F chord with a G on top, take your third finger off the D string to let it ring, and you'll be as close as you can be to it on a six-string guitar: I claim my £1,000.

† There's a touching moment in a recent profile where McCartney and his touring band pause in rehearsal to try and figure out what he does on bass at the end of the first verse, half a century later. Chris Heath, 'The Untold Stories of Paul McCartney', *GQ* (11 Sep. 2018), https://www.gq.com/story/the-untold-stories-of-paul-mccartney.

A Hard Day's Night, contributing to its overall coherence. These include the title track and 'I Should Have Known Better', both in G; 'Tell Me Why' and 'Any Time at All', both in D; 'Things We Said Today' and 'I'll Be Back', both in A minor (the former decisively, thrillingly, and the latter uncertainly, slipping in and out of the major); and the two side one ballads, 'If I Fell' and 'And I Love Her', in different keys but sharing a lilt that owes something to bossa nova.

The Latin feel is made explicit by the claves on 'And I Love Her', but is only hinted at in 'If I Fell' – when the Brazilian singer Rita Lee covered it, a little percussion was enough to bring it home.* The feeling of sand between the toes is new to the Beatles' own songs, and for all that they had spent the summer of 1963 performing in resorts as glamorous as Blackpool, Margate, Llandudno and Rhyl, travelling to Miami in February 1964 was – like any Briton's first sight of dazzling sun – a revelation. 'Miami was like paradise,' McCartney recalled. 'We had never been anywhere where there were palm trees.'[81] Busy prepping their second *Ed Sullivan Show* performance, they enjoyed a solitary day off – but some of the sand stuck.

The intro to 'If I Fell' is one of their most elusive bits of songwriting, a little Escher staircase. The first twenty seconds are a summary of everything that was different about the Beatles at this point. Lennon's singing at its least mannered, and the resolution into the home key of D is a delight, McCartney's harmony intensifying the ingenuous, open feel. It's a cousin to the opening phrases of 'Strawberry Fields Forever', and as with that song Lennon's initial home demo shows that the essential complexity was there from the start. (The opening to 'Strawberry Fields' can be heard half an hour into the film *Eight Days A Week*, where he idles the eerie descending measure on a melodica in a

---

* Both in English, and in Portuguese translation as 'Pra Você Eu Digo Sim'.

hotel room, perhaps only half-noticing at the time.)

Lennon and McCartney were already providing hits for artists in the UK,* but the songs from *A Hard Day's Night* fanned out across the world. 'And I Love Her' was recorded by the Wailers in Jamaica, and by Count Basie in the States. 'I Should Have Known Better' reappeared as 'Menina Linda' in Brazil, given Portuguese lyrics by Renato e Seus Blue Caps. Peter Sellers, imitating Olivier, brought hilarious kink to the gently suggestive lyrics in the title song, which was quickly recorded by the Supremes and Ella Fitzgerald.

The Beatles had borrowed extensively from girl groups and Motown on their first two albums, but the scale of their success meant that the tribute was swiftly returned. The Supremes recorded three songs from *A Hard Day's Night* for their third album, *A Bit of Liverpool*. But their lovely unrecorded cover of 'Eight Days A Week', performed on Shindig in 1965, is the one that joins the dots. It locates a lilt in the original that sounds perfectly idiomatic, and which could have served as a single release of their own (had they needed it – they had five consecutive US number ones in 1964, and a run of four more between 1966 and 1967).[82]

'I'll Be Back' concludes an album dominated by Lennon, fulfilling his early role as leader of a band he had at last – as he always promised – taken to the top. Still alternating between major and minor, it reprises the thread of departure and return that runs through side two. The Beatles *were* working like dogs, and they were constantly away, always on show: 'I'll Cry Instead' betrays this (not wanting to cry in front of other people), the dreaminess of 'Things We Said Today' is rooted in distance, and for kids who had grown up with rationing, travelling the world for the first time, there were a whole lot of things to tell her when

---

* These included number ones for Billy J. Kramer with the Dakotas in 1963 ('Bad to Me'), and for Peter and Gordon in 1964 ('A World Without Love'); the Rolling Stones had recorded 'I Wanna Be Your Man', Ringo's number on *With the Beatles*, as their second single.

they got home – as well as a whole lot of things not to tell her. Lennon vows in the album's last verse to stop pretending, perhaps to his wife, perhaps to a lover, and perhaps – having gone potty over Dylan in Paris – to himself.

Compared to the breathless intensity and coherence of *A Hard Day's Night*, the Beach Boys' *All Summer Long* comes in and out of focus. This is partly because it continues the practice of padding out their LPs with novelty numbers (one that only ended with *Pet Sounds*), and partly because the push and pull between introspection and the drive-in has become almost comical. Brian's continuing experiments in sound and sensibility are accompanied by the interview excerpt 'Our Favourite Recording Sessions', while the album's most complex and delicate songs – 'Hushabye' and 'Girls on the Beach' – are each followed by car-themed throwaways in 'Little Honda' and 'Drive-In'.

The title song trades cutesy references to spilt Coke and miniature golf for musical mischief: it features marimba from the start, while in the break a solo fife marches in from goodness knows where, high above Wilson's chewy bass. Characteristically, however, the fun is shadowed – summer is almost through – and 'Hushabye' (best heard on live recordings, the screams adding poignancy to precarious opening harmonies) heightens the sense of something cloying and overripe, the faded end of August. It's always the last day of summer with the Beach Boys, nearly or already the end.

'Hushabye' is the longest song on the album, and still only lasts two minutes forty seconds. One of many Beach Boys songs set in bedrooms, mainly bedrooms with only one person in them, it prefigures the soporific themes Brian turned to post-*Smile*. There

73

are ominous rolls on the toms, and a beautiful, easy-rocking bridge at 1:14, like a breath, opening a door to the sound world of *Today!* But the song also points back to barbershop and the first album Brian ever bought, *Four Freshmen and Five Trombones*: the micro-crescendos, semitonal harmonic fades and dramatic swoops in the melodic line all fed the Beach Boys' strange and sumptuous sound.

As 'Hushabye' fades far away, it's 'Go!' We are back in Mike's world, getting around, this time going through the actual gears on a Honda motorbike. Casting off the slumbrous poetics of the previous song, it opens with the frankly resistible 'I'm gonna wake you up early, 'cause I'm gonna take a ride with you': Mike Love, forever pulling off someone else's duvet. It may be a palate cleanser between more complex songs, but this function was not without importance to the Beach Boys sound – and Love was an effective singer. The goofiness of a certain strain of rock and roll is never far from the surface – it also found expression in Brian's love of hipster slang – and Love's songs do sound like fun.

The album's richest track is 'Girls on The Beach', which blends the barbershop harmonies, soaring falsetto and doofus lyrics of classic mid-1960s Beach Boys. As the semitonal key change glides in mid-verse at 1:36, it's an ocean sunset at the moment the colours seem ready to explode. The texture is almost indecently pillowy. But listen to how hard the six-bar bridge section at 1:15 is sung: it's this attack – a vocal expression of Wilson's frequent imprecation to his session musicians to 'play it hard' – that stops the Beach Boys from being cloying.

8 August ANOTHER SIDE OF BOB DYLAN

The Beatles were playing in Hong Kong the night *Another Side* was recorded, and at the Futurist Theatre, Scarborough, the day after its release two months later. The Beach Boys criss-crossed the US in this period; they might be playing the HIC Arena in Honolulu, or a high school in Boise, or the home of the Kentucky State Fair in Louisville, where Dennis Wilson was knocked out by female fans and needed stitches.[83]

This was not yet Dylan's world, and for now he enjoyed a less crowded schedule. 'We think he's important enough to record whenever he wants to come to the studio,' producer Tom Wilson confided,[84] and Dylan completed most of the songs for *Another Side* whilst on an extended road trip from Paris to Greece with Nico, soon of the Velvet Underground. But his work rate could be phenomenal: Dylan recorded the whole album in a single session at Columbia Studio A on 9 June, fuelled by cigarettes, red wine and an admiring entourage. George Harrison later remembered feeling sorry for Elvis: 'He had his guys with him but there was only one Elvis. Nobody else knew what he felt like. But for us, we all shared the experience.' Perhaps it was the same for Dylan, who would soon hear the tapping not just of the raven at the window but of teenagers at the limousine door.[85]

The Bob Dylan who entered the studio on 7th Avenue that June evening was intent on shaking off his first artistic skin. Interviewed there by Nat Hentoff, he said he didn't want to write *for* people, but from inside himself.[86] There were to be no more finger-pointing songs. Anyone expecting Dylan to push on from 'The Times They Are 'a-Changin'' into planning committee mode would have been surprised to hear his voice crack with laughter at the end of 'All I Really Want to Do', before a boogie-woogie piano ushered in his first great shambly blues, the kind of song that was still punctuating his albums fifty years later. The times *had* changed, but in another direction.

Dylan's is an art both of deep mining and of skittish escape, and the canary was always at his side. He wanted to be heard the way he wrote, which was playfully, allusively, not with the law school intensity of people who would approve or endorse. In this he anticipated and fashioned the spirit of the decade: these were wearisome days for purists, who fared no better in the Sixties than puritans.

He had already changed his name, so he knew what it meant to move on. He knew what it meant to be an outsider even when you had found your way inside – his paternal grandparents had had to register as aliens when the country joined World War One – although he located this not in ethnicity, but in the land of his growing up. 'I was born in, grew up in a place so foreign that you had to be there to picture it,' he told *Rolling Stone* in 1978, describing the hallucinatory stillness of the eight-month Minnesota winters and the metallic air in high summer, all Indian spirit and the earth full of ore.[87] Even his home town was a mobile thing: a generation earlier Hibbing had been moved two miles south to accommodate a new iron mine. The Sellers Hotel fell off the rollers, swerving off the road near the detention hospital in January 1921; it sounds like Laurel and Hardy in the cold country, it sounds like one of his songs. The newspaper quoted L. Pocket, apparently still in charge of moving operations: 'It is a total wreck.'[88]

In the same *Rolling Stone* interview Dylan summarized the theme of his art movie *Renaldo and Clara* as alienation, explaining that to free himself and be reborn, a man 'has to go outside himself'. And so he escaped not once but serially, lighting out like Huckleberry Finn into whatever territory he could inhabit and be inhabited by until the canary cried again.

Jewish writers have speculated on how Dylan's background influenced this. In *Rock 'n' Roll Jews* Michael Billig positions him as 'an outsider posing as a dispossessed insider', claiming a tradition that was not his own. It was this, Billig suggests, that allowed him to transform it – but he needed 'to keep moving – to keep wandering – as if fearing exposure'.[89] Benjamin Kerstein echoed this in July 2020, turning over Dylan's assertion in 'I Contain Multitudes' that he is just like Anne Frank (and Indiana Jones, and, in a rhyme that would make a dead man smile, the Rolling Stones). As a Diaspora Jew, he suggests, Dylan can 'stand outside, take it all in', whilst also being obliged to wear masks, play with his identity, be quick on his feet and retain 'that sense of play and humor that has kept the Jews alive across so many centuries of being strangers to everyone but themselves'.[90]

If you were to come to *Another Side* via the Byrds, who covered three of its ten songs on their first album (and another, 'My Back Pages', on their fourth), it might sound like Dylan's live performances in later years: wilfully uninterested in melody even when it lay in plain sight, more curious than beautiful. Where the Byrds' music is rendered poetic by sheer beauty, Dylan's poetry here reveals its beauty only in sparks. 'All I Really Want to Do' satirizes the act of rhyming, even of singing, yodelling back to the more playful delivery of his first two albums.

Another Side contains some of Dylan's best poetry, if that's what you want to call it. It reads like a typewriter come to life, punched direct from his fast-turning mind, but the writing is still disciplined. The cast of characters who would parade through his next two albums, from the 'motorcycle black Madonna' to T. S. Eliot, are still to come. Instead he is playful and reflective, finally getting young the old-fashioned way, obsessing over his feelings through the filter of erotic encounter. Dylan's sensuality can be underestimated, and the imagery on the album is strikingly physical, from the 'cliffs of your wildcat charms' in 'Spanish Harlem Incident' and Ramona's 'cracked country lips', to 'her mouth was watery and wet' in 'I Don't Believe You'.

Dylan's caring wasn't spent, and he poured his reserves of empathy into one more protest song. 'Chimes of Freedom' swerves the broadside narrative for something wilder, more ancient, biblical and beat, tightening strings of internal rhymes into a conclusion which – after a litany of refugees, underdogs, rebels and rakes, but also, tellingly, poets, painters, and lovers – embraces 'every hung-up person in the whole wide universe'.

It's a grand and generous vision, but including poets and painters among the world's misunderstood proved prescient. Dylan's prickly father figures in the folk community were spooked by the new songs, and the inevitable open letters followed: Irwin Silber of *Sing Out!* called his new songs 'inner-directed', 'inner-probing' and 'self-conscious' – which was spot-on, except that he didn't mean it nicely. Silber was perhaps closer to the money when he queried Dylan's entourage and identified a little cruelty in the writing.[91]

The writer David Horowitz (today a staunch conservative) went further in *Peace News*, leaving for posterity a clanging assessment of *Another Side*, which he called an 'unqualified failure of taste and self-critical awareness'.[92] Dylan was made of stern stuff, and would face down the public's scorn when he went on the road in 1965, but he was not immune to criticism. Decades later, he told *Rolling Stone* that modern critics accusing him of plagiarism were 'the same people that tried to pin the name Judas on me. Judas, the most hated name in human history!'[93]

The accompaniment is deliciously approximate and often out of tune, betraying the single evening's recording. The album is not without its longueurs: 'Ballad in Plain D' *is* plain, a barbed mea culpa sketching the end of his relationship with Suze Rotolo. But with *Another Side*, Bob Dylan flipped all expectation not just of himself but of the genre. If Dylan's topical material could reasonably have been interpreted as impetus to do or say something, these songs compelled the listener to think and feel.

The Beatles and Dylan meet for the first time, in NYC

With *Another Side* in the can, Dylan holed up in the Hudson Valley, staying for now at his manager Albert Grossman's house. Doug Gilbert took weeks of photos of him smoke-streaming new songs into a typewriter in the White Room above the Café Espresso on Tinker Street, lolling in the summer sun with local kids, playing bass with John Sebastian, and showing Allen Ginsberg how to play his Benares pump organ.[94]

At the end of July, he played the Newport Folk Festival in the last glow of the folk community's undiluted acclaim. Murray Lerner's 1967 film *Festival!* gives us an insight into that time: watching Pete Seeger introduce him so affectionately at the topical songs workshop ('Where is he? Bob? You were sitting back there'), then sitting expectantly on the stage with folded hands, long as a Parmigianino Madonna, one can see why it was both warm and constraining to be part of that world. Seeger sits pensively and taps his foot as Dylan sings a new song, 'Mr. Tambourine Man'. There is an impish quality to Dylan at this point, playing with his audience's expectations before they began to wash back. The music critic Dave Marsh excludes from the folk police Seeger himself, who smiles broadly when he rises at the song's conclusion: 'As a supremely astute judge of song quality, he knew well that Dylan's new songs were marvelous, even if they weren't about what they were supposed to be about.'[95]

Bob Dylan met Johnny Cash at Newport in late July, jamming with him in a crowded motel room after the festival closed. Cash had taken 'Don't Think Twice, It's All Right' around the country, and played it in his set on the Saturday night: 'I'm so honoured I can't – hi, Bob – our good friend Bob Dylan, we'd like to do one of his songs … we've been trying to tell the folks about Bob.'[96]

Cash *was* trying to tell the folks, and not only about Bob: in a sense he was taking up the younger man's mantle of protest. He had just recorded *Bitter Tears*, a concept album of songs themed around the Indigenous American experience. When DJs and radio stations declined to play 'The Ballad of Ira Hayes', Cash addressed them in a full-page letter in Billboard: 'Where are your <u>guts?</u>' he asked, acknowledging that the Ira Hayes song was strong medicine. 'So is Rochester – Harlem – Birmingham and VietNam,' he said, bracketing the growing conflict overseas with inner city riots and civil disorder at home. 'Classify me, categorize me – STIFLE me,' he declared, 'but it won't work.'[97]

He could have been speaking for Dylan, and the admiration was mutual. Dylan told Cash he had once hitch-hiked to see him play in Duluth: 'I didn't just dig you,' he told Cash, 'I breathed you.' Dylan offered him the song 'Mama, You Been on My Mind', recording into a tape machine set up by Joan Baez; Cash included it alongside 'Don't Think Twice' and 'It Ain't Me Babe' on the 1965 album *Orange Blossom Special*, and – as the Newport party ended – honoured Dylan with the gift of his guitar.[98]

The Beatles, having toured Australia and New Zealand in June and a string of British seaside resorts in July, returned to the US in August. The scale of their touring operation, with its motorcades and hotel room sieges, grand entrances and perilous exits, dwarfed the length of the set. It lasted a dozen songs at best, already twice as many as they had played on their British tour with Roy Orbison the previous summer. On the last weekend of August they played at Forest Hills in New York. Dylan drove down from Woodstock in a station wagon to meet them at the Delmonico Hotel, where his penchant for plonk prompted an apology for the ages from Brian Epstein: 'I'm afraid we only have champagne.'[99]

Some of the Beatles' encounters with people they admired – Elvis, for example, and the Supremes – could be stiff and awkward.

This one could easily have been the same: the group had recorded 'I'm A Loser' a fortnight before, and Lennon might have bristled on meeting a peer whose influence he was now channelling in song.* But it proved to be an enjoyable and even life-changing evening, partly because of the nibbles Dylan brought to the party.

The Beatles were no strangers to uppers, which had helped them through their gruelling Reeperbahn residencies, but their recreational drug of choice was whisky and Coke. In this respect they were well behind the aromatic and psychedelic curve of the West Coast, where the future Byrds were snacking on joints and chocolate milk. Dylan had been introduced to weed at college, and had taken acid for the first time that April[100] – coincidentally or not on the tour where John Sebastian, moved to tears by the singer's performances, recalled that 'all of a sudden, this second-ary spirit jumped out of him'.[101]

Now it fell to Dylan to turn someone on, and, as McCartney later admitted ('rather a coup'), no valet to the doors of perception could have carried more cachet.[102] Having sent out for cheaper wine, Dylan turned down the offer of purple hearts and suggested marijuana instead: doors were locked, jambs were stuffed, curtains were drawn. And at length, the initiation began.[103] They were like kids at school, high up in a hotel getting high, moving to a bedroom to get further from twenty cops on the doors. They were like kings at court, with Lennon getting Starr to test the first joint for him and McCartney having an associate write down his deepest thoughts. 'I was just a proud and happy *shadchen*,' recalled Al Aronowitz, who had set up the meeting, 'a Jewish matchmaker, dancing at the princely wedding I'd arranged. Buttons popped off my shirt.'[104]

The first three Beatles albums are all about momentum, and this would not be stopped in its tracks by marijuana. But

---

* By January he was telling the *Melody Maker* that Dylan dug the song. 'Beatles say – Dylan shows the way', *Melody Maker*.

the drug's invitation to pause and savour the moment in its full weight and absurdity began to tow their creativity in new directions, from the drag in the songs recorded *Beatles For Sale* that autumn, to the single 'Ticket to Ride' the following spring. Like all pleasures it could also lead to indolence, which is one reason the *Help!* album would tread water. The tenor of Dylan's music was impacting on their songwriting, and also in subtle ways their song choices: the rhythm and blues covers diminished in favour of rockabilly and even country: 'Act Naturally', Ringo's number on *Help!*, was originally a hit for Buck Owens.

As for Dylan, his work on *Bringing It All Back Home* would contain both ironclad blues and – influenced by the Beatles' work on *Beatles For Sale* – butterfly pop. And while he had given the Beatles a taste for weed, reinforcing the influence of his more inner-directed writing, they gave him something in return: a glimpse of big-time fame. Soon he would occupy hotel suites on his own account, and his gnomic persona hid a human being who could make decisions as daft as anyone else's: he would buy a house with countless bedrooms after visiting John Lennon's in 1965.[105] Buttons were popping in all directions.

The Delmonico meeting established the first influential relationship, or relational influence, between the three artists. Lennon and Dylan had more than music in common, and it was natural that they should become friends of sorts, though this was a dynamic where neither could – as they usually did in relationships – dominate the other. Lennon had been to art school and always drew. Dylan, in addition to the prose poem sleeve notes (introduced on *The Times They Are a-Changin'*), increasingly painted. Both wrote books in this period, although only Lennon's were published at the time. *In His Own Write* had come out in spring 1964, and he left the penultimate day's filming on *A Hard Day's Night* to attend a Foyles literary luncheon held in his honour.

He flubbed when asked to stand and make a speech: 'You've got a lucky face,' he told the person next to him, sitting straight back down.[106]

Lennon had loved *Alice's Adventures in Wonderland* as a child, and the absurd wordplay sparked his own. McCartney had a facility for melody, but Lennon, no slouch with a tune himself, had one for words. When a glass breaks before a take of 'You've Got to Hide Your Love Away', he immediately scats 'Paul's broken a glass, broken a glass' before finding perfect nursery rhyme rhythm: 'Paul's broken a glass a glass, a glass he's broke today'. Lennon later admitted that his stories were more personal than his songs at this point, crediting Dylan for the more subjective music that followed: 'not by any discussion or anything but just by hearing his work'.[107]

September to December 1964

		Bob Dylan	Beatles	Beach Boys
1964	Sep			
	Oct			[19] BEACH BOYS CONCERT [26] 'Dance, Dance, Dance' *[28/29] Recording T.A.M.I. Show*
	Nov		[27] 'I Feel Fine'	[9] 'The Man with All the Toys' [9] THE BEACH BOYS' CHRISTMAS ALBUM
	Dec		[4] BEATLES FOR SALE	*[7] Brian Wilson marries;* *[23] Wilson has his first breakdown*

Harder sounds began making it to the top of the UK charts: the Rolling Stones took 'It's All Over Now' to number one in July, and the Kinks did the same with the sputtering and distorted

'You Really Got Me' in September. Martha and the Vandellas enjoyed a huge summer hit with 'Dancing in the Street', a tougher-sounding Motown production. 'I Feel Fine' reflected the heavier impetus in these records, maintaining the Beatles' momentum as the competition intensified.

Capitol Records were unfailingly generous with Beach Boys albums, releasing *Beach Boys Concert*, recorded in August, less than a month before their *Christmas Album*. The Beatles were also recorded live in August, but the tapes from the Hollywood Bowl were only released on record in 1977. Both recordings are characterized by waves of screaming that break on each new song, singer and middle eight: that the Beach Boys can hold their harmonies is as remarkable as the Beatles managing to keep the beat.*

^{24 August} **When I Grow Up (To Be a Man)**, ^{26 October} 'Dance, Dance, Dance'

'Dance, Dance, Dance' opens with an urgent bass riff, snapping up the sleigh bells that were hanging round the studio during sessions for the *Beach Boys' Christmas Album*. But the interest tails off quickly, despite the presence of harpsichord and castanets, and the song features one of the hastiest key changes in pop.

It *was* only two months since their last single, 'When I Grow Up (To Be a Man)'. Here the harpsichord sounds organic, and the blend of words and harmony elevates sentiment to poignancy. A whole lifetime is captured in two minutes of bright-sounding pop, the singers anticipating the future even as it slips through

---

* These were the only non-compilation Beatle albums released in the first flush of my infatuation. After Lingasong's lo-fi (but fascinating) *Live! at the Star-Club in Hamburg, Germany; 1962*, released in April 1977 in one of the most unimaginative album sleeves ever printed, *The Beatles Live at the Hollywood Bowl*, which appeared a month later, was almost a deluxe edition. This time the aural interference is not the sound of bottles breaking, but the caterwaul of sound from the audience, the Beatles punching and rasping through the racket, just.

their fingers. The changes serve and intensify the lyrics: the major verses, sung solo, are full of truisms, but the questions accumulate weight against the minor chords and shifting harmony lines of the chorus – 'Now I'm young and free, how will it be?' – with 'free' held in query up top and the question repeated insistently in the lower voices.

In a terrific coup, the song starts counting up the years, which feels like counting down one's life: fourteen, fifteen, sixteen, seventeen after half a minute, before a surfy but tonally ambiguous break arrests the tally. But the numbers return – eighteen, nineteen, twenty, twenty-one, a Commendatore counterpoint – and dominate the coda. 'Won't last forever,' the lead reflects, as if we didn't know by now. In my early twenties I used to tell myself that youth would finally end where the song finally fades, barely audible, at thirty-one, thirty-two, thirty-three – thirty-three; it felt like plenty of time.

28/29 October **Recording T.A.M.I. Show**

Like their discography, the Beach Boys' film appearances were oddly out of synch. They had been filmed in April singing the title song for *The Girls on the Beach*, but this wasn't released until May 1965. They did feature prominently in something more important, though: the groundbreaking *T.A.M.I. Show*, a concert performance filmed in Santa Monica at the end of October and presented by surf pop pioneers Jan and Dean. 'I Get Around' is even quoted in the theme tune.[108]

As the cream of Black and white American talent gathered on the US West Coast, the Beatles were engaged at ABC cinemas in the UK's West Country. They missed the opportunity to associate with idols like Chuck Berry and Smokey Robinson, leaving their Chelsea boots to be filled by Gerry and the Pacemakers – guitars held tight to their chests as if straps were still subject to rationing – and Billy J. Kramer and the Dakotas. Only the Rolling Stones from Liverpool (as erroneously tagged in the theme song) make the British Invasion look like a thing.

The *T.A.M.I. Show* is an astonishing document, live and raw. The voices of the Miracles crack and reach; bikini-clad dancers hop about as if the stage were covered in smouldering popcorn. Everyone – performers, dancers, audience – smiles. Pacemakers and Dakotas aside, the show's sensuality is striking, as is the diversity of performers, singers and fans. For these were dark and dangerous days. Ron Howard's documentary *Eight Days a Week* places the Beatles' second US visit against the backdrop of the Freedom Summer Murders;* in September the group refused to play a show in Jacksonville if it was segregated, and by the following year's tour this was stipulated in their contract. Progressive intent was expressed in the casting and visual framing of the *T.A.M.I. Show*, concluding with a tableau of singers and dancers in what David E. James describes without obvious restraint as 'joyous biracial terpsichorean abandon'.[109]

Watching footage of the Beach Boys in concert is always curious, and their songs would only get harder to perform as Brian stayed home to work on more intricate ideas. They are all shapes and sizes, with just their stripy shirts to unite them; only Dennis would have been cast in a rock and roll band. Brian is gangly and has a tentative air, tristesse behind the half-smile. The slighter Mike Love apes the go-go dancers like it's the office party, and the group only looks halfway iconic when their faces are framed for 'Surfer Girl'.

The film is famous for James Brown's dazzling performance of 'Please Please Please', his stage show captured in all its dotty drama. Brown was in mid-season form, having won at craps and

---

* The bodies of civil rights activists James Chaney, Andrew Goodman and Michael Schwerner, murdered in Mississippi in late June, were found in early August.

tarried with one of the dancers that day, and the blood drained from Jagger's face as he watched from the wings.[110] But encouraged by Marvin Gaye, who told them to 'do your thing – that's what I do,' the group responded gamely.[111] The Stones were learning fast, and their cover versions were becoming transformative. Bobby Womack's 'It's All Over Now' is changed from a loose and shuffling blues (of the kind Dylan favoured) to a reverb-drenched groove with a clamorous chorus.

The what ifs for the *T.A.M.I. Show* are tantalizing. As well as the Beatles it might have featured Sam Cooke, alive in late October but murdered before its release, or even Elvis, dozing on the sand of so many movies just down the road. His latest, *Girl Happy*, had wrapped that July. The soundtrack album featured songs like 'Fort Lauderdale Chamber of Commerce' and 'Do the Clam', and Presley, who had inspired a generation, suffered the indignity of having his vocals mastered at the wrong speed. The craft in his singing means that it's rarely uninteresting, but the material and production here are so thin that it's painful to hear. In 'Puppet on a String' he admits to being helpless, concluding wanly: 'you can do 'most anything to me.'

Somehow he roused himself from this torpor to create the gospel album *How Great Thou Art* in 1966, but his career-defining *TV Special*, also masterminded by *T.A.M.I. Show* director Steve Binder, was still four years away. Sponsored by the sewing machine giant Singer, it only became known as the Comeback Special because it worked so well.

27 November '**I Feel Fine**'

We last heard the Beatles at the end of *A Hard Day's Night*, fading, fading, 'I'll Be Back'. When they returned it was with their hardest-sounding single yet: 'I Feel Fine' is an expression of musical and personal confidence that reflects the initial rush of their rise to global fame. Starting with a held bass note and a moment's feedback which in truth sounds like an electric razor, the circular riff leads to a swinging rhythm that simply dances on the hi-hat, Ringo's tour de force drumming cemented with a lovely off-the-beat route out of the guitar break.

They were candid about their influences: the riff originated in Bobby Parker's 'Watch Your Step' and the rhythm in Ray Charles's 'What I'd Say'.* Today Parker would have received a songwriting credit, even if it was not an active collaboration. 'I was flattered,' Parker said later, 'but I still had back in my mind that I should have got a little more recognition for that.'[112]

But the Beatles didn't just lift. They move the riff down one and then two steps in the intro before landing in an exceptionally mobile groove. The harmonies in the bridge are joyous, leading straight back to the hard-kicking verse. There's no iconic story behind 'I Feel Fine', and it isn't about anything beyond the excited feeling it conveys, but sometimes with the Beatles that was enough.

The bluesy B-side, 'She's a Woman', survives on the intensity of McCartney's vocal and the contrast of a lovely middle eight that turns out to be only two bars long; only a couple of dropouts midway through the track betray the speed at which they were working. Above all these are dance records, in ways that the Beach Boys' most recent single, 'Dance, Dance, Dance', kind of wasn't.

4 December BEATLES FOR SALE

The Beatles tended to leave their singles off their albums. It was a generous approach at a time when albums were often sold on

---

* They had covered Charles' 'Hallelujah I Love Her So' in Hamburg, and 'I Got a Woman' live at the BBC in August 1963.

the back of hit singles ('two hits and ten pieces of junk', as Phil Spector put it), and it leaves a single-sized gap on some of their best LPs. They were confident they had enough material to keep the albums up to scratch, but this wasn't always true. 'I Feel Fine' would have taken up some of the slack on *Beatles for Sale*.*

A fan buying the record in December 1964 and mistakenly playing side two first might have been concerned. It soars in on 'Eight Days a Week', with its always-been-there melody, glorious harmonies, throaty Lennon lead and innovative, droning middle eight (unusually, there's no guitar solo). But from there the quality tails off dramatically.

Buddy Holly's slight 'Words of Love' sounds lovely, the three-part harmony and chiming twelve-string sounding much more like the Byrds – who were only now signing a record contract – than anything on *A Hard Day's Night*. But the arrangement is uncharacteristically misjudged, the instrumental break lasting twice as long as it should. Carl Perkins' 'Honey Don't' is slighter still and not awfully well sung: it features two instrumental breaks, and here and elsewhere there are rough edges on display: a hasty bit of double-tracking here, a stray guitar note there. 'What You're Doing' is the first great mid-period, mid-tempo McCartney song, the harmonies lying under the lead, a mood he would revisit on *Help!*. But another Carl Perkins cover, swamped in reverb, sounds exhausted.

Side one is a different story. They're at their gentlest on the deceptively breezy McCartney ballad 'I'll Follow the Sun', the brightness in McCartney's voice masking the steel in the lyric.†

---

* 'We Can Work It Out' and 'Day Tripper' would have made *Rubber Soul* even better (although one can't say the same for 'Paperback Writer' and *Revolver*), while the thought of 'Penny Lane' and 'Strawberry Fields Forever' on *Sgt. Pepper*, and 'Hey Jude' on the *White Album*, is tantalizing.

† It's a good example of the invention and economy of Beatle expression: the guitar break is only four pick strokes, sliding up the ladder of intention the song has established; there's a little descending arpeggio behind Lennon's tender harmony on 'so my love I must go', but only the second time round.

They're at their most raucous on the two ecstatic rock and roll covers, 'Rock and Roll Music' and 'Kansas City/Hey-Hey-Hey-Hey!' – and at their most perverse on 'Mr. Moonlight' (contrary to received wisdom, this isn't an anomaly in their catalogue; their willingness to stretch tonal coherence to breaking point yielded some of their most imaginative, as well as some of their dullest, music*). But they're at their most original on the opening three songs: 'No Reply', 'I'm a Loser' and 'Baby's in Black'. The dynamic contrasts in 'No Reply' are almost expressionist, a threatening diminuendo in the second verse leading into a thunderous chorus, the on-the-beat handclaps from The Supremes' 'Baby Love' put to darker use in the bridge.

'I'm a Loser' maintains the intensity musically and lyrically: the harmonies are bright, the words and delivery (unusually for Lennon, not double-tracked) confessional. It's the last time we hear his folk-style harmonica on a Beatles record, and the teeth are almost blown out. 'Baby's in Black' is something strange, casting the folk song 'Johnny's So Long at the Fair' in a black veil. It should be a throwaway, but the mood is so powerful that it transcends the form, a boat borne on the choppy waves of George Harrison's tremolo-armed guitar, rowing out to some dark island.

 9 November **THE BEACH BOYS' CHRISTMAS ALBUM**
7 December **Brian Wilson marries**, 23 December **Wilson has his first breakdown**

Christmas came early for Beach Boys fans, and even earlier for the group, who had recorded the bulk of their seasonal LP in June. The album was conceived as a response to Phil Spector's *A Christmas Gift for You*, released in November 1963,† and represents the most

---

* 'Tomorrow Never Knows' and 'I Am the Walrus' belong in the former category, 'Yer Blues' and 'Helter Skelter' in the latter.

† Brian Wilson may or may not have played piano on Spector's Christmas album, which was released on the same day as *With the Beatles*.

explicit link to the Four Freshmen sound in the Beach Boys' catalogue. Brian Wilson was now in a position to engage their arranger Dick Reynolds, and his sumptuous orchestrations on side two add snow-sparkle to the harmonies. A stately, melancholy 'We Three Kings of Orient Are' bears the weight of the mystery (they had recorded a straight-faced 'Lord's Prayer' as the B-side to 'Little Saint Nick', released as a single a year earlier), and a full-on 'Blue Christmas' features a pendent solo lead from Brian.

The Beach Boys are pictured decorating a tree, Dennis reaching for the final touches. But when Christmas arrived, it toppled. The Beach Boys were booked on the kind of short-stop tour that Elvis undertook in his decline, snaking from the Gulf of Mexico to North Carolina. Brian was overworked, playing too many roles: he had just married his seventeen-year-old girlfriend Marilyn, and, like the Beatles, been introduced to marijuana. Now he broke down on the plane as it left LA for Texas, two days before Christmas. It was the 173rd of 179 Beach Boys concert appearances in 1964; that night's Houston show was the last he would make until a brief return in the summer of 1967. It was the decisive moment in Wilson's transition to full-time writer and producer. The Beach Boys engaged first Glen Campbell, and then Bruce Johnston, to replace him in the touring group.

A 1966 interview with the photographer Earl Leaf yields a detailed and gruelling account of a breakdown in which, Wilson says, he was coming apart.[113] He describes himself as constantly on the move, 'producing, writing, arranging, singing, planning, teaching'; the Beatles' success, meanwhile, had 'eclipsed a lot of what we'd worked for'.[114] No wonder he felt mixed up and overworked. Abandoning Houston for home on Christmas Eve, he unburdened himself to his mother, Audrey, for three hours: 'Generally I dumped out a life-long hang-up.' Troublingly, Wilson notes three subsequent breakdowns, the last only a fortnight before the interview.[115]

While Beach Boys fans enjoyed their *Christmas Album*, members of the Beatles Fan Club received their second Xmas flexi disc, a raggedy four-minute recording in which the group mess with a prepared script and conclude with a snatch of 'Oh, Can You Wash Your Father's Shirt?' They made seven of these discs, and they provide a loose counterpoint to the band's development. The first two were scripted by press officer Tony Barrow using the slang du jour ('we had no idea of all the gear things in store for us', reads John in 1963, his accent slipping in a dozen words from Scouse to Transatlantic and Welsh), but were enlivened by the Beatles' complete lack of old-style showbiz smarm – in 1965 Lennon thanks the fans for the 'playing cards made out of knickers'. At times it's hard to believe Peter Sellers isn't in the room; they start out with Goonish voicings and by 1967 sound like Monty Python. That year's recording, wrapped in a sepia collage of Victorian photos, is by some distance the most elaborate, and the only one to contain anything like an actual original song, 'Christmas Time Is Here Again!'

Somewhere between the richness of the Beach Boys, the inventive directness of the Beatles and the arch poetics of Bob Dylan, new territory had emerged, like a volcanic island that tips the waves.* All three had a sense of humour and a sense of themselves, even as the scope of their endeavours spread beyond expectation. Throughout 1964 the Beatles had been asked when the bubble would burst, to the point where it had become a joke. Neither they nor the others had anything to fall back on, had they needed to. But there was no sign of a lull in sales or ideas, so they kept moving.

---

* The island of Surtsey, for example, appeared south of Iceland on 14 November 1963 in an eruption that lasted until 5 June 1967.

1965: CONVERGENCE

The new land was fertile. The Byrds were poised to alight, the Stones to unbutton their blues, and the Kinks to tiptoe between the tea cosies and antimacassars. But the immediate impact of the Beatles' worldwide success in 1964 was a copycat phenomenon not unlike the American folk boom they had just busted. As the *T.A.M.I. Show* indicated, most of the beat groups in their immediate wake were awkward by comparison: stiff in their suits, goofy with their matching guitars, caught in the headlights of TV appearances that came too soon.

There was no shortage of them. In the week *A Hard Day's Night* was released the Animals and the Rolling Stones held the top two spots in the UK singles chart, but countless now forgotten groups lurked beneath, from the Applejacks and the Merseybeats to the Fourmost and the Migil Five. National variants appeared, whole subgenres: France had yé-yé, and Brazil iê-iê-iê, both after the chorus to *She Loves You*. In Spain Los Brincos adopted the new idiom more imaginatively than most of their British counterparts, while Poland's own Beatles were Czerwone Gitary. In Uruguay Los Shakers cycled breezily through all the available chords in 'Rompan Todo'. Even in America the new groups favoured Anglophile names like the Buckinghams, the Beau Brummels and the Beefeaters (the nascent Byrds) before the scene began to generate its own, stranger currents.

The implications of the new music varied. The Beatles' music reflected and amplified shifts in personal, social and sexual freedom in Western Europe, but Los Brincos and Czerwone Gitary, and Brazilian singers Roberto Carlos and Erasmo Carlos, all laboured under dictatorships. Dylan no longer addressed social change directly, but African American artists increasingly did: this development can be traced in Curtis Mayfield's singles with the Impressions, from 'It's All Right' in 1963, to 'Keep on Pushing' in 1964, to 'People Get Ready' in 1965.*

January to May 1965

		Bob Dylan	Beatles	Beach Boys
1965	Jan			
	Feb			[15] 'Do You Wanna Dance?'
	Mar	[8] 'Subterranean Homesick Blues' [22] BRINGING IT ALL BACK HOME		[8] THE BEACH BOYS TODAY!
	Apr		[9] 'Ticket to Ride'	[5] 'Help Me, Rhonda'
			Lennon and Harrison take LSD for the first time	*Brian Wilson takes LSD for the first time*
	May	*[9] The Beatles see Dylan live in London, before hanging out at his hotel*		

A decisive change occurs in the early months of 1965, and it's here that the mid-sixties sound is forged. Sparkling electric guitars replace acoustics at the heart of the mix, while the distinction between uptempo rockers and slower ballads elides in a distinctive

---

* As the Impressions' lead singer and songwriter, Curtis Mayfield was building a catalogue of melodic, conscious Chicago soul that would influence a generation of artists including The Band, Jimi Hendrix, and the Wailers: the licks that introduce Al Kooper and Mike Bloomfield's 'The Weight', and the trills in Hendrix's 'Little Wing', and the close harmony singing of the Wailers and a host of Jamaican peers, are all from the Mayfield-era Impressions playbook.

mid-tempo groove. This can be heard in the Rolling Stones' 'The Last Time', in the Beatles' 'Ticket to Ride', and in the Byrds' 'Mr. Tambourine Man'.

The charts now read like maps to the emerging culture as much as lists of bestselling records: also on and around the UK Top 20 when 'Ticket to Ride' is released are 'For Your Love' by the Yardbirds (a harpsichord-driven pop song which riled the group's guitarist Eric Clapton because it wasn't 'pure' English suburban blues), 'The Last Time' by the Stones, 'I Can't Explain' by The Who, 'Stop! In the Name of Love' by the Supremes, and 'Nowhere to Run' by Martha and the Vandellas. The sound of soul music continues to harden, with Stax Records challenging Motown from Memphis. Everywhere is the sound of tambourines; it's as if no record can be passed for pressing without one.

8 March '**Subterranean Homesick Blues**'

Dylan fans had waited seven months – an age in the pop world at the time – before 'Subterranean Homesick Blues' came out in early March, followed by *Bringing it All Back Home* a fortnight later. They weren't necessarily pleased when it did, and it wasn't only fusspots who were perplexed. There's a poignant moment in the film *Dont Look Back* [*sic*] when a teenage girl in Liverpool asks nervously if he will be singing 'The Times They Are a-Changin'', as the new songs don't sound like him. 'Oh, you're that type,' Dylan responds warily, signing an autograph, before explaining kindly that he wanted to let his friends play with him. 'It just doesn't sound like you at all,' she pursues, 'it sounds as if you're having a good old laugh.' Dylan smiles and replies: 'Don't you like me to have a good old laugh once in a while?'[116]

'The Times They Are a-Changin'' had just charted as a single in the UK, so the confusion that May is understandable.

'Subterranean Homesick Blues' sounds like a juiced-up hoedown, rattling at the seams. It sure isn't folk, but it isn't pop either, more a hard rain of words landing somewhere between the City Lights poets and Howlin' Wolf. It's also funny, and angry – 'Twenty years of schoolin' and they put you on the day shift.' As on 'Maggie's Farm' this works on two levels – protesting against injustice in society, but also against injustice to Bob Dylan: 'They say sing while you slave and I just get bored.'

Monday, 8 March was the first day American ground troops arrived in Vietnam, and the day after the Bloody Sunday of the first Selma to Montgomery march. Dylan's engagement remains but is now refracted, and the song is an impressionistic response to chaotic times. The attendant message of wariness is coherent enough: 'You don't need a weatherman to know which way the wind blows' is the pay-off, and the rhyme is with 'fire hose', used extensively by police against civil rights protestors.

John Lennon was shaken up by the song. It was his turn to wonder if he could compete, and he quoted the 'parking meters' line in one of his last interviews, for *Playboy*, in 1980.[117] By merging the Beat in his words to the beat in a band, Dylan had shown that a scattered, non-linear lyric could cohere on a subjective level, an idea that would take time to be fully realized in Lennon's own songs. As with rock and roll, Lennon responded intuitively to the *sound* of Dylan's records: 'You don't have to hear what Bob Dylan says, you just have to hear how he says it' is as much analysis as quip.[118]

The B-side, 'She Belongs to Me', is one of Dylan's prettiest recordings, closer to a pop song in feel, loosely but deliberately arranged; one might dance to it, discreetly. It's a good place to appreciate his timing: inexact on guitar by session musician standards, his vocals pop on every beat. It's also a good place to grasp why English was, like Italian for opera, the perfect medium for rock and roll.* Listen to the clusters of single-syllable words – don't-look-back – and the energy derived from pairing two-syllable ('walking antique') and three-syllable ('hypnotist collector') words. There's a light dusting of the curious and the exotic – trumpets for Hallowe'en, an Egyptian ring – and anyone listening to the song a fortnight later with the new album in hand might have interpreted it as a love poem to the elegant woman by his side.

The track has a band feel, and it wouldn't have been made without the influence of the Beatles. But it's far from being noisily electric. The bass guitar propels, the lead enlaces. It's almost the sound of a group rehearsing in an apartment with unamplified vocals: the affront to folk is in the groove, and in the way the music now inclines towards the wider world. In any case, a much more commercial recording of a Dylan song was already in the can.

○

Unlike our other artists, the Byrds arrived fully formed in the mid-1960s. The immediate catalyst in their case was not rock and roll and not even Dylan, but the Beatles.

Roger McGuinn and Gene Clark met in July 1964. Both were from the Midwest. McGuinn grew up in Chicago, where his artistically minded parents wrote a successful book called *Parents Can't Win*. Clark was raised with twelve siblings in Tipton, Missouri, his childhood a melange of Catholicism, wild country and disturbing events.

They both passed through the mighty wind of the folk revival. The studious McGuinn had enrolled at Chicago's Old Town

---

* English is a stress-timed language, so that even two-syllable words like 'artist' and 'again' have a single, beat-friendly emphasis. Italian, which is syllable-timed, accommodates better the less rhythmic, essentially melodic nature of opera.

School of Folk Music as early as 1957, while the sensitive but intractable Clark was plucked out of Kansas City for a year's tenure with the New Christy Minstrels in 1963. But it was the Beatles that shook them free. McGuinn quit working for Bobby Darin at the Brill Building in New York, and Clark jumped the Minstrels. Clark heard 'She Loves You' and 'I Want to Hold Your Hand' on tour in Canada, and again in Norfolk, Virginia, where Chuck Berry's trip to the 'Promised Land' begins. 'I played them all night long in this little coffee shop. I flipped out,' Clark recalled. 'And I quit the Christies the next day and went back to LA to find a way to start a group like that.'[119]

McGuinn had started including Beatles songs in his act at the Troubadour in LA, to the irritation of folk audiences, and it was when Clark heard him singing 'You Can't Do That' that he realized they could. Next to join was David Crosby, a richer strain of rebel raised in Santa Barbara and – via Les Baxter's Balladeers – another alumnus of the folk boom. He added the magic dust high harmony that made the 'Byrds sound' just as much as McGuinn's twelve-string ring.

They all went to see *A Hard Day's Night* when it reached US movie theatres in August, now with drummer Michael Clark in tow, talent-spotted on the street for his hair. They dug what Crosby described as their insouciance, by which he meant their pulling power. So did everyone else: when in October the group released a single on Elektra as the Beefeaters, Columbia Records – tipped off by none other than Miles Davis, and eager for an in on the British invasion – offered them a single shot.[120]

The song their manager Jim Dickson chose for them, 'Mr. Tambourine Man', had been written by Dylan in spring 1964. But it proved difficult for its author to record. The Byrds heard an outtake from the *Another Side* session which featured approximate harmony singing on the chorus (an idea they refined in their own arrangement). Dylan then recorded a version at the piano for his publisher, which appears on *The Bootleg Series Vol. 9* and sounds curiously weighed down. Another attempt during the sessions for *Bringing It All Back Home* was made with drums and tambourine and later released on the twelfth *Bootleg Series* LP, but Dylan's timing is too fluid to accommodate them: he aborts the take, saying with justification: 'The drumming's driving me mad'. Even the Byrds' first work on it is stiff, the lovely harmonies and jangling twelve-string electric hamstrung by a rattling military snare.

Dylan's song, played by a group who wanted to be the Beatles, needed a final ingredient: it turned out to be the sound of the Beach Boys. Only McGuinn's guitar was used when they came to record the song, and they sang to the same crack back-up as the Beach Boys and the Ronettes before them: top picks from the Wrecking Crew, including Leon Russell and Hal Blaine. The arrangement, inspired by 'Don't Worry Baby', contained two stunningly original hooks in the first eight seconds – McGuinn's iridescent twelve-string figure, and the bassline that slides up five tones beneath it.

Each time we hear the chorus, McGuinn and Clark double up on Dylan's tune, achieving a drone-like tone. But Crosby's delicious harmony effectively becomes the lead, changing Dylan's pensive barefoot poem into something radiant. The bass burbles, reverbed guitars peck on the beat: the sound is both gentle and groovy, a new taste for new times. Repeating the stunning opening in the fade reinforces the flawless conception, but the single was delayed by Columbia's release schedule. On 8 March, with the first yet to appear, the Byrds were already recording their follow-up single – an act of faith on the part of their manager.

15 February '**Do You Wanna Dance?**' , 8 March **THE BEACH BOYS TODAY!**

Four of the musicians who recorded 'Mr. Tambourine Man' with the Byrds on 20 January were also working with Brian Wilson on material for the *Today!* album. It was preceded by the Beach Boys' first single of the year, a cover of fellow Californian Bobby Freeman's calypso-flavoured 1958 hit, 'Do You Wanna Dance?'. The production is monumental for such a modest song, featuring three electric rhythm guitars, electric mandolin, electric bass, grand piano, Hammond organ, drums, timpani, two tenor saxophones and one baritone. These are rendered obscure by the mono mix, and the song – which explodes into the chorus – feels a little off-kilter, as if the whole thing might topple over in a crash of wood and sparks and saxophone keys. The B-side, 'Please Let Me Wonder', is by contrast exquisite and perfectly balanced.*

Marshalling such forces on songs like 'Do You Wanna Dance?' meant that when the material truly warranted the attention, Wilson was ready. 'Please Let Me Wonder' was the first song he worked on after his breakdown, and the first he wrote on marijuana. It starts out sounding like 'Don't Worry Baby'. But it breaks down at 0:18 into a fully internal world, at last free of the cars and surfboards that had served to shield Wilson's emotions in the high school canteen of their previous work. 'Now here we are together,' sings Brian, as if to himself, or anyone who might truly hear; 'Please forgive my shaking,' he continues, 'can't you tell my heart is breaking?' The choruses carry a clever reversal, the backing vocals ('please let me wonder') melting in from the

---

* 'Please Let Me Wonder' is still extravagantly scored for a pop song: horns and percussion aside, there are two twelve-string guitars (electric and acoustic), two pianos (upright and grand), two organs (Farfisa and Hammond), and a vibraphone. Craig Slowinski, 'The Beach Boys – The Beach Boys Today!: Please Let Me Wonder' (2007/2008), http://www.tiptopwebsite.com/custommusic2/craigslowinskicom.pdf, p. 78.

verse to take the lead before resolving on a wistful ninth chord.

Brian was like the player-manager in a football team, both one of the boys (Beach Boys archivist Craig Slowinski details an outtake for 'Dance, Dance, Dance' in which Brian and Mike venture an alternate lyric: 'I'm gonna fuck, fuck, fuck, right on the spot'[121]) and the guy responsible for making things happen on time. He was the impresario convening the talent, and the composer writing twenty chords into a B-side. That he was producing musicians and sessions of this complexity and calibre was remarkable enough; that he had to boss around the bunch of young guys that made up the band while handling his oppressive father left him thoroughly stretched. Murry's meddling is captured for posterity on outtakes from the 'Help Me, Rhonda' sessions in January where, barging in drunk, and noting that he's *also* a genius, he tries to coach the Beach Boys in a more syncopated style: 'Quit screaming,' he advises one of the era's most expressive vocal groups, 'and start singing from your hearts.' 'Are you going now?' replies Brian quietly. 'We would like to record under an atmosphere of calmness.'[122]

'Help Me, Rhonda' – not only released on different albums, but in different versions, and with different spellings – was released as a single in tandem with *Today!* Sung by Al Jardine, it has an irresistible hook (the unusual name is part of the fun), all repetition until the hopeful, unromantic pay-off: 'get her out my heart.'*

Today! is another mishmash, collating singles from the previous year as well as the results of the January sessions. But the decision to programme the rockier tracks on side one and the ballads on side two adds coherence and even gravity to proceedings, contributing a sense of something deepening and darkening, like rhododendrons at dusk. 'Kiss My Baby' matches 'Please Let Me Wonder', replete

---

* The album version is lighter and lacks the iconic 'a-bow-bow-bow' in the chorus that helped make the single the group's second number one smash; the most obvious difference between the two versions is a curious repeating fade on the album cut, in and out, a production idea that for once fails to pay off.

with clopping temple block, tinkling bell-tree and deep horns; the impassioned 'In the Back of My Mind', sung by Dennis against a full orchestra, out-doping Sinatra, was a stunning album closer – or would have been, if it hadn't been followed by two minutes of aimless chat with a disc jockey.

Paul McCartney's admiration for *Pet Sounds* is well-documented, but it's hard to imagine the music on *Today!* failing to impress the group. The Beatles' use of additional instruments had been largely confined to piano and handclaps to date, and *Today!*, with its oboes, cellos and French horns, exhibited a production world far beyond their scope or ambition at this point.* Only Phil Spector, Johnny Franz (producing Dusty Springfield and the Walker Brothers) and the songwriting and production teams at Motown were operating in similar territory to Wilson. Spector's records were beginning to sound more Gothic, the vocals receding ever further into the mix. Wilson's production is both lighter and more surprising, much less string-heavy, with unusual percussive and decorative touches that enter the space like swallows in a courtyard. The ghost of the hop is still tangible in the reverbed guitars, and even when oboes and lush strings introduce 'In the Back of My Mind' the echoing clip-clop percussion and pizzicato, combined with the closeness of Dennis's vocal, distance it from the upper circle.

This sense of complexity with a light touch, combined with the intimacy of the storytelling, can be compared to the sound Lamont Dozier and brothers Brian and Eddie Holland were perfecting at Motown with the Supremes. 'Stop! In the Name of Love', which feels orchestral, is produced using exceptional economy of means: the additions to a standard backline are organ, vibraphone and baritone sax, the momentum derived from James Jamerson

---

* They would start to expand their palette in 1965, from the B-side to their next single ('Yes It Is', featuring volume pedal) through the use of flutes, wooden percussion and a string quartet on the *Help!* LP, to harmonium on 'We Can Work It Out' and sitar on 'Norwegian Wood'.

pumping the bass through the chorus. Even 'I Hear A Symphony' eschews strings, with vibes, horns and piano driving the song up through the keys as the chord changes descend, a brilliant illusion.

22 March BRINGING IT ALL BACK HOME

The sleeve to *Bringing It All Back Home* expresses luxury, sensuality and recherché taste: Dylan, caressing his grey Persian cat Rolling Stone, shares a chaise longue with a woman in a scarlet jersey dress. She coolly smokes a cigarette, while he looks like a cross between a James Bond villain and a kid who has lucked out with the boss's wife – which in a sense, given that the photo shoot was held in Albert Grossman's Bearsville home, and the woman was his wife Sally, he had.

Scattered about are clues to his current influences, including – in addition to Dylan's own last album – LPs by the Impressions, Robert Johnson, Ravi Shankar, Lotte Lenya and Eric Von Schmidt; a pamphlet from the Earth Company; and, on the mantlepiece, the first and only edition of Ira Cohen's *Gnaoua*, an esoteric collection of Beat writing published in Tangier. Only a fallout shelter sign at the edge of the circle blur suggests the broader context of tension and protest that had once been his canvas.

Two matched pairs of songs open the album, tempest and tender, with 'Subterranean Homesick Blues' and 'She Belongs to Me' followed by 'Maggie's Farm' and 'Love Minus Zero/No Limit'. The latter's slashed title alone is thrilling, and the song leaps through a compact set of enamoured verses like a dog through a wet field. The pace and playing on 'Love Minus Zero/No Limit' closely echoes the feel of the Beatles' 'No Reply', and we know Dylan was still listening in. When that spring the journalist Maureen Cleave asked how he could be sure the kids understood his music, he replied by quoting 'I Feel Fine': 'They told me, don't you remember that song, "she said so?"'[123]

The clattering 'Outlaw Blues' is followed by 'On the Road Again' with its tremoloed guitar and piercing United States Marine Band, throwaway songs that push harder into rock and roll. 'Bob Dylan's 115th Dream' begins with a great-sounding line about riding on the *Mayflower* before breaking down in uproarious laughter. Off he takes again through colony and republic, a 136-line picaresque of violence and deceit played for literary and contemporary laughs – some of his funniest lines are in this song: 'I said "You know, they refused Jesus, too" | He said "You're not him!"'* The delivery is relentless, a handful of blue notes rattling gaily over moments of loose scansion, and the song reaches a fine payoff as the narrator finally makes his getaway from America by boat and finds that the captain is called Columbus: 'I just said, good luck.'

'Mr. Tambourine Man', which opens side two, finds Dylan on a different shore: free of the bullies and shysters in '115th Dream', unharried, unhurried, tumbled and changed. This time the ship in the song is a sensory transport, the 'I' Dylan's *other*, in such surrender to the muse that it dissolves presence and intention. Don't take any of it too seriously, I'm not even here, you're only chasing my shadow. Forgetting about today until tomorrow is a plea, not a promise. The ethereal feel had been hard to achieve, but the spare arrangement and informal dialogue between the guitars are at last perfectly matched to the lyric. And Dylan's song about a tambourine, in a year when tambourines were everywhere, didn't even feature one.

The difficulty for Dylan was that these astonishing songs demanded to be taken seriously: how else was anyone meant to

---

* The terrain is not so far from the dark vision he would sketch from the St. James Hotel years down the line in 'Blind Willie McTell'.

listen to 'Gates of Eden'? The first line uproots us with its eerie move from tonic {I} to minor dominant {v}: the dominant should be the chord of return, but here the minor suggests separation, the 'bed that is never mine' of the eighth verse. The words don't quite cohere but instead threaten magnificently, building like bad cloud. There's another defence of subjectivity at the close, when after a stream of cowboy angels and hermit monks, he hears out his lover's dreams unedited and unparsed: 'With no attempts to shovel the glimpse | Into the ditch of what each one means.' The glimpse is fortune, interpretation penury: these are songs that need to be sensed rather than analysed, not picked at but taken in whole.

'It's Alright, Ma (I'm Only Bleeding)', with its urgent, sinister accompaniment and streams of four- and fivefold rhymes, unfurls like the kind of folk narrative the song's acoustic arrangement dimly echoes. Here are specifics to the amazing weariness, a rain of disdain for advertising signs, party platform ties and – best of all – 'flesh-colored Christs that glow in the dark'; bright youth walking through the money-swollen world and finding it hollow. This time the manifesto comes tinged with paranoia (the guillotine is a long way from open letters in the press), but the cumulative effect is stunning, a panoramic of how America felt, or how it felt to be an artist in America, or how it felt to Bob Dylan to have America in him.

The pendulum at length swings back to love, love deliquescent and en depart, the song itself the wounded raven. Dylan had recorded the whole of side two on a single January day, and would sing the songs hundreds, thousands of times more. A few brave souls would cover 'Gates of Eden' and 'It's Alright, Ma' in time, but in 'Mr. Tambourine Man' and 'It's All Over Now, Baby Blue' Dylan had written two more standards. Artists as diverse as Earl Scruggs, Gregory Isaacs and William Shatner followed the

Byrds to 'Mr. Tambourine Man', while the dramatic high-sitting melody in 'Baby Blue' appealed to singers including Dion, Van Morrison and – more approximately – Roky Erickson of the 13th Floor Elevators.

9 April **'Ticket to Ride'**

The Beatles beat the Byrds to the jangle, just. 'Ticket to Ride' came out three days before 'Mr. Tambourine Man': droning and shapely, it marks the start of a new phase of development in their work. Lennon's lazily nasal yet still impassioned vocal complements perfectly the thunderous rhythm, the combination of McCartney's high harmony and shaken tambourine on the bridge offering only temporary respite from the drawn-out *dooown*s and *awaaay*s. The sound is heavier, the percussive focus moving from Beatlemania's ride cymbal to the toms, the bass dancing through the bridge. The only real hook is the abrupt coda with its falsetto 'my baby don't care', which sounds like a joke that made musical sense. The song works because of tension and feel, not tune and form, as the Carpenters' 1969 version, complete with church bells and harp, makes painfully apparent.

The Rolling Stones, meanwhile, could argue that they had beaten both the Beatles and the Byrds to the new sound. Finally writing their own hit, they took the looping, lolloping 'The Last Time' to number one in the UK charts in March. The timelines here are also close, probably too close: recorded by the Rolling Stones in January but not released until February, the Beatles would have needed to hear it in the studio, or been given an acetate by their friendly rivals, for it to influence 'Ticket to Ride'.*

After being judged too green to play on their first single, the Byrds now had to step up to recording the bulk of an album,

---

* 'Ticket to Ride' was recorded eleven days before 'The Last Time' was released.

predictably called *Mr. Tambourine Man*. Fortunately, in addition to the stained-glass harmonies, they boasted a gifted and prolific songwriter. 'I Knew I'd Want You' and 'Here Without You' surge with Gene Clark's distinctive spirit: deep melancholy dressed up as romance. Five of the album's songs were written or co-written by Clark: it gave him status, which did not sit easy with him, and money, which did not sit easy with them. He was able to sustain the strain for less than a year.

The groove of 'The Bells of Rhymney' is so similar to 'Ticket to Ride' that it again seems the recordings must have spoken, but in this case too it's unlikely: the Byrds had played their song at Ciro's at March, and would have had only five days to obtain and digest a UK copy of 'Ticket to Ride'. It came out in the States on 19 April, five days after they had recorded 'Rhymney'.

It's as if tiny nudges in the culture were pushing artists into similar space so they could project as well as reflect the music their peers were making. The musicians were largely self-taught, operating on instinct within small-scale and repetitive musical structures. But they were as attuned to a new idea as Mozart would have been, and as able to adapt it to their needs, although without the levels of theory or craft that notation and longer structures demand. All the Byrds knew, Chris Hillman has said, was that they wanted to copy the Beatles.[124] Immersing themselves in the emerging aesthetic, they were gifted enough to produce something new, like elements reacting to produce a new compound.*

The Kinks, labouring on Pye Records and sounding as if they were recorded not for a Dansette but on one, exemplify this. *Kinda Kinks* includes their most interesting single to date, 'Tired of Waiting for You', but is otherwise a mishmash of shape-shifting

---

* Chemistry teaches us that such reactions rarely produce exactly the same atomic configuration: 'Elementary Chemical Reactions', *Technical Tutoring*, http://www.hyper-ad. com/tutoring/chemistry/Elementary%20Chemical%20Reactions.html. This is more common in rock and roll, as a listen to *Nuggets: Original Artyfacts from the First Psychedelic Era* will confirm.

pop and tinny rhythm and blues à l'anglaise.

But they too were moving through the gears. Their next single, 'Set Me Free', introduced their characteristic descending scale motif, while 'See My Friends' is even stronger, besting the drone in 'Ticket to Ride'. Again, it's possible the latter was an influence, but it seems unlikely; Davies had been inspired by the chanting of Indian fishermen heard en route to Australia in January, and the Kinks had already tried to record it.[125] The dragging accompaniment and strange, repetitive lyrics – 'layin' 'cross the river' – establish a dark mood in keeping with the song's inspiration, the loss of a sister.*

○

The music was starting to rush, leaving behind some of the platforms that had sustained its first flush: the Beatles made their last appearance on ITV's *Thank Your Lucky Stars* in March, and recorded their last BBC radio session at the end of May. The young men jumping daft in suits were now getting stoned on the set of *Help!* in exotic sunglasses, suede and corduroy; the Cavern Clubs and Gaslight Cafes were forsaken, their alumni too famous to walk the streets.[126] But as fame compressed their world into limos, suites and island retreats, it found them interesting company: the rich, who have always known how to have tremendous fun in private, and artists from other fields, welcomed them into the fold like Warhol's superstars for as long as they were sufficiently diverting.

There was an intimacy to the scene that allowed groups to hang

---

* Davies' song rivals the Yardbirds' comparatively feeble 'Heart Full of Soul' (also released in July) at the birth of raga rock. Posterity remembers the Yardbirds' guitarists better than their records; having featured harpsichord as a lead instrument on 'For Your Love', they first recorded 'Heart Full of Soul' with a sitar player. Dissatisfied with the timing and attack, Jeff Beck replicated the sound on guitar with the help of his new Tone Bender fuzz box.

out at clubs like the Bag O'Nails in London, or at Ciro's in LA, or at gallery openings. Sometimes they hobnobbed in hotels. Art school curiosity, at the heart of so many of the English bands, found new impetus. It helped that marijuana was less dulling, and LSD more surprising, than the heroin or cocaine that later slowed music and inspiration to a crawl. Dylan and the Rolling Stones both mocked the Chelsea girls that they encountered in New York or London; the Beatles were less immediately descriptive, and new tastes and milieus were instead refracted through the music.

April Lennon, Harrison and Brian Wilson take LSD for the first time

Half of the Beatles, and all of Brian Wilson, took LSD that spring. It's a shame that no *Carry on Tripping* film was made to commemorate the circumstances in which John Lennon and George Harrison encountered the drug. They were turned on not by some far denizen of the counterculture, but by a London dentist named John Riley who slipped it into their coffee, without asking, after a dinner party.

Accompanied by Lennon's wife Cynthia and Harrison's fiancée Pattie Boyd, both Beatles recalled a curious vibe that made them keen to leave: 'I think he thought that there was going to be a big gang-bang,' recalled Harrison, 'and that he was going to get to shag everybody.' Relax and float downstream: when they made it to a club the lift light kaleidoscoped into fire, and Harrison felt afterwards as if centuries of experience had been gained in half a day. Once they were back in Esher and the others had gone to bed, Lennon imagined he was driving Harrison's house, which was a big submarine.[127]

In contrast to the Beatles' haphazard experience, Brian Wilson's first acid was – according to his friend Loren Schwartz – 'a clean, pure and correct dose'.[128] 'He had the full-on ego death', noted Schwartz approvingly. 'It was a beautiful thing.'[129] But even with pure dosage and an experienced and attentive companion, a trip was unpredictable. The beautiful thing – a 'religious experience' as Wilson himself recalled a year later, teaching him patience and understanding – led within days to auditory hallucinations that never left him.[130]

In March Dylan joined the Byrds on stage at Ciro's on Sunset Boulevard, haunt – in publicist Derek Taylor's contemporary account – of 'a thousand glamorous ghosts'. It was old Hollywood in decay, but the venue revived as 'Mr. Tambourine Man' climbed the charts that spring, its varied clientele captured by Taylor at the dawn of the hippy scene: 'wayward painters, disinherited sons and heirs, bearded sculptors, misty-eyed nymphs and assorted oddballs'.[131]

9 May The Beatles see Dylan live in London, before hanging out at his hotel

When Dylan reached London the following month, the Beatles came to his first Albert Hall show before visiting with him and Allen Ginsberg at the Savoy Hotel. Lennon invited Dylan to dinner in Weybridge, and in Dylan's recollection they 'played some stuff into a tape recorder'. It got no further than the ideas for songs they promised, like school-leavers in the days before email, to send each other in the post. 'He said he sent me things,' Lennon recalled, 'but he got the address wrong and it never arrived. Maybe that's why we get on well – we're both pretty disorganized blokes.'[132]

The Beatles were in the final days of filming *Help!* when they learned they had been awarded MBEs. Their award was in the Civil Division, adjacent to Scipio James Robinson (for political services in Petersfield), William John Marshall Robinson (for services to the poultry breeding industry of Northern Ireland), and Phyllis Mayland Smith (lately Chief Superintendent of Typists, Ministry of Defence, Royal Navy). 'It doesn't make me any more respectable,' protested McCartney that summer. 'I'm still a scruff.'[133]

Like Dylan, Lennon was defensive of his muse: the spiky responses both made to journalists were protection against sentimentality and cliché. When an interview about the MBEs turned to rags and riches, he wiped a mock tear from his eye. Asked if living in domestic splendour had affected their writing, Lennon replied: 'No, it's easier to write with cushions than on pieces of hard bench.'[134] Ginsberg found the Beatles almost impenetrable, 'so unsure of their minds and speech' despite their fame and power.[135]

It wasn't so much that they were unsure, more that they absorbed new experiences through the filter of their group dynamic. They worked together, but for years they also socialized together. We're so used to the narrative that we don't bat an eyelid, but it's curious that this is how people encountered them: the Beatles in whole or in part, like a married couple. When Lennon was depicted a year later drifting between Weybridge and London in his chauffeured car on a cloud of unused presents and gadgets, he brightened at the rumour that one of the Beatles had been spotted in Oxford Street. 'One of the others must be out,' he said, as though speaking of an escaped bear.[136]

June to August 1965

		Bob Dylan	Beatles	Beach Boys
1965	Jun			
	Jul	[20] 'Like a Rolling Stone'	[23] 'Help!'	[5] SUMMER DAYS (AND SUMMER NIGHTS!!) [12] 'California Girls'
	Aug	[30] HIGHWAY 61 REVISITED	[6] HELP!	
		[16] *Dylan visits the Beatles in New York after Shea Stadium*		
			[22] *In Portland the Beatles meet the Beach Boys*	
			In LA they [24] *trip with the Byrds and* [27] *meet Elvis*	

Philip Larkin's famous line* about sex starting between the end of the Lady Chatterley ban and the Beatles' first LP ('rather late for me') is often taken as a proxy for the dawn of the Sixties. But in truth it took longer, as Dylan would recall half a century later: 'If you were here around that time, you would know that the early Sixties, up to maybe '64, '65, was really the Fifties, the late Fifties.'[137]

The Fifties as an experience and media construct had pivoted around mid-decade with the crossover success of rock and roll, and so it was for the Sixties now. The music of July 1965 confirms this, signalling another shared and transformative cultural experience. 'California Girls' and 'Like a Rolling Stone' sound different to what had come before, and there's a palpable expansiveness in these records which reflects the excitement of the moment.

---

* In his poem 'Annus Mirabilis'.

The music to 'California Girls' was inspired not by a day at the beach but by Brian Wilson's first acid trip: troubled by flashbacks to his parents, he sat down at the piano to compose himself. 'I was thinking about the music from cowboy movies,' he recalled. 'And I sat down and started playing it, bum-buhdeeda, bum-buhdeeda.'[138] A similar motif would resurface in 'Wouldn't It Be Nice', and as the idée fixe in *Smile*: 'Heroes and villains, just see what you've done, done.'

But this is not the first thing we hear: instead there is a miniature prelude, almost divorced from the song and its more famous girls. This opening is so stunning that it lingers like physical beauty, twenty seconds of marvellous driftwood plucked from a place of oceanic calm. It's Wilson's most imaginative piece of production yet, a simple repeating figure over a shifting B chord that accumulates deep bass and forest horns, melting away like the figures in a masque before a song of exceptional silliness. Not since Donizetti had such riches been lavished on something so insubstantial, and like the best bel canto the song achieves its own gravity via a combination of musical intelligence and sheer panache, the magical chorus feeling like a rallentando, whacked down on the beat, dragged by tambourines, the complexity of the start reduced to something almost primal.*

That so dense a landscape could be built from an appeal to truisms ('Everybody loves girls, right? Everybody loves California and the sun'[139]) may have suggested to Wilson what a lyricist more gifted than he and his cousin might provide. *Summer Days (And*

---

* The chord structure belies that apparent simplicity: where the verse uses a standard B major chord sequence, tautened by a ninth on the first change ('dig those styles they wear'), the chorus follows its own harmonic logic – just try playing it on a guitar. Driven by the massed voices, this makes it sound like a chorale, taking steps in and out of expectation.

Summer Nights!!) was the group's last album of original material before *Pet Sounds*, the two exclamation marks in the title a less than subtle nod to changing times. Brian Wilson would meet Tony Asher, an advertising copywriter, by the end of the year: ironically, 'California Girls' lives on as a kind of jingle in perpetuity.

5 July SUMMER DAYS (AND SUMMER NIGHTS!!)

The lyrics on *Summer Days* are at times ingratiating, and songs like 'Amusement Parks U.S.A.' and 'Salt Lake City' are more curious than splendid. But the album grows more interesting as it proceeds, and – at just under twenty-seven minutes – does not outstay its welcome.

The cover of the Crystals' 'Then I Kissed Her' is irresistible, surging like the sea, but romance turns queasy on 'Girl Don't Tell Me': 'your shorts, mmm | They sure fit you fine | I'll bet you went out every night | During your school time'. It's one of the group's most Beatlesque numbers, driven (unusually) by acoustic guitar, but the brief guitar hook sounds even more like the Byrds – which is possible, as it was recorded just over a fortnight after the release of 'Mr. Tambourine Man'. The song could have slotted right in on *Help!*, and Wilson explicitly recalled this as an example of the Beatles' influence on his work – specifically 'Ticket to Ride', which is quoted (in homophone form) in the line 'Girl don't tell me you'll wri-i-ite'.[140]

The mere mention of shorts makes the lyric more overtly sexual than any in the Beatles catalogue to date, and the contrast with today's pop, where profanities are vacuumed out for radio while remaining identifiable to anyone over the age of ten, is marked. Given that music was one of its most overt forms of expression, this bears out the idea that the permissive decade took time to take hold. The songs at this point are about love or sex anticipated, regretted or denied, but never about the act; the Stones' 'Let's Spend the Night Together' would smuggle in a first-verse reference to cunnilingus eighteen months later, obscured by the controversy over the title, but for now even the emblematic lemons and pies of the blues were gone.

'Let Him Run Wild', played at a curious, enquiring pace, is wooded with saxophones and percussion, exploding into the chorus like a burst of colour; the instrumental 'Summer Means New Love' leans towards *Pet Sounds* while not escaping, or wanting to escape, kitsch. 'You're So Good to Me', played with a Tamla tambourine on the beat, features a joyful, hard sung lead from Brian: the backing vocals are so perfectly attuned to the music that it's easy to forget how inane they are, high *la-la*s and low *doo-doo*s, drawing as direct a line to rock and roll as the cod-cathartic, piano-bashed 'I'm Bugged at My Ol' Man'. The latter has a troubling subtext given the family context ('he cut off my hair in my sleep' doesn't sound implausible), but ends on a note of humour inspired by Brian's love of the comedy album *How to Speak Hip!* – 'he doesn't even know where it's at'. The Beach Boys had even sophisticated their fun.

The last song on the LP is a cappella: 'And Your Dream Comes True' showcases the band's voices, barbershop harmonies shape-shifting like internal rhymes. 'One more summer,' they sing on a lavish cadence, 'and your dream comes true.' If Brian Wilson's dream had been to emulate the Four Freshmen, and then to rival Phil Spector, and now to outdo the Beatles, he was almost there. One more summer would suffice – but at what cost?

20 July 'Like a Rolling Stone', 30 August HIGHWAY 61 REVISITED

It's sonically gorgeous. That's the first thing about 'Like A Rolling Stone'. It starts with a snare crack before curling and unfurling around creamy organ, the sound of the band and the metre of the rhyme pulling Dylan's voice into a new shape, elongating the syllables, falling off the end of each verse into the irresistible chorus. How does it feel? Beautiful, like you never want it to end (Columbia initially judged its six minutes too long for single release). Nasty, too, when you dig the brilliant words, a pitiless takedown of a snobby society girl fallen on hard times. It's rock and roll set free in his music for the first time, one of Dylan's best ever bands digging into the end of each verse as if hauling trees from the earth.

It was his biggest hit until 2020's 'Murder Most Foul', and was only kept from number one at the start of September 1965 by 'Help!'; 'California Girls' sat at number 3. The single was backed with 'Gates of Eden' from *Bringing it All Back Home*, and the world had a month to prepare for whatever else Dylan now had to say.

It turned out to be something harsher than *Bringing It All Back Home*, musically and lyrically. There's no pop poesy like 'Love Minus Zero' on *Highway 61 Revisited*. The demi-monde prompts disdain, and the blues and rockabilly numbers kick out into ever more bizarre and populous territory, a deranged cartoon strip of outlaws, artists, graveyard women and Ford 10s loaded with lead: the atmosphere is loveless and lawless.

Dylan races off through the cut-up rockabilly of 'Tombstone Blues': the song traces a pitiless landscape in the wildest and scrawniest playing imaginable. The singer laughs at the start of the mournful 'Ballad of a Thin Man', but it's a joyless party, another takedown, the best verse the most restrained: 'You put your eyes in your pocket | And your nose on the ground.'

The tenderest moments on side one come on 'It Takes a Lot to Laugh, It Takes a Train to Cry', a smoke-voiced respite which shows Dylan's way with the sparest means: 'Now the wintertime is coming | The windows are filled with frost.' On a record thick with allusion and deceit, this glimpse of the hard country where he was raised is like a window opening for breath, an elemental handhold (like the Juarez rain in the first line of 'Just Like Tom Thumb's Blues') to help us navigate the chaos. 'I'm not a New Yorker,' he told Nat Hentoff in a *Playboy* interview published the following March. 'I'm North Dakota-Minnesota-Midwestern. I'm *that* color. I speak that way.'[141] On 'Queen Jane Approximately', an exquisitely weary and out-of-tune account of the vast disappointments that might lead a lover to the singer's arms, Dylan seems to be yearning for quiet too, offering himself up as 'somebody you don't have to speak to'.

Sides of records play like suites of music. Luis Buñuel wrote movingly in *My Last Sigh* of the perfect temporal weight of a cigarette, and the same can be said about each side of a vinyl album. I hadn't grasped that it was a single groove from edge to core until my daughter asked if it was so, and it's a marvellous thing: the sonic message unfurls in time like a trail of smoke, and is worth some care, like a glass of wine or a kiss.

Highway 61 is itself a single groove running from Minnesota's frost-filled windows (all the way from Duluth, in Dylan's time) to Louisiana, following the broad Mississippi down past Memphis, through the country of the Delta blues, past Robert Johnson's dark crossroads to New Orleans and the Gulf of Mexico, where Johnny Cash dumped his blues. Just as the title song relocates the Abrahamic sacrifice there, so 'Desolation Row' sucks into its twister characters past and present, real and fictional, sacred and profane.

To sit with a guitar and sing 'Desolation Row', a simulacrum of Western culture imperilled but set to the simplest and prettiest of melodies, is terribly moving. The mood is not hopeful but ominous, albeit streaked with images of beauty, like fishermen holding flowers, which are so incongruous they too become laced with misprision. A piercing Marine Band solo hails the poets, mermaids and insurance men into port, but it's not over yet: one last verse reasserts the privacy of the singer's singular vision, before, with the harmonica howling and the rhythm stumbling, the song at last runs out.

Part of the thrill of mid-1960s Dylan, and one never quite recaptured, is the sound of musicians still figuring things out – sometimes without pausing to tune up. These songs hadn't been toured and pored over. Chord charts for half the album were prepped by Dylan and Al Kooper over a weekend in Woodstock. There are rhythmic judders, and the musicians audibly try out new ideas as they go along. Kooper had never played electric organ before he sat down with the band to record 'Like a Rolling Stone', and found himself playing the changes a sixteenth note later than the rest of the band to make sure he got the chord right. A testy exchange ensued when Dylan asked Tom Wilson to turn Kooper up on the playback: 'Hey, now don't tell me who's an organ player and who's not.'[142] Mike Bloomfield arrived at sessions assuming Dylan wanted his signature string-bending blues, only to be told: 'Hey, man, I don't want any of that BB King stuff.' Bloomfield was nonplussed, but found his way in: 'I played the way that he dug, and he said it was groovy.'[143]

The tension with Tom Wilson led to his being replaced by the freewheelin' Bob Johnston, who was not going to stand on any kind of ceremony, least of all Dylan's: 'I never cared what he did in the studio,' he said. 'It was *joyous* to me. Whenever he'd ask me "What do you think?" I'd say, "What possible difference could it make, what I think?"'[144] Anyone reading Dylan's stream-of-something notes on the back of the record might have asked themselves the same question: angling the eye and mind away from the music, they discouraged literal interpretation of the more literal and interpretable words within.

Working with a full electric band, Dylan had now established how it felt to play with other people; the impetus he had
taken from hearing 'I Want to Hold Your Hand' in the winter
of 1964 was one he would never lose. Having been the last to
plug in, he now contrived to make the most exciting live music
of the era.

○

Between recording 'Like a Rolling Stone' and the bulk of *Highway
61 Revisited*, Dylan diverted from Woodstock to the Newport Folk
Festival for the last time. He sang solo at the Saturday afternoon
workshop, he sang pretty; Murray Lerner's *Festival!* captures him
being gawked at in a trailer, faces close to the glass, the crowd
chanting for more. He looks dazed one moment, amused the next.
A young woman raps on the glass, and he taps back. 'Where are
all my friends?' he asks playfully. 'They deserted me.' They aren't
among a group of boys outside, who ask cockily: 'Who needs him
any more? He's accepted, he's part of your establishment.'

Dylan was too elusive for that. The next day we see him
prodding circus swirls out of a Hammond organ in a polka-dot
shirt, jiving with Mike Bloomfield as an exasperated shirtless
soundman tells the band: 'It is essential that you get your levels
for your instruments and for your amplifiers and get them into
your heads.' They're still rehearsing the songs.

Forty years later Pete Seeger recalled his annoyance at not being
able to hear the words to 'Maggie's Farm', although the film
reveals them clearly enough – it's the tune and structure that are
rendered opaque, some of the changes missing, Dylan's monotone
lines cutting through the substance of the song like cheese wire.
To the audience the sound was distorted; Pete Seeger's father,
Charlie, who wore a hearing aid, was visibly distressed.

The crowd really does howl; you can smell the boos in the night air. Uncharacteristically, Dylan flubs his words a few times. Was he nervous at all? Hurt? Mad? It can't have been easy to be cat-called at home, and from the off the playing isn't quite on it. 'Like A Rolling Stone' starts out stronger, though the guitar and organ parts slip right out here and there; the playing is ugly and ragged, the rhythm uncertain, the song virtually falling to pieces at the end. Dylan takes off without ceremony, followed by Bloomfield, who is running his hands through his hair: the headline act had played for fifteen minutes. MC Peter Yarrow looks winded. 'Bob,' he gestures, 'Bobby, can you do another song, please?'

Bobby returns alone, with an acoustic, strumming the chords to 'Mr. Tambourine Man' before asking if anyone has an E harmonica, *anybody*, 'just throw them all up'. He is all shuffling charm, beholden only to himself for the number of measures between the verses, far from ingratiating but tender and giving, the mood now like the embrace after a lover's row. He sings 'It's All Over Now, Baby Blue', the boos for a short set, or a disturbing set, or a distorted set, or whatever it was, turned to cheers like water to wine.[145]

Seeger didn't take an axe to the cables, though he said he wished he could.[146] Forty years later, Dylan still insisted the crowd couldn't have been reacting to anything they heard. But he conceded he was hurt when he heard of Seeger's intention. 'It was like a dagger,' Dylan said. 'The thought of it made me go out and get drunk.'[147]

But Dylan chose to double down. Now in search of musicians he could take on the road, he was persuaded to check out a group called Levon and the Hawks on Toronto's Yonge Street. The Hawks were young and battle-hardened, but best known as a backing group: when after touring and writing with Dylan they struck out in their own right, they named themselves what people tended to call them anyway: The Band.

Dylan engaged two of them, drummer Levon Helm and guitarist Robbie Robertson, to join him at Forest Hills at the end of August. This time the reaction was even worse, prompting Robert Shelton to praise Dylan's composure in the face of 'the noisy young boors who ruined an artistically strong concert'.[148] Some threw fruit; others rushed the stage.[149] Paul Nelson bowed out as the editor of leftist folk magazine *Sing Out!* with a powerful defence of Dylan's new direction. He said the atmosphere at Forest Hills was febrile enough to be threatening if you chose to applaud – which he did.[150] 'I choose Dylan, I choose art,' he wrote. 'I will stand behind Dylan and his "new" songs.' Dylan returned the compliment with concert tickets for years.[151]

Robertson remembered it as 'kind of insane, people *hated* it – they didn't, like, disapprove, they violently hated it'.[152] Kooper quit after a second night at the Hollywood Bowl, alarmed by a tour itinerary which took in Dallas: 'I didn't want to be the John Connolly,' he said. 'I didn't want to be the guy next to him.'[153] Robertson was astonished when Dylan expressed satisfaction, describing it as a fabulous carnival: 'I thought, what's this guy on? Why in the world would you come to that conclusion after this experience?'[154] The rest of the Hawks now joined them: Rick Danko, Garth Hudson and Richard Manuel. Even Helm, a veteran of the maelstrom that was life on the road with Ronnie Hawkins, didn't make it past November. 'We were all in it together putting our heads in the lion's mouth,' Dylan said later. 'In my book they were gallant knights for even standing behind me.'[155]

The *Bootleg Series* recordings of him with the Hawks in early 1966 reveal a landscape swirling with Garth Hudson's organ, stung from bar to bar by Robbie Robertson's Telecaster, Dylan's voice the rain that changes the hills to silver. It's the last of rock and roll, as crazed as Jerry Lee Lewis's Hamburg stand with the

Nashville Teens, a small band pushed to the limits before amplification allowed musicians to drive volume beyond the scope of the music.

Highway 61 cohered fully as a rock and roll album, but it sounded very little like the Beatles, who admired Dylan, even less like the Byrds, who admired both, and only marginally more like the Rolling Stones, whose schooling in the electric blues (they had even recorded at Chess in Chicago) lent them a looser feel.

Dylan was riding his own train, speeding through a dystopian America peopled by anyone and everyone from Abraham to Bette Davis. In this sense, as Seeger recognized, Dylan was still commentating, 'trying to help us understand where we are, what we gotta do',[156] driving a wrecking bar into the hard soil of hypocrisy. In 'Tombstone Blues', the commander-in-chief calls the sun chicken for being yellow. In the title song a promoter suggests putting out bleachers, affordable seating for America's Pasttime, so people can settle down to watch World War Three. His songs continued to explore, albeit obscurely, the fissure between the American ideal and its prosecution. That summer there were riots in Watts, and the war in far Vietnam grew fat on bombs.[157]

6 August **Help!**

The Beatles were once more touring the world with their brief set. Noël Coward endeavoured to meet them in Rome, but could only secure an audience with Paul: 'The poor boy was quite amiable,' he reported, reserving from McCartney his judgement of the group as 'bad-mannered little shits'.[158] In Spain they played bullrings in the face of the Franco regime's distaste. In August they hit their high watermark as a live attraction by playing at Shea Stadium, brand-new home of the New York Mets. Over 55,000 fans were in attendance – a concert record until it was beaten by Led Zeppelin in 1973 – and they played through four specially installed 175-watt speakers.[159]

'Honoured by their country, decorated by their queen,' as Ed Sullivan declared,[160] they changed in the umpire's locker room and ran out of the dugout to a stage set up at second base. They were both horribly exposed and far removed from the crowd, who were confined beyond the outfield. The speakers were to no avail; the crowd was estimated to have made twice as much noise as the group. Dylan visited them at the Warwick Hotel after the show, and they spent the next day with him and visitors including the Supremes and the Ronettes. It sounds extraordinary, but it must have felt quite normal after the night before.

The *Help!* movie, now out on both sides of the Atlantic, looked great – there's a nice visual gag as the Beatles enter a pair of terraced houses that turn out to have been knocked through into a groovy pad – but the vibe wasn't the same as in *A Hard Day's Night*. By their own admission the marijuana meant they were no use after lunch, and even a scene with Frankie Howerd failed to spark, not making the cut. Filming in the Alps and the Bahamas was to all intents and purposes a holiday, and while their relentless schedule demanded one (the previous year's work hadn't ended until mid-January 1965, when *Another Beatles Show* wrapped at the Hammersmith Odeon) the musical world had started to catch up. They were to an extent, and by their own standards, marking time.

For years Beatles albums cost more than any others, whatever the format, and they were never discounted. Lavish remastering and deluxing initiatives over the last ten years have maintained the tariff, improved the already superb sound, and obliged Paul and Ringo, George and Giles Martin, and a train of distinguished Beatles writers, to revisit and reinforce a myth that traces a steady line of innovation and musical growth from release to release.

But as we have seen, there are blips – and *Help!* is an interesting example.

The mood is upbeat but a little static, the group not quite on automatic pilot but sounding more like an existing idea of the Beatles than they ever would again. The best of the soundtrack songs are McCartney's effortless 'The Night Before' and 'Another Girl', with their flawless harmonies and sparkling guitar. The sound here is full and warm, but the production touches elsewhere – flutes, volume pedal, bongos – feel thuddy. 'Ticket to Ride' aside, and with 'Yesterday' an awkward outlier, there's a hint of airlessness – the feeling, perhaps, expressed with greater vigour, in the title song.

'Help!' vied with '(I Can't Get No) Satisfaction', 'California Girls' and 'Like a Rolling Stone' for number one. The Beatles hadn't exactly taken their eye off the ball, but the game had changed.

22–27 August In Portland the Beatles meet the Beach Boys; in LA they trip with the Byrds and meet Elvis

Fortunately the Beatles were both sociable and curious, and the days were getting curiouser. When they reached Portland in August, Mike Love and Carl Wilson flew up from LA in the hope of meeting them; Steve Brown of KISN, who got them backstage, remembered them talking about girls, cars and places to live.[161] When Paul asked where Brian was, Carl replied: 'Oh, he's given up touring. He just stays at home, producing and recording our records.' McCartney replied that it was a good idea, which has the ring of truth.[162] Their encounter was sandwiched between two performances that day, and came after an engine on their plane had caught fire on the way into Oregon. This was the kind of scenario that prompted George Harrison to say that, in exchange for money and screams, the Beatles gave their nervous systems.* Allen Ginsberg was also in the audience, and wrote a commemorative but oddly unmemorable poem: 'hands waving myriad | snakes of thought | screech beyond hearing'.[163]

When they reached Los Angeles at the end of August, they rented a house up in the canyon, where there was respite of sorts. One afternoon two girls jumped from a rented helicopter into the pool, and a party in their honour was attended by the yesterday and today of Hollywood royalty, from Groucho Marx to Jane Fonda. Her brother Peter was there when Lennon and Harrison took LSD for the second time, accompanied by David Crosby and Roger McGuinn of the Byrds.[164] The day fed into the Beatles' music: McGuinn showed Harrison how he was approximating the sound of Ravi Shankar's sitar on guitar, and when Harrison got spooked by the acid, Fonda reassured him by saying that he knew what it was like to be dead – a phrase which both irritated and stuck with Lennon.[165] 'I'm having lots of laughs,' Lennon told Cynthia in a letter, 'but in between the laughs there is such a drop.'[166]

It was an eventful sojourn. Two days later they made the short drive to meet Elvis Presley at his Bel Air mansion on Perugia Way, falling out of the car stoned and laughing – 'just like a Beatle cartoon', as Harrison recalled.[167] Elvis was watching TV when they arrived and conversation was scarce, with the Beatles for once star-struck. 'If you damn guys are gonna sit around and stare at me all night,' Presley said, 'I'm gonna go to bed.' Now things loosened up: guitars were found and they began to jam. Marty Lacker of Presley's 'Memphis Mafia' remembered them singing Chuck Berry and Beatles songs, with Paul and Elvis taking turns at the piano. Priscilla found the Beatles shy but cute, with Lennon

---

* Pressed on a Beatles reunion in September 1980, Lennon asked: 'Why should the Beatles give more? Didn't they give everything on God's earth for ten years? Didn't they give themselves?' He was shot before the interview hit the shelves. Sheff, 'Interview with John Lennon and Yoko Ono'.

particularly quiet: he told Elvis that if he went back to making rock and roll records, they would buy one. The following evening, when some of Elvis's entourage returned the visit, Lennon told them he had been nervous, and to pass on the message that 'if it hadn't been for him, I wouldn't be here' – a message that drew a royal smile from its recipient.[168]

On their last day in LA, McCartney and Harrison dropped in on the Byrds at Columbia Studios, discomfiting the band as they worked on an uninspired cover of 'The Times They Are a-Changin''.[169] Gene Clark's stirring, surging 'She Don't Care About Time' was something else altogether, the song's hallways and staircases leading to a lover who sounds more wraith than real, waiting in a place of private disclosure 'out on the edge of time'. The hallways soon led to 'Eight Miles High' and acid rock: George Harrison requested an acetate, and later wrote to the group acknowledging their influence on *Rubber Soul*'s 'If I Needed Someone'. This was influence cycling back to the influencer, as Harrison was now picking up on the twelve-string guitar parts that McGuinn had initially modelled on his own.

'She Don't Care About Time' was squandered on the B-side to 'Turn! Turn! Turn!' in October, and left off the album of the same name. *Turn! Turn! Turn!* wound up weaker than *Mr. Tambourine Man*, and signalled the personality clashes and internal politics that would strip the Byrds year by year from 1966, leaving only McGuinn from the original line-up by the decade's end.

The Beatles just missed catching Dylan at the Hollywood Bowl, which they had just played themselves. Ingenuously admitting at a press conference that they were all fans, Lennon quickly backtracked: 'We saw him in Britain, and it was good, but we're not going to flog it.' Asked which band represented the biggest challenge, Paul demurred before mentioning The Silkie,[170] presumably for promotional purposes; Lennon had just produced their cover of 'You've Got to Hide Your Love Away'. It was a modest hit.

Meanwhile, a Mellotron had arrived at Lennon's house in Weybridge.

September to December 1965

1965		Bob Dylan	Beatles	Beach Boys
1965	Sep	[7] 'Positively 4th Street'	[1] *Paul and George drop in on a Byrds session*	
	Oct			
	Nov			[8] BEACH BOYS' PARTY! [22] 'The Little Girl I Once Knew'
		BEACH BOYS PARTY! features covers of Dylan and Beatles songs		
	Dec	[21] 'Can You Please Crawl Out Your Window?'	[3] RUBBER SOUL [3] 'Day Tripper'/'We Can Work It Out' [13] *McCartney takes LSD*	[20] 'Barbara Ann'

Two releases late in the year reflect back the music around them, although in different ways. *Beach Boys' Party!* is a covers album which sets contemporary songs (including ones by the Beatles and Bob Dylan) alongside their doo-wop influences. *Rubber Soul* – the Beatles snapping back into form after dropping the ball, by their standards, on *Help!* – shimmers with Byrdsy harmonies, exotic sitar and Motown rhythms.

The Beach Boys were preparing a very odd release, mainly for contractual reasons: Capitol wanted a Christmas LP. The album that made do – a set of largely acoustic cover versions overdubbed with revelry – is an incongruous staging point between *Summer Days* and *Pet Sounds*. But the song choices are fascinating, and the album – especially in the form of the 'uncovered and un-plugged' reissue – is a rare example of our core artists covering, or at least singing through, one another's songs.*

Brian introduces 'Tell Me Why' as his favourite Beatles song, and Dennis Wilson improves upon Lennon's recently released 'You've Got to Hide Your Love Away', his voice sounding like the back end of a Turkish coffee. Al Jardine delivers a brisk 'The Times They Are a-Changin'': he loved the Kingston Trio, and had advocated a folkier direction for the original group. They take off Dylan's more recent 'She Belongs to Me' on the sessions, but 'Blowin' in the Wind' is reverently sung, with a lovely jazzy, chorded intro. The harpsichord tone of the twelve-string guitar gives it a hint of baroque pop.†

The record reads as a pattern book for the Beach Boys sound, from the Beatles' hard-sung pop to jovial rock and roll and ballads including Boudleaux Bryant's 'Devoted to You', via the Everly Brothers; even folk would feature on *Pet Sounds* in the shape of 'Sloop John B'. *Party!* is a self-avowedly slight album. But thanks to the strength of the song structures of their youth – 'Mountain of Love' and 'Devoted to You' are as indestructible as Beethoven

---

* The Beatles played or toyed with a number of Dylan and Beach Boys songs during the sessions for *Let It Be* in January 1969.

† They also have a crack at 'Satisfaction', which was in the charts as they recorded the album, and they play it pretty much the way anyone might have played it in their first band. 'Ticket to Ride' is even sketchier, the sound of someone working out the chords – though they get further than the Beatles would with 'You're So Good to Me' or 'Lonely Sea' during the *Let it Be* sessions.

– it stands up better than a thousand yards of ponderous rock.

They performed 'California Girls' on the *Jack Benny Hour* at the start of November, ahead of a stiff skit featuring Benny and Bob Hope as would-be surfers in daft toupees. 'Looks like a couple of senior citizen dropouts,' says Brian, and in this company they kind of were. But nothing was stiffer than Mike Love's bizarre delivery, complete with moribund hand gestures; he wears an orange shirt with striped sleeves, but still looks like the guy who takes karaoke too seriously for it to be any fun.* They sing the song live, and without the orchestral prelude; Brian's high harmony on the first chorus is touchingly sharp.

22 November 'The Little Girl I Once Knew'

There was room for one more single before 'Barbara Ann' hit the stores in Christmas week. The sessions for *Pet Sounds* had already begun, and although 'The Little Girl I Once Knew' is a touch frantic by comparison, the arrangement betrays this. An instrumental version reveals how strange the music underneath is: muzak played punk, everything whacking on the beat.

It stands alone – for once the single wasn't recycled on an album – and DJs were nonplussed, interpreting the daring two-bar stop before each chorus as dead airtime. But John Lennon called it the best record he'd heard for weeks. 'It's all Brian Wilson,' he told *Melody Maker*. 'He just uses the voices as instruments,' adding – as the Beatles now knew – that he no longer went on tour, instead sitting at home 'thinking up fantastic arrangements out of his head'.[171] The conversation in Portland may have resonated with the Beatles as the year waned: there was no Christmas spectacular this year, but the group were still turning out in the nation's Gaumonts, Odeons and ABC cinemas.

---

* The author should know.

3 December **RUBBER SOUL** , 'Day Tripper'/'We Can Work It Out'

If *Party!* is one contemporary map of influence, a discovery made decades later is another. John Lennon's jukebox, a KB Discomatic which he bought in 1965 and stacked with favourite singles to take on tour, turned up at auction in 1989. The full line-up of the 45s is speculative, as Lennon's handwritten index card is incomplete and overwritten in places, but it's a tantalizing glimpse into his aural world at the time.

Early loves are reflected in the 'oldies' picks, from Little Richard to Arthur Alexander, but the increasing sophistication of Motown, and the grittier, heavier sounds coming from Stax, are represented in singles from 1965 – Smokey Robinson's peerless 'Tracks of my Tears', Wilson Pickett's 'In the Midnight Hour' and Fontella Bass's riff-driven 'Rescue Me'. Accompanied by Donovan's 'Turquoise', and the Lovin' Spoonful's 'Do You Believe in Magic',* the Discomatic is a mood board for *Rubber Soul*'s blend of ersatz soul, gentle acoustic tracks and enduring pop smarts.

Another single in the jukebox was Dylan's 'Positively 4th Street', released in September, a takedown song so dripping with rancour that it becomes gloriously life-affirming. The feel is so similar to 'Like a Rolling Stone' that it could be one of the 'same again' follow-ups conceived for the Four Tops or Supremes, and it made the Top 10 on both sides of the Atlantic; Canadians sent it to number one.

George Harrison also had a Discomatic, and shared its 'Fab Forty' contents with Tony Hall of *Record Mirror* in December 1965. Harrison has singles by the Beach Boys and Dylan: 'The Little Girl I Once Knew' and 'California Girls', and the version

---

* And/or 'Daydream' (a song they loved and acknowledged as inspiration for 'Good Day Sunshine'), which he added to the jukebox in 1966. The Beatles, *Anthology 2* (Apple Records, 1990).

of Dylan's 'Please Crawl Out of Your Window' that was erroneously issued as 'Positively 4th Street'. But the number of Stax records on his and Lennon's jukeboxes helps to explain the group's
growing interest in recording there.[172] Feelers were put out the
following spring, with Brian Epstein even visiting the studio in
Memphis. But financial and security concerns, combined with
George Martin's reluctance to record in the States, conspired
against it. 'George [Harrison] really knows his records,' concluded Hall, and he and the other Beatles did: the jukebox compilations stand up as well now as they did then.

These are songs that were in the group's ears as *Rubber Soul* was
drafted. The inventive beginning to 'In My Life' can be traced to
the Miracles' 'Tracks of My Tears'; 'Drive My Car' is driven on
the one, like Otis Redding's 'Respect'; 'Norwegian Wood' opens
with a pensive strum, like Donovan's 'Turquoise'. The sarky 'tit-
tit-tit' backing vocal on the chorus to 'Girl' was borrowed from
the 'la-la-la' quavers in the Beach Boys' 'You're So Good to Me'
(they assured George Martin they were singing 'dit-dit-dit'). As
we have already seen, Harrison tipped his hat to the Byrds for 'If
I Needed Someone', while 'Nowhere Man' has a distinctly Byrdsy
three-part harmony from the start. The album that signalled a
new level of creativity for the Beatles, one frequently cited by
artists as a defining influence, is itself highly receptive to the contemporary music around it.

It leads off with a thrilling riff, 'Drive My Car' driven by cowbell and tambourine, everything recorded hotter. The falsetto
'beep beep yeah!' is their catchiest hook since 'She Loves You', and
with McCartney's rock and roll voice now directed into original
territory and Lennon singing the harmony just as hard, the song is
better than anything on *Help!*

Lennon later stressed the attention the group had paid to track
sequencing, which is one reason the American albums, mixed and

matched from the UK releases and at least two songs short, are often unsatisfactory by comparison. *All their previous albums had begun with two faster numbers to create momentum, but 'Drive My Car' faded into something unexpected: a gentle but elliptical acoustic song thrumming with sitar, the whole reflecting Dylan's gentler mode on *Bringing It All Back Home*.

The roots of 'Norwegian Wood' went back to the winter, when Lennon had conceived it, and the spring, when Harrison had heard Indian musicians on the set of *Help!* at Twickenham Film Studios. It was the start of a lifetime's fascination and devotion for Harrison. And as the Yardbirds had chosen to remake 'Heart Full of Soul' with electric guitar that spring, 'Norwegian Wood' became the first western pop song to feature sitar – conveying a niche interest in Indian music to the mainstream. Harrison's playing is approximate to the point of comedy in the first take on *Anthology*, the concluding line jokily pushed way out of tune. But the final track, which has less drone, sounding less Indian but more liminal, is perfectly realized. Like 'We Can Work It Out', and later 'Hey Jude', it shows how a harmony line by either Lennon or McCartney could transform the feel of a Beatles song, the musical generosity transparent.

The album is full of delights, from the deliberate to the accidental. George Martin's baroque solo for 'In My Life' was painstakingly recorded at half speed and sped up to sound like a spinet; he worked during the group's lunch break so he could present them with the idea as a fait accompli. But the curious, almost imperceptible slowing down in 'You Won't See Me'

* Track sequencing refers to the order of the tracks, complicated on a vinyl album because there are two sides and therefore two starts (and two endings) to the physical experience of putting on the record. Sequencing at its best is sensitive to mood, the need for variety, and the keys in which the songs are played.

The US albums were beyond the Beatles' control, as Lennon had noted in LA that August: 'We plan it, and they wreck it.' Jay Spangler, 'Beatles Press Conference: Los Angeles 8/29/1965', *The Beatles Ultimate Experience,* http://www.beatlesinterviews.org/db1965.0829.beatles.html.

presumably reflects the unbroken thirteen-hour session that completed recording for the album. Brian Wilson particularly admired this track, picking up on the drone-like high A in the last third of the song.[173] 'Girl' was recorded in the same session and is as immediate as torn lavender, Lennon's vocal prominently mixed and extremely beautiful, the intake of breath in the chorus at once soulful and dirty. It's one his best songs and recordings, aching with desire and a kind of unlocated sorrow conveyed more by the music than the words. Perhaps this is what children hear in the music of the Beatles: it sounds like their own yearnings, but also embodies what they imagine the adult world to contain.

'The Word' is glorious, the high D on 'word' again sustaining like a drone as the song progresses; the organ now sounds biting and distorted, rather than ponderous and heavy. To an extent they were doing with contemporary soul what they had first done with rock and roll, channelling the feel while changing up the chord structures and adding their distinctive harmonies, but as always there were other influences. 'Michelle', conceived as a joke song, floats on harmonies so perfectly judged that it winds up musically sincere despite itself; by the end of the song the music has overflowed its generic limits, hinting at vespers.

When the 'Red' and 'Blue' compilations came out in 1973, Lennon lamented the stereo mixes, perhaps noticing them for the first time: 'If you mix something in mono and then try and fake it,' he said, 'you lose the guts of it.'[174] Even on the 2009 remasters, *Rubber Soul* sounds anaemic in stereo, revealing too much of the working and not enough of the punch. Heard in mono it's gritty, grating in the odd moment of guitar or organ, warm to the touch like cooked-up speaker valves.*

---

* Mono is a subtle thing, and doesn't work well through headphones, but play it loud through a Bluetooth speaker and you get a feel for how the music was designed to sound.

'Day Tripper' and 'We Can Work It Out' were released as a double A-side on the same day as *Rubber Soul*, and deserve to be heard alongside the LP. 'Day Tripper' is closest in feel to 'Drive My Car', with a more serpentine riff, and Lennon's vocal is as raw as it was on 'Twist and Shout' – the song even reprises the ascending *ahh*s. There's not much to it in terms of song structure, but the character in the singing, the craft in the arrangement and the enduring *joie de vivre* carry the day. In 'We Can Work It Out' the harmonium swells are marvellously tactile, the rhythmic change in the chorus dragging against the flow and ending (at George Martin's suggestion) in waltz time.[175] What is it, a ballad? Not really. A dance tune? Nope. Pitching us into the middle of an argument, the song marks a contrast in personality and message that is not as simple as it might appear. McCartney's lyric sounds accommodating but is in fact accusatory, asking for an admission of fault without offering one. Lennon's is detached – life is short, there's no time – but there's pathos in the youthful perspective. It lasts just over two minutes, creating a specific sonic landscape they would never revisit. Again, it sounds better in mono: in stereo one can see the joins; the dish separates out into its ingredients.

Two weeks later both sides of the single were featured in a Granada TV special, *The Music of Lennon & McCartney*. They were the only Beatle performances, albeit mimed, in the show. The George Martin Orchestra leads in with a medley based on 'I Feel Fine', best described as peppy, and incorporating for no obvious reason the opening to Tchaikovsky's *Piano Concerto No. 1*. John and Paul skit with just sufficient energy on an assortment of cover records, from Ella Fitzgerald to Honor Blackman.

Compared to the energy of the *T.A.M.I. Show* it's tame stuff. Peter and Gordon manoeuvre cautiously between static models as they sing their hit version of Lennon and McCartney's 'World

Without Love', the most dynamic feature of the set a staircase. 'A Hard Day's Night' is mangled at considerable length by jazz organist Alan Haven, who grooves wildly at the keyboard as if wrestling a steer. And the humorist Fritz Spiegl leads a frock-coated string ensemble in a parody of 'She Loves You' and its B-side 'I'll Get You'. It is made to sound like a movement from a Mozart string quintet, and a period-correct modulation into the minor would have raised a smile from any classical music buffs in the viewing audience. But it must have been a long wait for the Beatles' young fans.

The sheer confidence of the Beatles at this point is exemplified by the promotional films they made that November for 'Day Tripper' and 'We Can Work It Out'. Ringo spends more time sawing his way out of a train carriage prop than shaking his tambourine, while Lennon has McCartney in fits of giggles, at one point imitating the bass player's trademark 'oooo' head-shake. Their new album was being cut for pressing that very day.

Rubber Soul is an unusually precise snapshot of artistic intent in its UK format, with only one song ('Wait') recorded outside a single month's worth of late autumn sessions. The arrangements, for all that the album featured sitar on one song, are spare. They were still recording the basic tracks live at this point. There is film of their 1994 reunion at George Harrison's home, Friar Park, where they reprise their old roles: McCartney making the best of it, Ringo happy to be playing, and Harrison decidedly equivocal. But seeing these three middle-aged and not obviously stylish men playing through a handful of rock and roll covers is one way to be reminded that they were once a bunch of guys making music with their hands and feet.

The cover looks autumnal, the distorted perspective tinged in pinewood greens and earthy suede, the proto-psychedelic typography rendered in russet.* After the high jinks of *Help!* the Beatles look reflective, their mouths *sfumato*: the collage of thoughtful faces, overhanging leaves and cigarette smoke on the back cover intensifies this.

Rubber Soul drew on the world outside, but the final tracks don't sound much like their prompts. Otis Redding's 'Respect' uses only major chords: the tension is derived from the verses operating outside the tonic, moving from the dominant {A} to the subdominant {G}, so that the move home to the tonic {D} in the chorus comes as a release. 'Drive My Car' is played in the same key, but achieves a different kind of release by dropping to the relative minor Bm {vi} for the chorus; the bright harmony singing is angular, and the arch piano triplet after 'Baby you can drive my car', which seems to say 'if you know what I mean', offers an urbane counterpoint.

Donovan's 'Turquoise' is played on two chords. There is none of the variation found in Lennon's melody to 'Norwegian Wood', never mind the lovely modulation from major to minor tonic {I} at 'She asked me to stay', which acts like the unexpected vertical shot in a Hitchcock film: we know this isn't going to end well. So the Beatles were right when they said they had achieved something new on the record: this was adaptive influence in full flow. 'You don't know us now if you don't know *Rubber Soul*,' said Lennon, while McCartney called it 'the beginning of my adult life'.[176]

○

Three days after *Rubber Soul*, the Byrds released *Turn! Turn! Turn!*. The album is clad in gorgeous sea blue, but it's a fitful

---

* 'If you tap into a rubber tree then you get a sort of globule,' explained Charles Front, who designed the lettering, 'so I started thinking of creating a shape that represented that, starting narrow and filling out. I was paid 26 guineas and five shillings.' Lisa Bachelor, 'Iconic Beatles artwork under the hammer', *The Guardian* (17 Jun. 2007), https://www.theguardian.com/artanddesign/2007/jun/17/art.thebeatles.

effort: there is a gulf between the refined gloom of Gene Clark's 'Set You Free This Time' and the derivative 'Wait and See'. The latter feels patched from the slighter songs on *Help!* and runs out of inspiration completely in the chorus. But 'Set You Free This Time' unfurls in lines that alternate rapid and elongated syllables, fading out in harmonica that strengthens the debt to Dylan's gentler work on *Bringing It All Back Home*.

'She Don't Care About Time', the Gene Clark song that had so impressed George Harrison in the studio, was consigned to a B-side and left off the album in favour of leaden Dylan covers and McGuinn's maudlin 'He Was a Friend of Mine'. Two other Clark songs suffered the same fate, and a much better album could have been made.* There was depth and craft to the Byrds, coupled with curiosity and enduring oddness, which would allow them to survive their loss of their most gifted songwriter in early 1966. But they could never replace Gene Clark's songs, which would keep coming over the years as he tumbled through the cracks in his make-up like a rock down a ravine. 'Oh! Susannah!' comes as a relief as the album closes, the tune played for laughs like a raga: the nonsense words ('it was so hot, I froze to death') take on an acid hue.

Rock in this early phase had a whimsical side: there are traces of humour in 'Michelle' and 'Girl' on *Rubber Soul*; there is exaggeration in the Beach Boys' backing vocals which draws a direct line back to rock and roll; and Americans in 1965 were vulnerable to the blend of the winsome and the gormless found in Herman's Hermits' 'Mrs. Brown, You've Got a Lovely Daughter' and 'I'm Henry the Eighth, I Am', both of which reached number one in the US, although not, to its credit, in the UK.[177] Stronger than this tendency, fortunately, was a growing impetus in favour of self-expression, which would transform the genre.

---

* It can be constructed from the 2000 reissue.

●

There was competition between the bands; there was competition within them. 'Imagine two people pulling on a rope, smiling at each other and pulling all the time with all their might,' George Martin said of Lennon and McCartney. 'The tension between the two of them made for the bond.'[178] Our artists were now explicitly responding to one another's work, and if their most interesting albums of the year had been paintings, they would have made sense in the same show, in the way that the distinct personalities of impressionist painters coalesced around a shared spirit. But there was no movement, because there was no manifesto. The absence of an artistic credo allowed instinctive writers to carve out new space on their own terms, but the musicians soon found themselves caught between being sold as acts (which is what the Beatles' tours determined) and being seen as artists (which is what the style of Dylan's sleeve notes declared).

Rumblings in the counterculture had gathered pace in 1965. Drop City, a proto-hippy commune housed in home-made geodesic domes, took shape in rural Colorado as a live-in art concept.[179] The International Poetry Incarnation was held in London in June, and marked a passing of the torch from the Beat generation (including Allen Ginsberg and Lawrence Ferlinghetti) to the emerging hippy scene. Flowers were handed to the crowd as they entered the Royal Albert Hall, which rapidly filled with 'marijuana smoke, flying paper darts and foliage'.[180] In October, a thousand San Francisco hippies partied at Longshoreman's Hall to Jefferson Airplane, fuelled by LSD supplied by the 'artisan of acid', Augustus Owsley Stanley III. The illustrator Stanley Mouse followed the siren call to San Francisco, where LSD in his view brought a generation out of the dark ages: 'It cured the 1950s.'[181]

The Merry Prankster narrative of domes and dope and Acid Tests, which crossed over into the mainstream as flower power, coincided with one of activism and struggle. Malcolm X was assassinated in February 1965. Free speech, the free press, sit-ins and teach-ins all played out against the background of the escalating war in Vietnam. Three Americans self-immolated that year in protest against it, one beneath the window of Robert McNamara, Secretary of Defense at the Pentagon.

Briefly, public taste coincided with artistic experiment in an atmosphere of tolerance, but the period of grace would end as drugs and casual sex, hitherto the pleasures of the few, threatened to become the pastime of the many. 'I don't want that sort of filth here,' complained the general manager of the Royal Albert Hall after the Poetry Incarnation. 'Would you send your teenage daughter to hear that sort of thing?'[182]

'Satisfaction' had already been censored when the Stones played it on *Shindig!* in May, the tape clumsily scrambled at the line 'trying to make some girl'. When Lennon reflected on it all the following spring, observing that the Beatles had more meaning to young people than Jesus, his words were used to provoke a reaction that echoes to this day in the culture wars. But for now, the consensus held. We could work it out, like the Beatles said.

Couldn't we?

1966: EXCHANGE

London was now in full swing: 1966 was the year of the Kinks' 'Dedicated Follower of Fashion', and of Antonioni's *Blow-Up*. In ascent was San Francisco; on the third day of the year, the Thelin brothers opened their Psychedelic Shop in Haight-Ashbury, complete with a meditation room.* In February, the boutique Granny Takes a Trip opened in London.

But the mainstream changed only gradually. The work of social realist photographers tells us this. Family photos tell us this – my parents' car (their first, as it was for many in that generation) was no elfin sports vehicle but a sturdy Hillman Minx in battleship grey. The numbers of Americans using LSD for the first time peaked not in 1967, but – rising sharply – in 1972.[183] And the record at number one when I was born in September 1965 was Ken Dodd singing 'Tears'.

The bestselling car in the UK was now the Austin Morris 1100, a car with all the lithe grace of a pet rabbit. Consumer culture had more widespread influence than the counterculture, and the old world went on, its structures and hardships largely enduring. In my mind as a teenager absorbing the wider world of the Sixties from afar, it seemed the whole world must have been dressed by spring 1966 in Ray Davies' polka dots and stripes. But Pathé's Cup Final footage from that year shows only modest change from the years before. The community singing at Wembley no longer

---

* In November it was shut down for selling Lenore Kandel's *The Love Book*; by October 1967 it was gone, the hippie movement, they said, dead. 'The Psychedelic Shop Gets Raided', *Bay Area Television Archive*, https://diva.sfsu.edu/collections/sfbatv/bundles/210733.

makes the cut, but the band of the Royal Marines still marches on at half-time ('Liverpool fans would have preferred the Beatles,' the voice-over had noted suavely the previous year, 'but – that would have been taking sides.'). Only a portly man running across the pitch, pursued by policemen who miss him with a botched rugby tackle, hints at a loosening of the national belt (or, more plausibly, a bottle of Haig). The tone in these Pathé newsreels, which were admittedly on their last legs – sidelined by TV, they barely lasted the decade – is still one to cheer a weary post-war nation: 'Wembley, great Wembley,' declares the voice-over. Everything is 'great', including perfectly ordinary shots and saves.

The bestselling US single of 1966 turned out to be a song released in January, Staff Sergeant Barry Sadler's 'The Ballad of the Green Berets', hailing 'men who mean just what they say'. Sadler could walk the talk, having served briefly in Vietnam, but his story took a strange turn. On discharge he moved to Nashville, shot dead his lover's ex-boyfriend, and – after serving twenty-eight days – wrote a pulp fiction series about an immortal mercenary named Casca; he wound up being shot in the head in a taxi in Guatemala City. As Sadler's biographer concedes, 'The Ballad of the Green Berets' wouldn't have been a hit a year later,[184] as the musical culture began to reflect, after fifty years of world wars, Korean and now Vietnamese wars, a yearning for peace.

In 1966 it reflected just as strongly an appetite for kicks. The sting in the sound of the Rolling Stones and Dylan now influenced American bands whose encounters with LSD, arcane philosophy and astute marketing departments led to the first avowedly psychedelic albums. In the sleeve notes for *Nuggets: Original Artyfacts from the First Psychedelic Era* in 1972, Lenny Kaye summarized a 'changeling era which dashed by so fast that nobody knew much of what to make of it while it was around': his compilation includes 'Pushin' Too Hard' by the Seeds, the vocal spat over pixie-like organ, arpeggio guitar chords and a fuzz lead, and the 13th Floor Elevators' only hit, 'You're Gonna Miss Me', ominous and bubbling, from January. Their first album, *The Psychedelic Sounds of the 13th Floor Elevators*, would appear in October, followed by the Blues Magoos' *Psychedelic Lollipop* in November. That same month, the Beatles began work on 'Strawberry Fields Forever', twelve months after recording 'Michelle'. The momentum was irresistible.

January to June 1966

		Bob Dylan	Beatles	Beach Boys
1966	Jan			
	Feb	[14] 'One of Us Must Know (Sooner or Later)'		
	Mar	[22] 'Rainy Day Women #12 & 35'		[21] 'Sloop John B'
	Apr			
	May		[30] 'Paperback Writer'	[16] PET SOUNDS
		[2] Dylan and Lennon and McCartney play each other acetates and work in progress from BLONDE ON BLONDE and REVOLVER		
			[17] Bruce Johnston plays PET SOUNDS to Lennon and McCartney in London	
		[27] Dylan visits Lennon's house and they are filmed riding in a limo by D. A. Pennebaker		
	Jun	[10] 'I Want You' [20] BLONDE ON BLONDE		

Many of the tropes of Sixties style can be dated to 1966, which saw the arrival (as the V&A Museum puts it) of 'the miniskirt proper', and of Paco Rabanne's manifesto for '12 unwearable dresses in contemporary materials'.[185] Perhaps surprisingly, when our musicians chose to make music in their own contemporary materials, the public still elected to wear it.

The level of exchange in the counterculture – of ideas, drugs, attitudes – coincided with and fed a spirit of adventure in the musical community. This sponsored the wild experiment of The Beatles' 'Tomorrow Never Knows', Dylan's exquisitely elongated meditations on *Blonde on Blonde*, and the sonic ambition of the Beach Boys' *Pet Sounds*. All of these were in the can by the end of April, and two key meetings took place in London the following month: the Beatles and Bob Dylan played each other acetates of their new songs, while Bruce Johnston, the Beach Boy who joined to take Brian's place in the touring group, arrived in London with a pressing of *Pet Sounds*, in search of the Beatles.

●

Rubber Soul impressed Brian Wilson as much as 'Be My Baby' had two years before: he called that the greatest pop record ever made, and *Rubber Soul* the greatest album.[186] It spurred him on when making *Pet Sounds*, although the two records are not much alike. Where Wilson's work feels like a suite of music in the same emotional key, the Beatles alternates driving rock with gentler and more exploratory, even whimsical songs. But it was the US version of *Rubber Soul* that Wilson heard, and this had been re-cast, like all other Beatles albums to date, according to Capitol's whims and market instincts.*

---

* *Rubber Soul* was their ninth official album release in the States (it was only their sixth LP proper), and technically the nineteenth album an American Beatlemaniac could have bought in two years.

This time they wanted an album that sounded more like folk rock. So the album Wilson loved, and which prompted the most fertile phase of the groups' mutual exchange, was not the organic artistic statement he thought it was. Influence was in a tangle: the Beatles' latest work was jumbled up to make them sound more like the groups (especially the Byrds) who they had influenced in the first place. Each side of the US version opened with a song held over from *Help!*, while 'Drive My Car', 'Nowhere Man' and 'If I Needed Someone' (ironically, the song most directly influenced by the Byrds) were omitted.

The notion of a musical album as something closer to its roots in photo albums – something informal that might be rearranged – challenges our sense of the rock canon, though it's at the heart of playlist culture. The idea of Capitol execs sitting down to figure out how they can improve a Beatles album seems even odder. But the twelve-inch LP was only eighteen years old. As recently as 1946 Columbia had released Sinatra's first album, *The Voice of Frank Sinatra*, as eight tracks on four 78-rpm records stored in an actual book-style album; with one track per side, the listener could enjoy it in any order they wanted.[187] Nor were pop records yet seen as complete artistic statements: *Sgt. Pepper* was the first Beatles album not to bear an advertisement for EMITEX, the company's proprietary record cleaner.

The US *Rubber Soul* has its admirers. All Music's Zac Johnson finds it 'earthy and textural': without 'Drive My Car' and 'Nowhere Man', he writes, it's warmer and 'more organic'.[188] And it is this coherence that Wilson embraced: *Rubber Soul* to Wilson's ear 'was like a folk album by the Beatles that somehow went together like no album ever made before'.[189] It's worth noting that the second side of the Beach Boys' *Today!*, released nine months earlier, had also conveyed thematic unity. *Rubber Soul* expressed something he was already aiming for, chiming as much with his vision of his own work as with the originality of theirs.

Sometime Beach Boy David Marks suggested that *Rubber Soul* gave the 'introspective, melancholy' Wilson permission to express himself.[190] Like Dylan hearing the Beatles in early 1964, this points to an influence of potential rather than example. In Dylan's case it meant pursuing the experiment he had already made with a backing band, although he didn't adopt the harmonies that were so key to the Beatles sound. In Lennon's case, it meant absorbing the scope and free association of Dylan's extensive lyrics and applying this to highly subjective but pared-down songs that sounded unlike the source. Influence is less rooted and more mobile than example, and this, in imaginative hands, creates the conditions for a step change. The riches of *Rubber Soul* drove John Cale and Lou Reed to work harder at their new band, but what they made as the Velvet Underground was quite different.

Influence by example had characterized the also-ran Beat groups in 1964, and produced in the derivative early writing of the Rolling Stones and Small Faces a distinctive but limited English rhythm and blues that couldn't match the Motown and Stax songs that inspired it. But in 1966 the influence of potential can be traced in 'Eight Miles High', on *Aftermath*, and in 'Sunny Afternoon', where the Byrds, Rolling Stones and Kinks respectively become something other to themselves. 'Hey Joe', similarly, was a West Coast garage standard – recorded by the Leaves, Love, the Standells, and the Byrds on *Fifth Dimension*. It kept being replicated until Jimi Hendrix transformed it into something luxuriant, heady, inarguable.

'Eight Miles High' appeared in mid-March, just as the Mamas and the Papas made number four in the charts with 'California Dreamin''. The two West Coast styles, druggy acid rock on the one hand and gentle folk rock on the other, would dominate the scene over the next eighteen months. Gene Clark had shared his initial idea for 'Eight Miles High' with Brian Jones of the Rolling Stones, and the song wound up being co-credited to both Roger McGuinn and David Crosby. Diverse influences were once more in play: the Byrds had been listening to a tape of Ravi Shankar and John Coltrane on the tour bus, and McGuinn's strange, spattering guitar part was his attempt to emulate the saxophonist.*

The Rolling Stones, too, were transformed by the influence of possibility. They had started to write in earnest the previous year, but behind the stunning singles their albums were still ramshackle affairs. The Beatles had riffed 'rubber soul' from 'plastic soul', a phrase Paul McCartney said Black American musicians used for Mick Jagger,[191] and *Out of Our Heads* from summer 1965 featured some of the most ill-advised covers imaginable. Jagger just about gets away with Don Covay's 'Mercy, Mercy', but then takes on, and takes off, three of America's all-time great male soul singers: Marvin Gaye ('Hitch Hike'), Otis Redding ('That's How Strong My Love Is'), and – to add insult to injury – Sam Cooke ('Good Times'). It's a shocking sequence, Jagger's voice feebly pitched in half-baked imitation.

On *Aftermath*, released in April 1966, Jagger was now fully himself – although that turned out to be a curious melange. In 'Mother's Little Helper', punctuated by abrupt sitar lines, his accent in the brief chorus alone combines cockney notes ('mother's little 'elper'), the plastic soul accenting of the covers ('helps her ahowwn her way'), and a hint of cod-aristo camp in the rolled 'r' of 'thrrough'. The social observation here is sharp and empathetic (something which cannot be said of 'Stupid Girl'); at 'minimoise your ploight' he sounds like the Artful Dodger, which in a sense

---

* When they saw an actual coal train, they broke up in 'cosmic giggles'. John Einarson, *Mr. Tambourine Man: The Life and Legacy of the Byrds' Gene Clark* (Backbeat Books, 2005), p. 82.

he was, pocketing from all and sundry with an impish charm that disguised the theft.

The album is by turns laddish, coquettish, menacing and delicate, eclectic to an extent that *Rubber Soul* hadn't been: it evidences direct borrowings (sitar and fuzz bass had both featured on the Beatles' latest LP), formal adoption (using more minor chords in their songwriting, which the Beatles had done from the start) and a new sense of freedom, a wider tonal palette prompted by the Indian and baroque stylings in the air.

16 May **PET SOUNDS**

For all that *Rubber Soul* is remembered as a groundbreaking work, the progress remained organic and the means were still modest. *Pet Sounds* was more of a leap, a complex and compassionate work of art let down only by the cover, where much of the available space is taken up by a goat's backside. It is also, for all its sonic integrity, a compendium of contemporary musics – taking in the Beach Boys themselves, Sinatra, easy listening, surf music, Hawaiian reverie and folk sea shanty. Revisiting it for this book I smiled and cried, as we can at our own stream of words in a counselling session, the weight of it both improbable and deeply felt. It is a startlingly interior record, draining the listener of emotional certainty as much as it returns it in lyric empathy and melodic grace.

On Wilson's next project, *Smile*, the many constituent parts – including the overt use of humour – would lead to overload for writer and listener. Here the incongruity of the gentle Bahamian folk song 'Sloop John B' at the end of side one instead yields simplicity, the intrusion of grits and corn enough to bring the heart's ship briefly to shore. The song is delightful and energizing in Wilson's hands, but it is also (literally) a bad trip, aching with the desire for home. In a sense that brief and picaresque narrative anchors the whole album: the rest, like the ebb and flow of possible endings at the end of 'You Still Believe in Me', is experienced in waves that both calm and alarm. Having taken the song far beyond the Kingston Trio's chaste calypso, the group made a promo video complete with visual gags, Monkees-style choreography and, mainly, the band falling in and out of a dinghy in Wilson's swimming pool.

In memory the album is lush, opulent, orchestral. The two instrumentals, with their exotic stylings, perhaps suggest this. But in the raw it is mercurial and compact. At times it sounds as if the voices of the other Beach Boys – or on the instrumental 'Pet Sounds' itself, the brass – are being sampled from elsewhere. Listen to how economical the drum part is in 'Sloop John B', Hal Blaine hitting downbeats on the first chorus, 'unheard of', he recalled, 'just downbeats', before the rhythm changes to hard-hit eighths on snare and floor tom.[192]

The detail is applied with marvellous assurance and tact. Soundscapes we have remembered for years turn out to be mere moments, like the subtle brass accents at the end of 'You Still Believe in Me'. Ideas that hint at indulgence, like the oboe under-pinning the vocal line in 'I'm Waiting for the Day', or the string lines in the instrumental 'Let's Go Away for Awhile', are never overplayed. 'God Only Knows' was recorded with an a cappella coda, but was then stripped back to Carl Wilson's limpid and affecting lead. Even the decision not to include 'Good Vibrations' on the album makes sense; the sheer emotional rush would have unbalanced it.

The singer Helen Shapiro points out that the lyrics, too, are straight to the point. Tony Asher would be indiscreet about Wilson when interviewed in the 1970s, but one can see in the *Pet Sounds* episode of *Classic Albums* the charm that must have reassured his co-writer.[193] 'Tony was a very mellow person,' recalled Wilson, 'he wasn't a real peppy guy, he was kinda low key.'[194] Having bumped into each other at Capitol Studios, where Asher was recording advertising jingles, and with the Beach Boys away on tour in Japan, they got together for writing sessions at Wilson's Bel Air home.

Asher's lyrics, driven by a copywriter's instinct for concise communication, are far less ambitious than Van Dyke Parks' on *Smile*. Time has returned them to his world: 'Wouldn't It Be Nice' has been used to advertise washing powder, chocolate and (at the time of writing) mobile telephony services. The tunes are whistleable – I found 'I'm Waiting for the Day', not the most obviously catchy song on the record, on my lips one recent Sunday morning. Bellini was famous for his long melodic lines, and Brian Wilson may be given the same praise. The melody here is a stream that lasts for forty seconds, allowing for some repetition; the slower melody in 'Wonderful', from *Smile*, develops freely for twenty. Paul McCartney was one of Wilson's only contemporaries to match this; the melody in the verse to 'Yesterday' is almost as long, and may well have influenced him. (Bellini goes further: the glacially slow melody to *Norma*'s 'Casta Diva' advances across one and three-quarter minutes, demonstrating not only the limits of such comparisons but also why enjoying classical music is not an easy step from baroque pop.)

The primacy of melody in the Beach Boys' music is one reason it has been so hard to emulate. There are more gifted arrangers than there are inspired composers, and Wilson himself says he built the songs around the melody: 'I would write the melody then I would try to make the arrangements kind of like surround the melody,' he explained.[195] This sounds unenlightening, but is actually key. As the arrangement became more central to the listener's experience in these months, it remained secondary to the artists' compositional process: 'Strawberry Fields Forever' would be furnished in the studio, but it was written on an acoustic guitar.

The sense of interiority is intensified when we hear *Pet Sounds* in mono, where sound is not left and right like space but near and far, like memory. This develops on side two following the round at the end of 'God Only Knows', palpable in the almost maddening quantity of wooden and metal percussion, rattling like obsessive thought until it feels as if one is in a jar being shaken, or caught in the deep water of the waves and being spun. 'I Know There's an Answer' was initially and presciently written as 'Hang On to Your Ego', which could be a lifelong challenge for people who used LSD. 'I didn't know what an ego was at the time,' recalled Al Jardine of the struggle between Wilson and Mike Love, who disapproved of the lyric. 'But I learned very quickly.'[196]

Finally the tumult recedes, 'Caroline No' conveying in stark melodic lines that most familiar and intractable of human experiences, the loss of happiness. The constrained and repeated melody first resolves to the major ('oh Caroline *no*') before bursting onto the E♭ m {vi} of you break my *heart* – a chord which, surrounded as it is by sixths, sevenths and ninths, startles with its simplicity. The tide is out again, the wood blocks now broken glass rounded off by ocean: a brief sonic coda shakes us back, an idea extended by the Beatles at the end of 'Strawberry Fields Forever'.

Recordings of the *Pet Sounds* sessions show Brian Wilson in full control of his resources: calm yet decisive, fair but firm. He is quick to accept a suggestion from the piano that they shorten the accented break down in 'God Only Knows', but later says of the same section: 'So many lags or screw ups in the first half of that thing all the time, let's go.' When Wilson complains that the first high horn line is too jerky and that it should be slurred, the horn player responds: 'I did slur it, but it's a harmonic, you know,' which makes everyone laugh except Brian. He's marshalling his own resources, moving the bass clarinet in a little bit here, cajoling the kettledrum player there. But he hasn't played in an orchestra, he doesn't know the details of each instrument's range the way a trained composer would. Instead he bristles: 'Let's go, please, come on.' There was more than a little of Murry in his eldest son, and studio work is as much stamina and discipline as inspiration: 'One good strong take and we've got it,' he says, introducing take twenty. 'Let's put out.'

'Brian was between a hipster,' Bruce Johnston would recall, 'and one of your famous British generals that was tough. He was tough. He demanded everything from everybody.'[197] Nick Venet, who produced their first album, recalled that Wilson would work for hours on end, irrespective of cost. 'I used to think he was crazy,' said Venet, 'but he was right.'[198] One of the tape master boxes from the *Pet Sounds* sessions is marked 'not bad, Dad!!'

Just as Dylan had been allowed to record when he was ready, Wilson was now at liberty to record where he wanted. *Pet Sounds* was made at four different Los Angeles studios: in Studio 3 at Western; at Gold Star, where Spector worked; at Sunset Sound Recorders, and at CBS Columbia, which had the only one-inch eight-track in LA, allowing for double and triple vocal tracking. Venet credited Wilson with liberating West Coast producers and musicians, but at a cost: speaking in 1971, he speculated that the industry would now have been 'more equipped to handle a Brian Wilson, set up a lifestyle for him so that he could live and work without ever worrying about going broke'.[199] They said the same of George Best, that he would have been looked after better now, that they would have seen the signs, but brilliance is not easily managed: Maradona, fourteen years younger, lived only six months longer.[200]

The self-taught Wilson was able to lead trained musicians

because he had the strategy for the completed song in his head and was able to communicate it to the players without scores. Passing round handwritten and often untitled chord sheets, Wilson would move from the rhythm section to the guitars, pianos and horns, singing parts and defining rhythms, working the chart in the room before going into the control room.* Was he a genius? Al Jardine says he has a 'special receiver', while Bruce Johnston settles for 'so gifted'. Wilson himself demurs, saying that genius is being clever, good at something, like (he says this with a touching lack of irony) Albert Einstein.[201]

From being a band famous for songs about girls and hot rods, the Beach Boys (or specifically Brian Wilson, who was even credited as solo artist on a single release of 'Caroline No') had made a masterpiece. Wilson himself knew that the album was different to what had gone before, telling *Melody Maker* in March 1966: 'It's all been like an explosion for us.'[202]

It attracted mixed reviews from its peers, although not from Lennon and McCartney: Mick Jagger liked the production more than the songs, while Pete Townshend judged it overly remote. It didn't sell as much as Capitol wanted or expected. 'The record company in America really let him down,' said Bruce Johnston. 'All of a sudden this can't do anything wrong guy was made to feel he had done something wrong, and started losing a little of his confidence.'[203]

[17 May] Bruce Johnston plays PET SOUNDS to Lennon and McCartney in London

Lennon and McCartney were able to form an opinion of the

---

* The charts were not perfect. Bassist Carol Kaye admitted that the seasoned musicians discreetly rewrote them: 'We admired Brian so much,' she recalled, 'we'd quickly do it and not say a word.' 'On the Issue of Brian not Writing his own Charts: Carol Kaye as related to Gus Russo', *Cabin Essence*, http://www.cabinessence.net/essays/owncharts.html.

album earlier than most. The Beatles had already recorded 'Paperback Writer', a Beach Boys homage of sorts, before they heard *Pet Sounds* a day after its US release. Today the album would have been delivered by armoured car to captive journalists, but in 1966 the newest band member, Bruce Johnston, brought a pressing to London by aeroplane on the off-chance. He immediately hit it off with Keith Moon of the Who, with whom he did the rounds of TV, music press and the clubs; the pair then arrived late for the Who's own concert, sparking an onstage brawl among the group.

It was Moon who introduced him to Lennon and McCartney at one of their regular clubs, the Scotch of St James, and they agreed to come to the Waldorf Hotel, where Johnston had secured a record player, to hear *Pet Sounds*. 'We played it through, and then we played it again,' Johnston recalled. 'They were so polite and cool.' They were also receptive and thoughtful – in one account heading straight for the nearest piano, where they 'began playing chords and discussing a song with each other in a whispered conversation'.[204] This sounds hagiographic, but London had at any rate welcomed the messenger. 'I almost got knighted because I brought this great work I had nothing to do with,' recalled Johnston, whose initiative now encouraged EMI to get behind the album. It was a bigger hit in Europe and the UK than it was at home.[205]

Sessions for *Revolver* were well under way, but 'Here, There and Everywhere' was written soon after they heard *Pet Sounds*, and its gentle sound world (complete with a pensive introduction) reflects this. But the album would have more of an impact on McCartney's writing on 'Penny Lane' and *Sgt. Pepper's Lonely Hearts Club Band*, in pulsing rhythms that echo 'God Only Knows', and via Wilson's use of inverted chords (where the bass plays something other than the root note, subtly reframing the parent chord).* More broadly, as with the influence of *Rubber Soul* on *Pet Sounds*, the record inspired resolve and trepidation in equal measure. 'Oh dear me,' McCartney remembered thinking, 'this is the album of all-time. What are we gonna do?'[206] The tables had been turned.

As a fellow bass player, and the group's most fluent melodicist, McCartney was the main conduit for Wilson's work: 'I played it to John so much that it would be difficult for him to escape the influence,' he said of the sessions for their next album. 'If records had a director within a band, I sort of directed *Pepper*. And my influence was basically the *Pet Sounds* album.'[207]

^{2 May} **Dylan and Lennon and McCartney play each other acetates and work in progress**
^{27 May} **Dylan visits Lennon's house and they are filmed riding in a limo by D. A. Pennebaker**

May was a month of meetings: it had started when Dylan caught up with the Beatles in London. This time, in a tantalizing scenario, they played each other acetates from their forthcoming, unnamed records, in the company of Brian Jones and Keith Richards.†

Dylan had with him acetates of *Blonde on Blonde*, and the Beatles were keen to play him work in progress from *Revolver* – including 'Tomorrow Never Knows'. But while the night can be seen as an historic summit, it was also the point at which Dylan's

---

* These are known as slash chords to pop and jazz musicians; the slash divides the main chord from the bass note. A good example is the beautiful D/A – a D chord with an A in the bass – that begins 'God Only Knows'. Try it on the piano: D to B minor is obvious; D/A to B minor is magical. The bass note problematizes the home key, echoing the doubt in the words of the song. 'I may not' under a straight D chord sounds a little undercooked, but the A in the bass already aches for the B minor.

† A working title for *Revolver* was 'Abracadabra'; as they came to mix *Blonde on Blonde*, producer Bob Johnston turned to its author and asked: 'What do you want to call this?' Howard Sounes, *Down the Highway: The Life of Bob Dylan* (Grove Press, 2001), p. 205.

investment in the Beatles' music began to wane. His own influence on them had been absorbed, and now manifested obliquely in music he didn't care for. They had taken what they needed, even if it was a slow-acting drug, and were now prepared to work more freely. In Lennon's case this meant narrowing the gap between the associative technique he used in his prose, and the more conventional approach he took to lyrics.*

Conversation opened with uneasy-sounding banter about screaming girls. Dylan had been more screeched than screamed at since the autumn, and perhaps didn't appreciate how weary the Beatles had become of touring. Public image was evidently on his mind, and his reaction to 'Tomorrow Never Knows' was an obvious mask for whatever he did or didn't make of it. 'Oh, I get it,' he deadpanned. 'You don't want to be cute any more.'[208] It was too late for the meeting to influence *Blonde on Blonde*, but Dylan took an ascetic view of the more experimental production, and he was no more impressed by the sound of *Sgt. Pepper* the following year.

Lennon in turn took against Dylan's '4th Time Around', which he interpreted as a dig at the expense of 'Norwegian Wood'. Both songs are in E and share the ¾ time signature, and when Dylan asked what he thought, Lennon replied that he didn't like it. 'I was very paranoid about that,' he admitted later. 'I mean he wasn't playing any tricks on me. I was just going through the bit.'[209] (The Beatles would have heard it again at the Albert Hall at the end of the month, rubbing salt into any wound. They didn't hear 'I Wanna Be Your Lover'; recorded early during the *Blonde on Blonde* sessions, and quoting directly from their own 'I Wanna be Your Man', it went unreleased until 1985. The exuberance might

---

* 'I used to write a book or stories on one hand and write songs on the other,' Lennon explained in 1968. 'Dylan taught us a lot in this respect.' Jonathan Cott, 'John Lennon: The Rolling Stone Interview', *Rolling Stone* (23 Nov. 1968), https://www.rollingstone.com/music/music-news/john-lennon-the-rolling-stone-interview-186264/.

have made the playfulness more apparent: 'I don't wanna be hers,' sings Dylan, 'I wanna be yers.') Dylan's song might as well have come from Donovan's 'Turquoise'; it sits somewhere between that and 'Norwegian Wood' in terms of melodic interest.

The acquaintance endured for now. Lennon invited Dylan to his house at the end of the month, when the pair were filmed in a queasy encounter by D. A. Pennebaker. Brilliant but not academic, wary of engaging on an intellectual level with analysis that might compromise their own creativity, they shared a sense that they could see through anyone and everything. This made it hard for them to see each other, a dynamic captured in the footage of them together in the back of a chauffeur-driven limo. Both wear dark glasses, and conversation is uneasy; Dylan looks especially fragile. A year earlier his road-trip companion Nico, no stranger to the morning-after look despite her eternal cheekbones, had already said he looked terrible, 'like a handyman'.[210]

What may have been a semi-scripted conversation gets nowhere, partly because Dylan is fading by the minute: 'Come, come, boy, it's only a film,' says Lennon. 'Come, come, pull yourself together. Another few dollars, eh? That'll get your head up.' Dylan was sufficiently ill by the end of the ride to need helping to his room; Lennon joked that it was the last they would be seeing of him.[211]

Dylan rallied for that evening's performance at the Albert Hall, the last of his world tour. The Beatles – cute or not – were supportive enough to boo from their box when the audience jeered Dylan, and to send him a supportive message after the show. 'The booing didn't matter,' they wrote, 'the music did.'[212] They also said they would see him at his hotel, but Dylan was finally spent. When they arrived he was nowhere to be seen, and Grossman and Robbie Robertson attempted to revive him by drawing him a bath. Robertson describes in his memoir, *Testimony*, how

Dylan almost immediately sank down into the water and nearly drowned. There was to be no all-nighter this time.[213]

Taken together, these May meetings signal a realignment in the trajectory of our narrative. The artistic and personal relationship between Dylan and the Beatles had been fruitful, especially when it came to Lennon's songs, but was now fraying; George Harrison would be the one to reconnect with Dylan later in the decade. There had been less personal contact between the Beatles and the Beach Boys to date, and none with Brian Wilson himself. Musically, the Beach Boys had responded more to the Beatles than the other way round. But this was about to change, with McCartney now to the fore.

30 May **'Paperback Writer'**

I'm still thrilled by the knowledge that I was alive when these records were released. I was less than a year old, but – even if I didn't encounter the music at home – I must have heard snatches of them from transistor radios and passing cars. Waking at dawn on summer mornings thirty years later, when my son was the same age, I would drive to Chiswick House and push him around the walks, entering the great empty conservatory with its camellias and cool iron, the belly of a contented ghost. I didn't know it then, but I was close to a crack in time: this is where the Beatles had recorded promo films for 'Paperback Writer' and 'Rain' exactly thirty years before.

The films were made to provide access that the band were now reluctant to grant in person; the first frame of 'Rain' shows Ringo walking away from a gateway where schoolchildren are crowding. The mood is, in keeping with the music, a sort of sinister pastoral. McCartney still displays a badly chipped front tooth from a moped accident in Liverpool at Christmas 1965. He had been in the company of Tara Browne, whose fatal car accident a year later at the end of 1966 is commemorated in 'A Day in the Life'.

Free of recording fees or standard hours, the group began to make EMI's Abbey Road studio their home. It was a kind of laboratory where new machines were built and new techniques developed; technicians still wore white coats when setting up equipment, and a dress code for staff was only abandoned in 1969.[214] In what would become a working and workable practice for the next eighteen months or so, culminating in 'I Am the Walrus', the countercultural impetus outside the studio dovetailed with a sort of potting shed ingenuity and can-do spirit within, compensating for the hotter American sound they had sought to find in Memphis.

When John Lennon said that he wanted to sound like the Dalai Lama singing from a mountaintop, Geoff Emerick – on his first day as chief engineer for the group – made sense of it by imagining the scene on nearby Highgate Hill, an accommodation which is in its own way more surreal.[215] Lennon loved the sound of double-tracked vocals, but not the chore of doing them; Ken Townsend invented automatic double tracking (ADT) to compensate. The curious and delicious sounds on the Beatles' psychedelic recordings (around forty songs between April 1966 and October 1967) reflect a mix of invention and improvisation grounded in musical ideas, developed within the constraints of four-track recording and flown under the radar, as far as possible, of Abbey Road's formal policy: to put Lennon's voice through a Leslie speaker they had to break into the circuitry.[216]

The 'Paperback Writer'/'Rain' single reflects this. Handwritten session notes detail efforts to boost the bass via limiting, compression and 'filters in Mr Cook's pad'; trying the jangle box through a Leslie speaker; and the use of ADT on the remix. 'All having a good time,' it records, although Ken Townsend got a rap on the knuckles for messing with the impedances. Even the mastering was different: the louder bass sound they had achieved risked making the needle jump, so to cut the lacquer they used 'a wonderful new machine just invented by the backroom boys', as if it were a Sopwith Camel.[217]

These were the first songs the public heard from the *Revolver* sessions, released between *Pet Sounds* and *Blonde on Blonde* at the end of May. *Revolver* would sound no more like *Pet Sounds* than the latter resembles *Rubber Soul*, but 'Paperback Writer', an oddly overwrought and unbalanced single, sounded – with its layered a cappella opening and elaborate backing vocals – as if it might.

In truth the sound is harder than anything the Beach Boys or the Beatles themselves had yet produced. The stereo mix, still crudely split at this stage with bass in the right channel and guitars in the left, is pretty messy. The B-side, 'Rain', is both more sonically coherent and more experimental: there is varispeeding in what would become a characteristic Lennon vocal sound, a thrilling drum part, and some novel backwards phrasing at the end. Overall the single's sound is hard, angular, crashing: more complex than the garage rock by the Standells and Leaves in the US charts, but heavier than much of the gentle pop in the UK chart it briefly topped in June – including the Mamas and the Papas' 'Monday Monday', the Kinks' 'Sunny Afternoon' and the Lovin' Spoonful's 'Daydream'. Only the Rolling Stones' 'Paint It Black', taking up the sitar from Norwegian Wood and applying it to something more febrile, compares.

20 June BLONDE ON BLONDE

It's tempting to see *Blonde on Blonde* as the end of an era, the last of Dylan's great trio of mid-1960s head records. But the album also looks forward. It was largely recorded in Nashville following unproductive sessions in New York, and guitarist Charlie McCoy and drummer Kenny Buttrey would feature on his next two albums, *John Wesley Harding* and *Nashville Skyline.*

Once installed in Nashville's Columbia Studio B, Bob Johnston and Dylan arranged the studio without baffles or distancing. The musicians ranged around on fifty-foot cables, their amplifiers set in adjacent rooms, and Johnston erected a glass booth for Dylan in the middle of the studio: 'He was in there with a table and chair – it was like his study.'[218] The record as a whole is more intimate and less uproarious than *Highway 61 Revisited*, anchored by 'Sad Eyed Lady of the Lowlands' over the whole of the fourth side. After the road blues of *Highway 61* it represents a return to Dylan making pop on his own terms, or shaping it to his own ends: as the historian Sean Wilentz points out, he starts to write middle eights on this album.[219]

Side three is a fertile place to explore this development. The lazy, piano-led 'Temporary Like Achilles' is essentially a muted blues. But the chords in the middle eight step down from G to its relative E minor {vi}, and then more soulfully up to a B minor {iii}, a change characteristic of Curtis Mayfield's writing for the Impressions: this anticipates the many songs on *Nashville Skyline* which explore similar space. Dylan waits the best part of two minutes before introducing this change. He's in no hurry, and later blows his harp over a languid repeat.

Robbie Robertson, one of Dylan's closest associates at this time, found the stream of words in the acoustic set he heard each night on tour hard going: 'It was too talky for me,' he admitted. 'I didn't want to listen to that many words from anybody – anybody!' Robertson played the Impressions to him, focusing on the mood and the sound quality, saying his music could be 'more soulful and simplified'.[220] *Blonde on Blonde* suggests that this was beginning to filter through.

'Absolutely Sweet Marie' has more than a hint of Motown in the drum pattern, and recycles the riff from the Byrds' 'Feel a Whole Lot Better' (itself lifted from the Searchers' 'Needles and Pins') on the organ. Shuffling the same pack of chords as 'Achilles', it takes an unprecedently pop turn for a Dylan song in the middle eight, moving from D {I} to the borrowed { ♭VI} B♭ in a way that would have slotted readily onto the Stones' *Aftermath*, and which Dylan later uses achingly on *Nashville Skyline*'s 'Tonight I'll Be Staying Here with You'. It's perfectly danceable; if a band had been booked for a rave-up and failed to show, and Dylan had stepped in, this song would have done the job – though he might have had to play it all night.

The next song, '4th Time Around', is the one that appears to quote 'Norwegian Wood' in its pretty, circling melody. According to Al Kooper, who raised an eyebrow at the similarity in the studio, Dylan claimed the Beatles had taken the idea from his own private, acoustic rendition of the song in the first place; if this happened it must have been in May 1965 – but Lennon had already started work on the song in February. [221] The song sounds sincere enough in its own right, and Dylan at least thought it worthy of twenty takes.

The LP opens with the eccentric 'Rainy Day Women #12 & 35', enlivened by what sounds like a marching band that has fallen on a consignment of Pusser's Rum. Dylan's delighted refrain, 'everybody must get stoned,' his voice ranging approximately in pitch like level meters surging on a console, took the song to number two, his biggest hit for the next half century. 'Pledging My Time' slows his trademark blues to a crawl, sloping out to harmonica that sounds like a guitar played through a reverb pedal. The pressure now drops even further, the volume is turned down, and 'Visions of Johanna' moves us like a panning shot from the streets to a loft – or if not a loft then your friend's bedroom in Tunbridge Wells, or your bare student room, or any close and conversational space full of the stamina and curiosity of youth. It's the sound of 2 a.m., the feel of a party thinning out, the beat before a kiss.

It's also kind of funky. *Blonde on Blonde* in this mode is a gentle thing, the warbling organ more a hand in yours than a wake-up call: the lingering bridges in 'One of Us Must Know (Sooner or Later)' and 'I Want You' are erotic handholds in a falling dream. Rather than a map of America in flames, its four sides sound like a way of being: tender, brilliant, boastful, full of characters that now feel tangible, relatable. Even Shakespeare, when he makes an appearance, is in the alley talking to some French girls.

It was the first rock double album, just beating *Freak Out!* by the Mothers of Invention, and is long enough to accommodate the eleven-minute 'Sad Eyed Lady of the Lowlands', the jaunty pop of 'I Want You' (which employs the descending scale that was as ubiquitous in the music of 1966 as the tambourine the year before), and leisurely blues songs. Robbie Robertson, whose service with the other Hawks on tour was not rewarded with many studio recordings with Dylan, brings piercing guitar to the rangy 'Leopard-Skin Pill-Box Hat'.

Dylan looks drawn and weary in the blurred cover shot, inscrutable as Rimbaud in Abyssinia. The drab colours of his skin, hair and suede coat merge with the background like an insect on a branch; in one of the gatefold shots he holds a pair of pliers to a portrait of a Victorian woman, as if ready to pull the teeth of the past. Elsewhere he lights a cigarette, rolls a joint, and is pictured at his Telecaster somewhere on the spring tour, heavy-lidded, his mouth pursed and defiant.

He had come to feed on and return the crowds' fury. May 1966 footage of him singing 'Like a Rolling Stone' in Newcastle shows him bawling the lines and gurning, squinting into the lights like a man who would be enjoying the colours on an LSD trip if he hadn't forgotten his specs.[222] The derision is palpable when he moves to the piano for 'Ballad of a Thin Man': there are cries for him to go home, switch the mike off, and Dylan plays the song with corresponding rage, flinging his left hand off the keyboard like a preacher. In the car he admits that it's hard to focus with all the booing, and wonders why people bought up the tickets so fast. But on some level his wariness of artistic safety kept the booing in perspective. 'You gotta realize,' he said later, 'you can kill somebody with kindness too.'[223]

The audience are divided, combative even. One man in heavy specs complains furiously that Dylan is faking poverty for his own gain: 'He's making a pile out of people then pretends he's poor.' It took some nerve to defend him: 'The words are good, all the songs are good, he's better than Donovan,' insists a teenager. 'An' he's better than Elvis Presley too.'[224] At this point he was, and his producer Bob Johnston gave the credit to the Almighty, saying Dylan had the spirit: 'Instead of touching him on the shoulder, He kicked him in the ass, and that's where all that came from.'[225]

Most double albums outstay the welcome not only of the format but also of the genre: *Blonde on Blonde* contains enough variety, and enough energy, not to. In Dylan's 1978 *Playboy* interview with Ron Rosenbaum, he famously characterized the album's sonic world as a thin, wild mercury sound. 'It's metallic and bright gold,' he continued, pursuing the visual metaphor until it tails off via Hopperesque streets at dusk into 'water trickling down a brook'.[226]

The first part of the quote has stuck because it's so acute: a thin, wild, mercury sound *is* what we hear on his biting recordings from 1965 and 1966, achieved with economical instrumentation perfectly matched to the musical intent.

Yet the album also has liquid warmth, a trickling counterpoint to the thin and wild which finds its fullest expression on side four. Dylan had married Sara Lownds in November 1965, and their first child Jesse was born in January; there was still a tumultuous tour to come, and it would take the motorcycle crash that summer to prompt a more domestic Woodstock lifestyle at Hi Lo Ha.* But 'Sad Eyed Lady of the Lowlands' already feels figuratively and literally like a slowing down, an investment of Dylan's river of imagery in one person. This is desire as a bottomless pit, the weightless descent of the untethered heart that attaches artefacts, details, looks and sounds, historical moments and geographical places to the obscure object. Dylan roused the musicians before dawn, having finished the song at the studio piano as they napped and played cards, and it was new to their ears. Charlie McCoy later said it was hard to master something so long and slow, and Kenny Buttrey remembers the weary musicians building again and again to what they thought *must* be the climax this time.[227]

'The song is like a painting,' Dylan said of 'Murder Most Foul' in 2020. 'You can't see it all at once if you're standing too close.'[228] 'Sad Eyed Lady' works in the same way. I don't know what he means by the kings of Tyrus with their convict list, waiting in line with their geranium kiss, and I don't care – but I could tell you how it feels. There's something about the span of history, the penetrating smell of a geranium flower, the sheer cosmic extent and physical hit of desire. But this is conveyed in image, not argument. Dylan later said that he didn't know what John Donne meant in describing a woman's breasts as Sestos and Abydos – 'but it sounds good. And you want your songs to sound good.'[229] The song is tender, but – thanks to the hard-cut lyrics reflecting the world's, the woman's, and the relationship's biography – never sentimental. It's also erotic. This love is tangible, rooted in bed linen, fabrics and metals, beginning with a mouth and ending in fingertips.

---

* There can be few addresses more delectable than Dylan's at Hi Lo Ha, Camelot Road, Byrdcliffe, Woodstock.

There is space in Dylan's music for lovers, and for loners and losers, and for singers. I've seen people's eyes light up to 'Jailhouse Rock' at a New Year's Eve party for recovering alcoholics, the ancient thrill of rock and roll still alive to hearts curtained for decades by Communism and alcohol; I've seen Polish aunties singing along to 'Hey Jude' in summer allotments thick with barbecue smoke and flowers, their smiles and shoulders softening to recollection. But Dylan's songs take you under.

You can't hear a song like 'Just Like a Woman' without wanting to play it, inhabit it, taste the words. I once got to perform it in a university play set in Warhol's Factory, reaching back for the Sixties at a time when most of its avatars were alive but its energy remote, the music they were making now thinned out by digital studio technology.* It's gorgeous to sing, the middle eight arriving a full two minutes in as a delicious prolongation, disrupted by a ninth bar to allow the phrases to repeat and linger. The lyrics retain a cruel bite tempered by longing and balanced with a hint, perhaps, of empathy, the recording fading out on some of Dylan's prettiest harmonica playing.

○

The West Coast was now a recusant outpost of the republic. Berkeley was in the vanguard of radical student politics. There were 10,000 people in attendance at the Trips Festival in January, and Ken Kesey held Acid Test parties all winter. The emerging sound was essentially folk rock (melodious, gentle) spiked with acid (trippy, mellow) and splashed with electric blues (heavy, visceral): like the Byrds, Jefferson Airplane had deep roots in the folk scene.

The Byrds' *Fifth Dimension*, released in July, was a jewel of exotic

---

* Nico was in attendance, just, when I saw Allen Ginsberg speak at Oxford in the mid-1980s, his squeezebox incantations ringing round the ancient walls.

promise floating in the summer air. While it retains breezy folk-pop in the Beatley 'Mr. Spaceman', it speaks to stranger dreams – of space, internal travel and, in its heady reading of traditional folk songs, memory. For the first time there were no Dylan covers, although these would return: he lingered in the group's DNA.

The title song is perfectly poised, drifting in on the magic carpet from the cover. The signature sound of their first two albums is subtly slowed in the echo, jazzy drums ranging around the kit, the lyrics sounding rational in Roger McGuinn's calm delivery but speaking of disruption and change. Falling through its own hole, the song – true to the West Coast scene – manages to convey both chemical alteration and natural healing: 'just be quiet and feel it around you.' The group's signature harmonies are held back until the chorus, with its message of beatific acceptance: 'I opened my heart to the universe and I found it was loving,' immediately followed by a challenge to the whole system: 'And I saw the great blunder my teachers had made, scientific delirium madness.' It's one of the most ecstatic and subversive songs of its era, an aural sugar cube anticipating Timothy Leary's famous invitation, via Marshall McLuhan, to 'turn on, tune in, drop out'. The playing – as with the Beach Boys, much more decisive in its constituent parts than the dreamy overall sound betrays – creates an echo chamber, less a thing to hear than a place to be. Van Dyke Parks, building a reputation as a songwriter and session player, plays spidery organ.

July–August 1966

		Bob Dylan	Beatles	Beach Boys
1966	Jul	[27] Dylan crashes out		[18] 'Wouldn't It Be Nice'
	Aug	[18] 'Just Like a Woman'	[5] 'Yellow Submarine'/ 'Eleanor Rigby' [5] REVOLVER	

If there was a sense of infinite progress in the music of the year, there was in the lives of its makers a hint of things spinning out of control. Friends and associates had been concerned for Dylan, who was subsisting on a diet rich in amphetamines. Brian Wilson was acclaimed as a genius in the press, a campaign masterminded by Derek Taylor which only added to the pressure. The Beatles were harassed and threatened in the Philippines and in the States, and were long out of love with live concerts when they gave their final one in August.

Having released no singles at all in 1964, Dylan put out five in 1965 and four in 1966, with a number two US hit in each of those years. But he was *hors de combat* by August, and there would be no new material for Columbia to release until December 1967.

[5 August] **REVOLVER**

For three college Septembers I worked on a hop farm, and passed time in the threshing shed by playing Beatles albums in my head from memory. From *Revolver* to the *White Album*, I can walk the grooves of any Beatle record as well as the garden I grew up in, with its elderberry bush and septic tank covered in weeds, its bramble and rhododendron banks. The silent exercise fails, memory falters in the noise of the machine. But these are the texts my mind holds fast, as a hundred and fifty years ago it might have done the Good Book. If I had to live on memory, this is the music that would sustain me.

The culture also walks our remaining records easily and often, its only revision in half a century to position *Revolver* higher than *Sgt. Pepper* (sometimes a lot higher, as in *NME*'s 2013 list where the former was placed at 2 and the latter at 87). *Sgt. Pepper*, with its extravagant sleeve, marks most obviously the moment when pop aligned itself with art, the Summer of Love in which it dropped a brief cultural high against which all summers since are measured. But *Revolver*, wrapped in black and white in the year of Carnaby Street polka dots, has a heady atmosphere all its own.

The Beatles, while they now necessarily occupied a social air pocket, were out in the world that spring – visiting clubs, seeing the Lovin' Spoonful at the Marquee, mingling with the Rolling Stones. Harrison had been put in touch with the Asian Music Circle; McCartney had been stimulated by the music of the Italian composer Luciano Berio and played his own home movies to the film director Michelangelo Antonioni, who was in town scoping the scene for *Blow-Up*.[230]

McCartney was immersed in a rush of artistic engagement and self-improvement. In contrast to Lennon's unhappy suburban suspension, waiting for something or someone to shake him out of his torpor when away from the group (it turned out to be the artist Yoko Ono, who he met in November), McCartney was 'trying to cram everything in, all the things I've missed'.[231] This included a radio production of Alfred Jarry's play *Ubu Coco*, which he heard in the car, and weekly lessons in composition from British composer John Gardner, which didn't last. 'It's just the notation,' he told Hunter Davies later that year: 'it doesn't *look* like music to me.'[232]

All of this fed into the sessions for *Revolver*, but only the references to Harold Wilson and Ted Heath in the first song are explicitly contemporary; there are few of the swinging London characters who populate the Stones' *Aftermath* or the Kinks' *Face to Face*. 'Taxman' and 'Dr. Robert' aside, the references reach back in time via the graveyard and the mock derring-do of 'Yellow Submarine'. This was in tune with the contemporary vogue for artists like Aubrey Beardsley (whose influential exhibition ran at the V & A that whole summer), antique clothes, and the art nouveau stylings that characterized Californian poster design. But it also means the album has aged extremely well.

For the first time since *A Hard Day's Night*, and in a landscape of greater scope and ambition, there are no weaknesses. Exercises in whimsy would wind up cloying or half-baked on *Magical Mystery Tour* and the *White Album*, but the album's lightest track, 'Yellow Submarine', is resourceful and energetic – displaying both the group's sense of humour and their versatile producer's readiness to muck in, drawing on his experience making comedy records.

The creepy count-in over whirring tape noise and coughing sets the tone from the very start: this music exists on their own terms. We can note the studio innovations that had crept in to date, arguably a little overplayed in liner notes and mini-documentaries as one set of re-releases replaces another, but here they can be *felt*. There's a succulent quality to *Revolver*'s tape distortion, varispeeding, humming drones and backwards sounds. The heat in the guitars, the leaping bass, the deeper thud of the kick drum (partly facilitated by a large woollen jumper): all serve to involve and absorb the listener.

'Eleanor Rigby' extends the sense of melancholy that had crept onto *Rubber Soul*. McCartney's plain singing and the sombre, close-miked strings sidestep sentimentality for something Gothic and stark, the echoing line in the backing vocal – which must have seen irresistible when it occurred to them in the studio – judiciously confined to the final 'lonely people' motif. McCartney had shared the opening line of the song with Maureen Cleave in March. 'If our bodies stayed young,' he added, 'our minds would have to stay young, and nobody wants that.'[233] It's a telling remark, and one that gives weight to the cross-generational empathy evident in his songs from this period.* The song is over in two minutes, the strings stepping down the final arpeggio like a last look into the grave.

'I'm Only Sleeping' sidles up like rain at dawn, hinting at glimpsed dreamworlds in the sour snatches of reversed guitar while also conveying the deliciously simple feeling of drowsing late. The backwards guitar line at the end segues ideally into the cascading sitar of 'Love You To', which in its half-minute introduction goes far beyond the modish use of the instrument in 'Norwegian Wood' or 'Paint It Black'. Anil Bhagwat's thudding tabla, one of two session credits on the LP, drives a sound composition so focused on the music that its working title, supplied by a recording engineer who had to call it something, was 'Granny Smith'. Harrison only visited India for the first time later that year, and this is a love song to a culture which would sustain him musically and spiritually for the rest of his life.

There is a special sense of expectation the first time we play a record, with the songs that open and close sides each carrying their own weight. Here the variety in the Beatles music, combined with clever sequencing, means that the album plays out like waves crashing and rolling back: the intensity of 'Love You To' is followed by the reflective 'Here, There and Everywhere',

---

* 'Eleanor Rigby', 'She's Leaving Home', 'When I'm Sixty-Four', and 'Your Mother Should Know'. *Sgt. Pepper's Lonely Hearts Club Band* was itself a fanciful ageing motif, positioning the group as old, or at least old-fashioned, and the *Magical Mystery Tour* film recuperates psychedelia into a remembered seaside world populated by variously garrulous, loveable and creepy older characters in locations ranging from the gentle to the seedy: the Beatles and their remote uncles and aunts.

its opening designed to emulate the sound of the Beach Boys on 'God Only Knows'. The mood is gentle, but the playing is far from tentative: the saturated guitar chords push, the triads in the backing vocals rise and fall, a cymbal crashes. Detail is sparingly applied, with the minor counter-melody played on guitar at 1:05, and a heart-stopping harmony below the melodic line at 1:55, both used only once.

'She Said She Said' channels the troubled mood of the Beatles' pool party with the Byrds and Peter Fonda the previous summer, percolating into a swirl of distorted guitar, varispeeded vocals and explosive drums. Fonda's repeated assertion that he knew what it was like to be dead irked Lennon at the time, but Fonda's words anticipate the theme of 'Tomorrow Never Knows', and the songs anchor the two sides of the album. 'She Said She Said' pivots on a moment of aching clarity: 'When I was a boy,' Lennon sings, finding his own theme in the muddled discourse as the rhythm seems to slow, 'everything was right.'

'Good Day Sunshine', the Beatles' own submission in a summer of sun-drenched records, rolls along charmingly on piano: its ending echoes the coda to 'She Said She Said', voices jangling in the round, while removing the song to another key – the first of four songs in a row, as Ian MacDonald notes, to do this.[234] 'And Your Bird Can Sing' lands on a subdominant A {v}, McCartney's bass chirping with satisfaction as the chord fades – easy if you know how.

'For No One' follows it like falling rain: there is another echo as the descending scale in the verse reprises the line from 'And Your Bird Can Sing'. McCartney claimed in a *Sunday Times* interview with Hunter Davies that September to have given up piano lessons, and with it learning to read and write music, three times.[235] His clavichord playing on 'For No One' shows how much he had learned. It's more than adequate, and a perfect example of 'good enough' craftsmanship in a pop song. Where greater facility might have led to trills and flourishes, McCartney's playing serves the song.*

For all the experiment with genre, form and recording technique, the songs on *Revolver* (as on *Pet Sounds*, where the tracks are only a little longer) are as concise as ever. The richness of the four songs at the start of side two, none of them much over two minutes long, disguises this.

'Dr. Robert' is a sarcastic companion piece to 'And Your Bird Can Sing', the guitar parts snarling beneath a lyric that gestures perhaps towards Dr Timothy Leary, or the dentist who had spiked their coffee with acid a year before. The thrills of drug culture are brought down to earth by references to the National Health Service. Many bands would later attempt to emulate the sound on this track; there is even an effects pedal for guitarists named after it. But few maintained the restraint of the Beatles' soundworld, which is full of light and air: it breaks down in a childish rhyme over sustained organ chords. Nor could they call on singers with such different styles; Lennon is dry and even Dylanesque at first, but it is McCartney's 'pushed' vocal style that makes the chorus, while the bridge contrasts so effectively because Harrison joins in, acting the words as well as singing them.

The brass accompaniment to 'Got to Get You into My Life', Stax via the bandstand, refracts that year's hard-hitting soul into a tone that is almost too bright to look at, as if a drug is beginning to kick in – a sensation which only accelerates on the final track, 'Tomorrow Never Knows'. This was the song that more than any other aligned the Beatles with the psychedelic underground, and in turn announced it to a mainstream audience.

---

* Speaking to Jonathan Cott in 1968, Lennon confirmed this, saying he had missed having a piano in India but confiding: 'My piano playing is even worse than me guitar. I hardly know what the chords are, so it's good to have a slightly limited palette, heh heh.' Cott, 'John Lennon: The Rolling Stone Interview'.

1966

'Tomorrow Never Knows' encapsulates the Beatles' engagement with the world and each other that spring. The germ of the song was Lennon's, but it was inspired by Timothy Leary's LSD manual *The Psychedelic Experience*: this he sourced at Indica Books and Gallery, a countercultural shop run by friends and financed in part by McCartney. The Beatles all had tape machines at home, but it was McCartney who led input on the tape loops; it was Harrison who proposed the drone effects on tamboura and organ; Starr's drums are practically the lead instrument.

The French pioneer of *musique concrète*, Pierre Henry, had in 1962 recorded *Le Voyage*, a ballet score also inspired by the Tibetan Book of the Dead. The comparison is instructive. Henry's work goes on and on, sounding as if traffic, birds and rodents have been caught in the plumbing of a large house, or in one's own guts after a heavy supper. It might prompt curiosity, but it is only tangentially an invitation to the senses, and barely at all to the emotions.

Henry's title references the journey of the soul in its transitional state, but also Baudelaire's 'Le Voyage' (1861), and indirectly Rimbaud's 'Le Bateau ivre' ten years later.* Here again the comparison with Henry's score is not flattering. Compare the thunderous drumming and terrific energy of 'Tomorrow Never Knows' with the dyspeptic bleeps of *Le Voyage*: the rapture of the symbolist journey is in the former. The Beatles were now making modern art that worked on a sensory level as effectively as the lyrics of Dylan, whose debt to Beat and symbolist poetry is more explicit. Ian McDonald described 'Revolution 9' on the *White Album* as 'the world's most widely distributed avant-garde artefact',[236] but 'Tomorrow Never Knows', with its esoteric

---

* Baudelaire's 'We saw stars, and waves, and sands' is echoed in Rimbaud's 'I saw starry archipelagos! and islands with wild skies.' Author's translations from: 'Nous avons vu des astres Et des flots, nous avons vu des sables aussi' (Baudelaire); 'J'ai vu des archipels sidéraux! et des îles | Dont les cieux délirants [sont ouverts au vogueur]' (Rimbaud).

primary reference point and use of tape loops to create a bizarre and disorientating soundscape, came first.

Klaus Voormann was frightened by the track when he heard it, and this is reflected in his sleeve art. Drawn from memory, it represents the group as a set of spiralling memories (is that Stuart Sutcliffe in there?), a tangle to get lost in, the Beatles crawling out of ears like a loose-limbed monster, in and out of hair. It was their old Hamburg associate's response to hearing the tapes in person, and – as a delighted Brian Epstein put it – a bridge to the unfamiliar record that lay within.[237]

Voormann's working method – 'scissors, scalpel and glue' – echoed the hands-on way 'Tomorrow Never Knows' was assembled, with technicians in lab coats positioned around the studios spooling tape loops onto machines with pencils. It was analogue art *in excelsis*. Compared to *Blonde on Blonde*'s drab blur, and the San Diego goats on *Pet Sounds*, the artwork and its genesis make the LP a complete artistic statement, the bold upper-case title lettering neatly reversed on the back cover.[238] Voormann himself appears in elegant miniature on the front, compensating for the nugatory fee he was paid. Thirty years later, having stayed friends with the group and played bass on some of their best solo work, he reassumed the position in his artwork for *Anthology*, his face discreetly aged.[239]

The Beatles' psychedelic recordings were not accompanied by an explicit programme of chemical realignment like the 13th Floor Elevators' debut LP (which the album liner notes describe as a 'quest for pure sanity'). But they were – given their pervasive influence, and a socially acceptable image that had held until now – more broadly subversive. McCartney had been the last of the Beatles to try LSD, in December 1965. His companions this time were not Dylan or his fellow Beatles but Tara Browne, his wife Nicky, and Viv Prince, late of the Pretty Things – who sounds like *The Tiger Who Came to Tea* in McCartney's description, polishing off whatever was to hand.

McCartney's reluctance to take acid had tested the group's all-for-one approach. But having given into curiosity, or peer pressure, or both, and in the kind of turnaround familiar to unlucky schoolchildren, he wound up being the one to take the rap. Interviewed for ITV in June 1967, and sounding more downbeat and defensive than usual (in fact very like Lennon), he attributed any bad influence on their fans to journalists' keenness to broadcast it.

McCartney was, and remained for decades, an enthusiastic toker. His first experience of marijuana in 1964 reads like a trip ('there are seven levels') and he described 'Got to Get You into My Life', begun on the second day of recording for *Revolver*, as his own 'ode to pot'.[240] His recent introduction to LSD may have played a part: like Brian Wilson, he remembered his first trip as a religious experience, opening his eyes 'to the fact that there is a God', as he told a journalist in 1967.[241] At any rate, *Revolver* did not contribute to the criminalization of LSD in the UK, which passed into law the day the record came out.

Seen as a series of number one singles across the US and UK charts, the music of that summer and autumn appears a level playing field, with songs like the Lovin' Spoonful's 'Summer in the City', the Kinks' 'Sunny Afternoon' and Donovan's 'Sunshine Superman' easily on a par with 'Paperback Writer'. But the corresponding albums remain comparatively thin. The Kinks's charming *Face to Face* is still the aural equivalent of a man in a bird suit jumping off a pier, while the Lovin' Spoonful's *Hums* is a rattle-bag of whimsy with one ear on the covers market.

o

Brian Wilson had carved out the space he needed. The group toured without him, and he worked on the records. The Beatles had no fallback; the creative core was also front of house. Their set list from Munich at the end of June, when they resumed touring after their longest break since 1960, features only three songs they might not have played a year earlier.* Even reading it one can sense the fatigue; it's a hodgepodge, with a song for each to sing, and something off most of their albums save the one they had just finished recording.

Rock and Roll Music
She's a Woman
If I Needed Someone
Day Tripper
Baby's in Black
I Feel Fine
Yesterday
I Wanna Be Your Man
Nowhere Man
Paperback Writer
I'm Down

Their first stop was Japan, where they received death threats relating to their appearance at the Budokan martial arts venue. They went then to the Philippines, where they incurred the wrath of Imelda Marcos: unaware they had been invited to a reception at the presidential palace, they woke up late to find that the event was being televised. They stayed put, and were badly roughed up at the airport on their departure. Landing in the UK in July, Harrison said they had come back for a couple of weeks' rest before going to be beaten up by the Americans – which, in a

---

* They played a fifteen-minute set at the NME Poll Winners Show at the Empire Pool, Wembley, on 1 May.

sense, they were. A campaign of Beatles boycotts in the South had been ignited by Lennon's remarks about Jesus, first made in an *Evening Standard* interview with Maureen Cleave in March[242] and now republished in a teen magazine.

The interview had already been quoted in *Newsweek* and published in the *New York Times Magazine*. But things only kicked off when *Datebook* circulated it to southern radio stations: Beatles records and memorabilia were burned at public bonfires. The response feels more tangible today than it did when I first read of it in 1977. It seemed then to come from a world that was long gone, but it now feels emblematic of reactionary fury, stoked in the Trump years and culminating in the invasion of the Capitol in January 2021.

Lennon was reduced to tears by the prospect of facing (and apologizing to) the press on arriving in Chicago, and their interview in August stands in sorry contrast to the joy of their first American tour two years before. Given all we know and feel about *Revolver* it's a strange sight indeed, the circus reduced to its mechanics, the bubble of bonhomie evaporating before their eyes, all weary ciggies and flowered flock. McCartney describes the record-burnings as 'a bit silly' and a publicity stunt, at which point they are asked if the 'Jesus' interview *itself* was a stunt to shore up declining popularity. It's the Beatles' own moment with the goats in the zoo, the artists cut down to size by a lack of attendant imagination.

Lennon apologized, in part 'for opening me mouth'. But he stood his ground on what he had said in the original context, pointing out that he wasn't comparing the Beatles with 'Jesus Christ as a person, or God as a thing, or whatever it is', and fielding adroitly a couple of questions calculated to make things worse. Alluding to death threats, record-burnings and radio bans, a reporter asks if they think they're being crucified: Lennon responds with a mirthless laugh and careful emphasis: 'No, I wouldn't say that at *all*.'[243] When they are asked to identify the most enjoyable thing 'about this adulation, this almost godhood on earth that you've achieved', Lennon spots the trap and cautions the assembled press: 'You all saw that.'

Harrison had touched on religion in his own interview with Cleave, asking how anyone could live with themselves as Pope with all the trappings of money and power, and saying the hypocrisy needed to be brought out into the open. 'Why is there all this stuff about blasphemy?' he asked. 'If Christianity's as good as they say it is, it should stand up to a bit of discussion.'[244] Here was the disproof. Ku Klux Klan members protested against the Beatles' appearances in Washington DC, and at the Mid-South Coliseum in Memphis, where a cherry bomb firecracker went off on stage during 'If I Needed Someone'. The *Daily Gleaner* in Birmingham, Alabama reported that a box of dust created by putting their records through a 'Beatle-grinder' would be presented to the group.[245] *Datebook* had led with a picture of Paul McCartney and his own contentious Cleave quote: America was 'a lousy country where anyone black is a dirty n*****'.[246] The same magazine had quoted Ringo Starr a year earlier saying that segregation was 'a load of rubbish'. Hatred wore the cloak of faith.[247]

There were more scares in store. An electric shock from a rain-soaked amplifier launched their road manager across the stage in Cincinnati, forcing them to postpone the gig and leaving them with a double header in different cities the following day: noon in Cincinnati, 8.30 p.m. in St Louis. Here there was another downpour, and the group played beneath a makeshift shelter. By now even McCartney had enough: 'It felt like the worst little gig we'd ever played at,' he said, 'even before we'd started as a band.'[248] In Los Angeles they were obliged to use an armoured car as a getaway vehicle when decoy limos failed to disperse the crowds; they had waited in an underground dressing room for two hours with no obvious way to escape Dodger Stadium. By the time they played their last concert gig at Candlestick Park in San Francisco, they had refreshed their set with exactly one song, 'Long Tall Sally' replacing 'I'm Down'. Once on the plane, George Harrison declared: 'Right – that's it, I'm not a Beatle any more!'[249]

They hadn't entirely lost their sense of humour. When asked in San Francisco if they took ideas from baroque composers, Lennon said he didn't know his Handel from his Gretel.[250] But some of the laughter jars. One question at the last press conference of the tour related to a *Time* article claiming 'Day Tripper' was about a prostitute and 'Norwegian Wood' about a lesbian. Asked what had inspired 'Eleanor Rigby', Lennon replied to general merriment: 'Two queers.'[251] Their own manager was absent from Candlestick Park, having been robbed overnight by an ex-boyfriend who then attempted to blackmail him over a suitcase containing pills, explicit photos and $20,000 in cash. Epstein's suitcase was recovered in a sting, but not its private contents; in 2019 it was sold at auction, a poignant lot empty of its hidden life, for £3,437.50.

Revolver, *Pet Sounds* and *Blonde on Blonde* would wind up locked in a cycle of perpetual influence on other people, but for now the cultural momentum was too strong for them to appear iconic. In different ways, each of the artists had been brought down to earth, the Beatles touring wearily against a backdrop of dissent, Brian Wilson let down by an indifferent record company, and Dylan – after a gruelling tour where many booed the music the culture would one day revere – by a Triumph. Joan Baez wrote of riding with Dylan that she always felt the motorbike was driving him, and his hard fall came at the end of July on a winding Woodstock road.[252] He was hurried to Doctor Thaler's house in Middletown, an hour away, and remained there for a month. Selma Thaler re-called her husband's patient as sweet and quiet, and she believed he had broken his neck. It was the recuperation he needed.[253]

1966–67: MUTATION

August 1966 to May 1967

		Bob Dylan	Beatles	Beach Boys
1966	Aug		[27] *Brian and Carl Wilson play Good Vibrations to McCartney in LA*	
			[29] *Their final tour gig in LA*	
	Sep			
	Oct			[10] 'Good Vibrations'
	Nov			
	Dec			
1967	Jan			
	Feb		[13] 'Penny Lane'/'Strawberry Fields Forever'	
	Mar			
	Apr	[24] 'Leopard Skin Pill-Box Hat'	[10] *McCartney visits Brian Wilson at the studio in LA*	
	May		[26] SGT. PEPPER'S LONELY HEARTS CLUB BAND	

The writing and recording of the Beach Boys and the Beatles reached new peaks of invention in this period, but they released fewer records. This left their record companies anxious for product, and for the first time our protagonists were anthologized: Capitol hurried *Best of the Beach Boys* onto shelves before *Pet*

Sounds was cold, and *A Collection of Beatles Oldies* plugged a gap at Christmas 1966. This was followed by *Bob Dylan's Greatest Hits* the following March.

The Beatles alone released new material in the first half of 1967. As they finished *Sgt. Pepper* in the spring, Brian Wilson was faltering over his *Smile* tapes, while Dylan turned to home recordings with the Band in Woodstock. The B-sides to 'Good Vibrations' and 'Leopard-Skin Pill-Box Hat' were prescient: 'Let's Go Away for Awhile', and 'Most Likely You Go Your Way and I'll Go Mine', respectively.

So it was the Beatles who communicated that surge in the counterculture that manifested in these months. Underground and in student rooms was the free press, with the *San Francisco Oracle* launching in September 1966, the *International Times* in October, *Oz* in its London incarnation in February 1967, and the *Chicago Seed* in May 1967: dazzling layouts in split fountain gradient, a plant growth of line illustration for the new age.

27 August **Brian and Carl Wilson play 'Good Vibrations' to McCart-ney in LA**
10 October **'Good Vibrations'**

The blend of sophistication and punch in the Beatles' sound-world was still only matched by Motown and the Beach Boys. The stunning productions of Holland-Dozier-Holland peaked in the second half of 1966 with the Supremes' 'You Keep Me Hangin' On', with its nagging, repeated E♭, and the Four Tops' ominous, shimmering 'Reach Out, I'll Be There'. The Beach Boys' 'Good Vibrations', pushing even further the limits and scope of the 45 rpm single, claimed the rivals' crown for the last time in November. Mixing the wildly expensive sixteen-track re-cording to mono, Brian Wilson felt a rush of power: 'A feeling of exaltation. Artistic beauty. It was everything.'[254] It was the last time he would be on top of his world, and, with the song topping charts around the globe, anyone else's.

McCartney and Harrison heard 'Good Vibrations' in August, ahead of its release, on a day off towards the end of the US tour. Derek Taylor had been the Beatles' publicist before moving to California and now worked for the Beach Boys, occasionally mixing up the bands' names. Aware that the backstage meeting in August 1965 had been hurried, and that Brian hadn't even been there, he arranged a soirée at his home. It was a beatific setting for what might have been a tense encounter. 'The lights were low in the house,' Taylor wrote, 'the Los Angeles basin twinkled blue, red-gold and silver, and we had *Glenn Miller's Latest Hits* softly on the record player.'

Perhaps learning from his experience with Elvis the previous year, the Beatle made his rival laugh by saying: 'You're Brian Wilson and I'm Paul McCartney so let's get that out of the way and have a good time.' Wilson responded warmly with, 'Would you like to hear a dub?' And so Wilson played McCartney his masterpiece, at the start of what became – as Derek Taylor predicted – a warm and lasting association between the two.[255] Lennon was a fan, and had telephoned Wilson to tell him how great *Pet Sounds* was.[256] But he was also moodier, by turns generous and cruel, and essentially an introvert. McCartney, although nobody's fool, was better placed to connect with Wilson. Typically the foil to Lennon in shared company, journalists knew McCartney to be more talkative and open on his own.

His reaction is not recorded, but we can at least go straight to the source. You have to be an accomplished pianist to play a score by Beethoven or Chopin, and recordings of their music made on instruments of their time, while often stimulating, can sound thin compared with the rich tones we are used to from modern pianos. You can fall in love with a painting in reproduction and experience dissatisfaction when face to face with the actual thing, surrounded by people, distracted by the lighting and the wallpaper and the ache in the back that comes gratis with admission to a gallery. Sometimes even the frame looks clumsy, weighing down the composition, pulling grace out of shape. With 'Good Vibrations' to hand, there can be no confusion.

For all that it cost so much and took so long, the song's impact is physical and immediate. Carl Wilson's bluesy 'I ...' over tiptoeing guitar figure and staccato organ draws us into a kind of vortex: we are far above surety, as if the ground has fallen away beneath our feet. It feels uncertain partly because we alight on a minor chord without knowing if it's home, and partly because – if it is home – it's a very unfamiliar one (D♯ minor is barely used in popular music). This, and the tiptoeing contrapuntal bassline, disguise what is a standard descending sequence, twice repeated before modulating to the relative major, and safer ground, of F♯. This is where the 'good vibrations' come in, accompanied by spectral theremin.

The music sits on this chord in a sort of refracted doo-wop for thirteen seconds, warbled by triplets on the cellos as if trying to generate lift-off – before at length lurching up a tone, and then another. Both of these might conventionally signal key changes – except that the last chord, a B♭, is used as the subdominant for a return to that pulsing D♯ minor. We are back where we started, and no wiser: the music is a maze.

Wilson's construction is both clever and serendipitous. The music remains sensational, like the doo-wop whose ghost inhabits that long F♯. But unlike the chords that so reliably underpinned rock and roll, the structure is now idiosyncratic and unpredictable. It is neither academic nor even entirely conscious, which is why it remains so fresh and odd, built on a whim, chord by chord, like the rickety railway rolled out of rhyme in Dr Seuss's *Green Eggs and Ham*. 'I don't know where but she sends me there,' sings Mike Love. This is our experience of the song, and it is also Wilson's compositional rationale: the muse is leading him.

There follows, at 2:21, a kind of false coda: we have settled via neat modulation in F, a place of calm, the ocean seen at the end of a long drive, an expression of the love Wilson maintains he always meant his music to convey. 'Gotta keep those lovin' good vibrations happening with her,' the voices sing, fading, and a harmonica keeps the melody going as the bass pulses. There is a sound offstage, a cough or a dropped stick, before an echoing a cappella seventh chord and brief return to the 'good vibrations' chorus. McCartney asked for the dub as a souvenir, but Wilson preferred not to part with it. 'He wasn't completely happy with the sound,' Taylor recalled.[257]

June 1966–May 1967 Sessions for SMILE

At the epicentre of the scene and steeped in its principal drugs and texts, from the I Ching and *Siddhartha* to Kahlil Gibran, Wilson was in 1966 at the zenith of his capabilities. 'Psychedelic music will cover the face of the world and color the whole popular music scene,' he told *Teen Set* magazine. 'Anybody happening is psychedelic.'[258]

The unrealized *Smile* project came to hang round the culture's neck, as well as Wilson's, and its eventual manifestation in 2004 turned out to be robust enough to maintain the myth. But for now it was business (stoned business, whimsical and extravagant business, but still business) as usual. Wilson was available to journalists, associates, friends and film-makers: footage of him singing 'Surf's Up' at the piano acts as a climax to the CBS TV show *Inside Pop: The Rock Revolution*, broadcast in April 1967. So the

Smile sessions are justly a part of our narrative, even if the album itself, properly speaking, is not. The 2004 edition was an assemblage of what Mark Linett describes as a 'largely unfinished, unsequenced' project.[259]

Wilson was overwhelmed partly by his cascading mental health – variously interpretable in Jules Siegel's contemporary account as excessive perfectionism, psychosis or cosmic hang-up.[260] But it was also the art he was creating at all-night sessions with Van Dyke Parks. Like the Italian lawyer crushed to death by his own papers, Wilson succumbed to the snowballing scale of his own tapes.* His segmental approach to recording and composition had worked on 'Good Vibrations', but when applied to hours and hours of music, open to assembly in infinite combination, it defeated him. *Smile*, even as finally completed by its own author, is a sometimes exquisite, fitfully moving but also enervating and even claustrophobic experience.

The *Party!* album aside, this is the only point at which Dylan's influence can be seen clearly in Brian Wilson's 1960s work. It came in at an angle, via the lyrics of Van Dyke Parks. Parks was not a professional lyricist, and Wilson was most struck on meeting him by his manner and syntax, writing in 2011, 'It reminded me a little bit about what Bob Dylan was doing.'[261] Parks, while resistant to the British Invasion, had been taken with Dylan's vocal style, and with his lower-case sleeve notes in the style of e. e. cummings: 'While it was transparently imitative,' said Parks, 'I thought it was a good position.'[262]

Accounts of their working process and the extent to which they shared a vision for the record differ. But whether it was conceived as a critique of Manifest Destiny, or as 'a far-out trip through the Old West', Americana with laughs, no one can accuse Wilson of not leaving his comfort zone (if indeed he had one).[263] A *Rolling*

---

* A 'news in brief' I read in the *Daily Mirror* in the 1980s.

Stone piece from 1971 notes that Wilson shared with his associate of the time David Anderle 'an admiration for Beethoven and Dylan'. Wilson 'seemed a little frightened by Dylan', wrote Tom Nolan in 1971, 'and Brian loved things that frightened him a little'.[264]

Frank Holmes's 'shop of smiles' album art as submitted to Capitol reflects Wilson's remembered idea of the album as something to spread happiness. But he also created, for six of the songs, images which according to Van Dyke Parks helped to orientate the writing.[265] These drawings are more crowded, oblique and suggestive than the shopfront; they have the faintly sinister simplicity of magic lantern slides. In truth the album is as eerie as it is jovial, and John Gast's painting *American Progress*, a nubile Columbia flying wraith-like above the land as settlers drive Indigenous Americans and buffalo west under a darkening sky, would have been as suitable a motif. (The original working title for the record was *'Dumb Angel'*.)[266]

The reconstructed album sparkles with tack piano, lowers with bowed bass, and is choreographed to the Beach Boys' finally tracked voicings.* At its best – on 'Do You Like Worms (Roll Plymouth Rock)' and 'Cabin Essence' – it has the spooky, sloping quality of Andrew Wyeth's painting *Christina's World*, or Catherine Storr's children's book *Marianne Dreams*: a world seen from a place of tremulous stasis.† David Anderle painted a portrait of Brian Wilson at that time which captures that sense of something still but off-centre, weighty but unanchored; it was true enough to its subject to spook him. Elsewhere, on 'Look (Song for Children)' and 'Holidays', the jangle box piano curdles, the primary colour themes grate and the whole becomes ominous.

---

* It is best heard as reconstructed from the original 1966–7 tapes for 2011's *Smile Sessions* LP.

† Wyeth's painting dates from 1948, Storr's book from 1958.

Wilson called his fragments 'feels'. Repeated, like the 'Heroes and Villains' piano motif, they suggest an *idée fixe* of the kind used by Berlioz in his opium-inspired *Symphonie fantastique*. Described by Leonard Bernstein as the 'first psychedelic symphony in history', it is also the sound of an orchestra galloping in frenzied search of a tune; there is no piece of music I want more to enjoy. 'You all know what an obsession is,' Bernstein tells his audience conspiratorially in his *Young People's Concert* on the symphony, 'it's something that takes hold of your mind and won't let go.'[267] This is in essence what was happening to Wilson as he worked on *Smile*: the ideas kept coming, but the structure that would make final sense of them did not.

There are thirty-four parts and tracks for 'Heroes and Villains' alone on the *Smile Sessions* box set. Even as edited for single release in July 1967, six months later than scheduled, it's a complex work: film of the Beach Boys performing the song live captures an undertaking both heroic and absurd. Mark Linett estimates that the album was spread over as many as seventy-five individual sessions spanning a year, meaning that when it came to reconstructing the original recordings, the task was 'much more like putting a film together than a conventional recording'.[268] Wilson's willingness at length to return to *Smile*, complete it, and even tour it, adds to his troubling biography a coda of great artistic and personal courage. But pop demands a laser focus, and it is not always in evidence here. Perhaps, after all, Wilson was correct at the time: there was something not quite right about the vibe.

The best of the album is summarized in 'Surf's Up', where the writing is as balanced as it is complex. The opening section cycles between (almost) equal but opposite chords which rely on the suspension in the bass for interest and resonance. If you can play a little piano, try singing the opening two lines of 'Surf's Up' over Gm7 or Dm7 chords without the bass notes: the melody is plaintive but the accompaniment relatively flat. Then sing it again, adding a D under the Gm7 – see the difference? – and then a G under the Dm7. The transformation is astonishing: suddenly there are multiple possible directions for these chords, although the song only briefly exploits the obvious ones, working instead in the unresolved space between keys.

The opening verses are in an implied D minor, before resolving at the end of the 'columnated ruins' section into what briefly feels like – on 'sleeping' – D major. This now feels like home, but Wilson changes key without warning to a remote A♭, introducing 'dove nested towers' (the lyrical echo of 'columnated ruins' providing a handhold for the disorientated listener). There is a profoundly gifted musical imagination at work here, animated by Van Dyke Parks' dream dissolve lyrics. It goes beyond conventional changes, melody and rhythmic expectations to create its own meaning but still speaks directly to the heart, the notes running up a semitonal scale to climax on 'too *tough* to cry'. The song finishes in another key, in another rhythm, in a separate section.

Despite the song's complexity, it's perfectly robust, surviving inept playing and scratchy singing that has to duck down an octave for the highest notes. The cadence on 'surf's up' is deeply moving, the repeated but still unanchored A♭6 chord leaving those resonant words floating on a reminiscence of earlier, easier Beach Boys music and suggesting the phrase 'time's up' – the 'young and often spring you gave' already given.

13 February 'Penny Lane'/'Strawberry Fields Forever'

The issue for the Beatles was now one of momentum, and to an extent of role and maturity. The old question about the bubble bursting hadn't gone away, but a new one was being asked, with ITN buttonholing the Beatles as they arrived at Abbey Road before Christmas to enquire – given their lack of interest in touring, and the difficulty of finding a suitable script for a third film – if they would continue as a group in the new year. The Beatles' line now was that they didn't want to keep doing the same thing, that they wanted to keep moving forward.

As countercultural attitudes and drugs seeped into straight society, the Beatles found themselves in demand as spokespeople – under fire for whatever ills they were supposed to have sponsored, and under pressure to propose solutions. Harrison was interviewed by the BBC in India in September, and McCartney for Granada's *Scene Special* in January 1967, and then by ITN in June (when he admitted to taking LSD).

Reminded in Tokyo the previous summer that they had attained 'sufficient honour and wealth', they were asked what else they wanted: 'Peace,' Lennon replied, before noting, when asked how much interest they took in the Vietnam War: 'We think about it every day, and we don't agree with it and we think it's wrong.'[269] This belies the myth that the Beatles were entirely muzzled at this point: his words echo those used by Harrison in his *Evening Standard* interview with Maureen Cleave: 'Anything to do with war is wrong,' Harrison had said in March 1966. 'They're all wrapped up in their Nelsons and their Churchills and their Montys – always talking about war heroes.' And so they remain.*

One message the Beatles wanted or felt able to convey related to personal and artistic freedom. The *Scene* special on which McCartney appeared, broadcast on Granada TV on 7 March 1967, focused on the counterculture and was groovily titled 'It's So Far Out, It's Straight Down'. As ever, he struck a diplomatic note: critics, he said, don't realize that the counterculture advocates something everyone wants, namely 'personal freedom to be able

---

* The UK's Brexit Prime Minister Boris Johnson authored in 2015 *The Churchill Factor: How One Man Made History*, ignoring the three million who served in the British armed forces alone, never mind anyone else.

to talk and be able to say things'. But not everyone wanted this, and if they did, they didn't all interpret freedom in the same way. 'It's dead straight,' McCartney pursued hopefully. 'It's a real basic pleasure for everyone, but it looks weird from the outside.'

Their latest single was one expression of that freedom. Lennon had already listed Liverpool locations from childhood in a long poem that ceded to the universal in 'In My Life'. But this time, perhaps because he was away from home, filming *How I Won the War* in Almeria, Spain, he focused on a single location: the Salvation Army children's home with the wild grounds and evocative name, Strawberry Field, where he had played as a child. Lennon remembered finishing the song on the beach: 'It was really romantic – singing it too – I don't know who was there.' [270]

One person who was there and who heard Lennon working on the song was the comedy actor Michael Crawford – his housemate during filming. The Beatle worked repeatedly on one sequence but remained enigmatic to his co-star: 'There was not a lot revealed,' Crawford recalled, a line worthy of his most famous creation, Frank Spencer.[271] There are a number of demo recordings of Lennon running through the song on guitar even before work began at Abbey Road, where the Beatles reconvened after their autumn break.

George Martin was unusually effusive about Lennon's gentle, acoustic run-through. For all that it evolved in the studio, becoming the first song they wholly rerecorded, its writer pitched it as a whole structure. This included the song's most surprising change, the F♯ {VI} chord that introduces 'nothing is real'.* The

---

* Having established a distant mood in the first change from the tonic A {I} to Em {v} , Lennon must have played with the descending scale on guitar from E, to open D, to – where? C♯ follows in the scale, but when played as a chord doesn't fit the melody he was sketching. Making that C♯ the dominant within an F♯ chord is a much odder change, but it allowed him to repeat the melody of 'Strawberry Fields' over the chord as 'nothing is real' with only one flattened note, to sinister effect. No wonder it took time to find the right sequence. 'Living is easy' plays out over another descending motif, through the major and diminished sevenths of an E chord.

other-worldly feel of 'Strawberry Fields' as recorded comes partly from the writing but also from the muted, cushioned production in the song's first minute, the clearest sound Lennon's own voice, the curious changes borne on Mellotron, pulsing organ and tape-saturated guitar.

Like 'Good Vibrations', 'Strawberry Fields Forever' blends more than one recording session, in this case a splice between two different takes of the whole song: a slower, gentler, version (take seven, cued by George Martin as if discreetly announcing an eccentric visitor at a formal party), and a faster, more sonically crowded version (basically take twenty-six). The first has the haunting Mellotron introduction; the second has the sunstruck brass, cascading swarmandal, backwards cymbal sucks and stentorian cello parts. It's impossible to imagine either without the other. An exact accommodation of differing pitch and speed was achieved by splicing the tape at one minute, where the sound gets busier, like a door opening to allow a crush of people into a room. The development lacks the introspective tenderness of the opening, but it makes more of the 'nothing is real' note in the lyrics, sounding both ominous and, ending on the key word 'forever', exultant.

'Penny Lane' is on the face of it a simpler proposition, apparently founded on a familiar rock and roll turnaround and playing with descending scale motifs. But here again are two of the instinctive compositional surprises that so delighted Bernstein: first, having started the song in B major, McCartney finishes the first line on a B minor chord, an unexpected parallel key modulation that makes us look over our shoulder to check our bearings. Then at the end of the verse, instead of suspending the F♯ {V} chord a second time, he goes down to E ('very strange'), using it as the dominant that facilitates a key change to A. This means that the sunny-sounding chorus is a tone *below* where we started, when a typical pop key change, usually at the end of a song, moves us *up* a tone.

Having gained our trust with that luminous opening phrase, the music has spun us round before winding up ('meanwhile back') to emphasize the musical point – home in B. This is what accounts for our experience of a song which seems so bright but in which something is out of place. As Ian MacDonald demonstrates in one of his most perceptive footnotes, there are also lyrical corridors between expectation and reality, the weather and the seasons mixing – compressed like early memories.[272]

The song is full of suspended chords, for so long a feature of Brian Wilson's writing and now decisively adopted by McCartney. Yet their writing lacks the cocktail lounge feel of Tin Pan Alley. Instead the defining motifs operate outside the familiar body of changes, but without discarding the sense of home – using the listener's expectation of return as part of the play.

○

By December 1966 the song 'Surf's Up' was almost finished; the album *Smile* was nearly complete; artwork had been prepared, and a potential track listing of twelve songs – minus 'Our Prayer', which Wilson always envisaged as the opener – was submitted to Capitol in December. But, as the late-rising Beatles trickled into Abbey Road to work nights that winter, Wilson faltered.

What he lacked at this point was a reliable support network, personally or musically. Wilson did not want for company; many on the canyon scene were only too keen to associate with the man now being touted by Derek Taylor as a genius. But it was a house, like his piano, set on sand. His mental health, already fragile, was undermined by drug intake; his wife Marilyn was still a teenager; his steadiest brother, Carl, was only a few months older than her, turning twenty just before Christmas 1966. Now as focused on the Beatles' 'religious' sound as he had been on Phil Spector, he became paranoid and frantic, shedding associates, in one case because he believed their girlfriend was affecting his brain via ESP. [273]

Meanwhile the Beatles had each other, George Martin and Abbey Road. The *Sgt. Pepper* album isn't flawless, but it reflects a collective work ethic that allowed for experimentation while still valuing focus. The Beatles had stopped doing Christmas shows, but they were recording at Abbey Road into the small hours of New Year's Eve. George Martin was willing to pump a harmonium to the point of exhaustion to get the right sound on 'Being for the Benefit of Mr. Kite!', yet he was impatient with experiment for its own sake, observing that the band needed to be 'a little more constructive' when McCartney interrupted sessions on 'Penny Lane' to produce a fourteen-minute tape collage for the Million Volt Light and Sound Rave at the Roundhouse. [274] But the esoteric side project fed the music, Martin and Emerick later meeting Lennon's 'smell the sawdust' brief for 'Mr. Kite' with an effects loop made of nineteen different pieces of tape, chopped up, thrown into the air and reassembled at random.

When Lennon was overwhelmed by the acid he had taken during a session for 'Getting Better', and George Martin innocently sent him up to the studio roof for some fresh air, McCartney and Harrison quickly rescued him. No single Beatle had to carry all the music in their heads at any one time; they worked as a group, still recording from the bottom up but with time to devote to overdubs and the novel techniques their ideas demanded.

It was a good time to be productive, for the psychedelic scenes in LA, San Francisco and London were starting to bear fruit. 'Light My Fire' wouldn't be a number one single until July, but it came out at the beginning of January on the Doors' first LP.

Jefferson Airplane's second album, *Surrealistic Pillow*, was in the can by Christmas, and released on the first day of February. The Velvet Underground's first and less immediately prominent album came out in March.

These days, new releases appear like midnight mushrooms on our streaming apps, and it's hard to know how quickly the Beatles encountered these new sounds. Certainly they were tuned into the London underground: McCartney and Starr saw the Jimi Hendrix Experience in January, as the dreamy, smoky 'Hey Joe' hit. The Experience made number three in March with the much wilder, effects-laden 'Purple Haze', and their debut album appeared just before *Sgt. Pepper*. Pink Floyd, working on their first album at Abbey Road, popped next door to watch the Beatles at work one night in March, and David Crosby, their summer friend from LA, was there when they taped the three-piano final chord to 'A Day in the Life'.[275]

The Rolling Stones, also close associates, released one stunning single and one curious album in January. 'Let's Spend the Night Together' was sufficiently provocative for the *Ed Sullivan Show* to insist they sing 'some time' together, prompting a series of camp eye rolls from Jagger. 'Ruby Tuesday', released beside it as a double A-side (like 'Penny Lane' and 'Strawberry Fields Forever'), was an opulent ballad. It develops the baroque feel of 'Lady Jane' with bowed bass and recorder, slow drum rolls on the chorus, a lovely coda, and one of Jagger's best vocals.

Jagger later blamed the bouncedown on *Between the Buttons* for muddying the sound. But the uncertain vocal and even instrumental tuning on songs like 'Back Street Girl' and 'She Smiled Sweetly' shows either haste or carelessness, contributing with shaky organ to what would be in today's idiom a (deliberately) detuned feel. The album sounds like someone walking through a market, running their hands over fabrics, smelling the joss sticks.

It ends on a little marching tune with Yellow Submariney brass, which may have in turn suggested the feel of the title track on *Sgt. Pepper*. An English version of Dylan's Mr Jones has wandered into a park as the bandstand honks into life: 'He's not sure just what it was | Or if it's against the law,' sings Jagger innocently, before concluding the record with a knowing 'evenin' all' from your trusty happening policeman.

There was more focus in evidence on the Byrds' *Younger than Yesterday*, released a fortnight after *Between the Buttons*. Free of maudlin folk tunes, still playful, and biting in places with acid rock lead guitar, it only falters on 'Mind Gardens': when Crosby's long-standing desire to write a song on one chord was given rein, it only demonstrated the limits of free expression. The flickering ennui of 'Everybody's Been Burned' is almost as minimal, but much more effective. Crosby's mountain stream voice unfurls over a modulating E minor chord, but it is the changes that animate the song and create the emotional tension, yielding a moment of spiritual resolution over major G and A9 chords – 'you die inside if you choose to hide' – before returning to a decidedly tentative 'I love you' on the minor: more resigned existential choice than romantic declaration.

'Mind Gardens', by contrast, is sung sententiously over an A minor drone. The faux-folk syntax 'there came winds' unwittingly sums up the enterprise, which has the effect – rare in psychedelic pop – of making one want to commit an act of violence. 'At that time everything was supposed to have rhyme and have rhythm,' Crosby recalled, as if he had solved a great mystery.[276] But instead of being liberated from form, we end up trapped inside a tiny component of it. Its only merit is to make the song that follows, a glittering cover of Dylan's 'My Back Pages', feel like heavenly breath after a night of asthma.

26 May SGT. PEPPER'S LONELY HEARTS CLUB BAND

The Beatles devoted five months to *Sgt. Pepper*, diverting to Knole Park at the end of January to film promo videos for 'Penny Lane' and 'Strawberry Fields Forever', and to Michael Cooper's Chelsea studio at the end of March to shoot the cover (they still showed up at Abbey Road that night to work on 'With a Little Help from My Friends'). For all the time they had at their disposal, the group worked with intensity and at times impatience. A busy George Martin was overlooked for the string arrangement to 'She's Leaving Home', but swallowed his pride to conduct the parts: the team ethic, tried to breaking point during sessions for the *White Album* the following summer, held for *Sgt. Pepper*. They all grew moustaches: seeing the first photographs of the new look in February, Joe Orton thought they looked like early twentieth-century anarchists.[277]

The record was completed in April and released in lavish gatefold at the end of the wettest May on record. The front cover is crowded as a late Victorian parlour, complete with ferns and municipal flower display. A Court Circular of lyrics in austere black Garamond covers the scarlet reverse; inside the yellow fold the Beatles sit large as life, gazing at you and me, as they envisaged it, with love.[278] A dreamy psychedelic landscape was commissioned for this space from Dutch design collective The Fool, but the palette would have clashed; their work was confined to the raspberry pink swirls of an inner sleeve.

The cover was designed by pop artists Peter Blake and Jann Haworth but populated with many characters of the Beatles' own choosing: Marlon Brando and Marilyn Monroe rub shoulders with Karl Marx and Karlheinz Stockhausen, Lewis Carroll and

Bob Dylan.* That the assembly contains clues (Lennon adored Lewis Carroll and admired Dylan), but also seemingly random deflections (Laurel and Hardy), reflects the way both the Beatles and Bob Dylan talked about their work at the time. The latter had cited as influences Rimbaud, W. C. Fields and the trapeze family in a circus.[279]

The album is full of rushes, from the laughter in the opening song to the *ahh*s in 'Lucy in the Sky with Diamonds' and the calliope loops in 'Being for the Benefit of Mr. Kite!', the sonic air sucked in and pumped out by turns, the music working like a series of reveals. The obscure and musically embedded emotional modes explored on 'Strawberry Fields' and 'Penny Lane' are here too: 'Fixing a Hole' hovers between major and minor, drifting deliciously 'where it will go'. In mono especially the guitars sting and the sitars buzz and the harpsichords sparkle, underpinned by stoic cellos, muffled toms and booming kick drum. Beneath the patina of Summer of Love associations this is still music played, and often sung, hard, the violins on 'She's Leaving Home' miked close to grating point. The first side works as an immaculate suite, going out on 'Mr. Kite' in a shower of dying circus sparks that are taken up by tamboura, dilruba and swarmandal at the start of side two.

Harrison had offered the truculent 'Only a Northern Song', which was justly held over until the *Yellow Submarine* soundtrack, and it was better to leave him to his own devices. No one else appears on 'Within You Without You', the Beatles' longest song to date at just over five minutes. It might in truth have been faded at three and a half, but the invitation to see 'beyond yourself', balancing the song's accusatory piety ('are you one of them?'), gives context to the affectionate, cross-generational vibe of 'When I'm Sixty-Four'. Here the insistent, elided backing vocals in 'older

---

* The only other contemporary singer featured on the cover is Dion (suggested by Peter Blake); the Rolling Stones are named on a sweater worn by a large doll.

too' and 'scrimp and save' nod back to the previous song's serpentine string lines. 'Lovely Rita' is filler to die for, McCartney's lead (as in 'She's Leaving Home') decorated by Lennon's beautiful, echo-laden backing vocal and ending on an eerie minor vamp.

There are introspective songs on the album – McCartney's 'Getting Better' and 'Fixing a Hole' look inward, and Lennon's 'Lucy' is a private vision – but no love songs as such. Instead there is companionship and community, seen through largely positive or forgiving eyes. The cheering audience is a link to the life they had left behind, and Ringo gets by with a little help from his friends (the other three Beatles stood by him at the microphone after a long night's recording to coax a lead vocal and final high note from the nervous singer). There is a sympathetic picture of family breakdown in 'She's Leaving Home', the daughter's elopement in search of love undercut by the banal identification of her suitor, who is 'from the motor trade'. The teams of circus performers in 'Mr. Kite', the uxorious narrator in 'Sixty-Four' looking forward to having grandchildren, the protective sisters sitting with Rita: all are people getting by in decidedly British, often mundane settings. They also echo that populous cover, the Beatles looking more like a team than ever before in their sherbet-coloured cod-military suits. Even the tailoring by M. Berman is carefully choreographed, the cuffs, piping and braiding mirrored in two paired sets.*

The mood finally sours with Lennon's 'Good Morning Good Morning', an eccentric collation of time signatures and section lengths where a moribund life is enlivened only by some half-hearted flirting, ending with a biting blast of lead guitar and a double time shuffle towards some kind, any kind, of release. The rockier reprise to 'Sgt. Pepper' reclaims the Beatles from their personas, all four singing in unison, taking in a classic one-tone

---

* The paired costumes are worn by John and George, Paul and Ringo, 'The Beatles - Sgt Pepper', *The Costumer's Guide to Movie Costumes*, http://www.costumersguide.com/cr_pepper.shtml.

hike of a key change, and finally expanding mournfully, like water running out of a neglected bath, into 'A Day in the Life'. They had known this would end the album, even as the final pieces fell into place.

Everything is muffled, contained, held back like tears. After the bravura of the brass band opening, this is sudden reality, death close to home, not someone in the papers but someone they knew. Its subject, Tara Browne, was not a lucky man who had made the grade, rather the son of the Fourth Baron Oranmore and Browne, and heir to the Guinness fortune. By comparison, they *were* lucky men who had made the grade, and it could have been them in the car – Harrison had driven himself, Lennon and their wives home from their first LSD trip in his Mini.

The line 'I'd love to turn you on' lands like a yearning for escape, but the hushed music leads unexpectedly to an even more extreme rush. The instruments in the orchestra ascend their own scales over twenty-four menacing bars, before landing a different singer in a different and unrelated key (E, not G) and not in wonderland but in mundane reality, a reverse rabbit hole. This soon disperses in dream, massed horns leading back into the verse via a squared-off major key turnaround – C-G-D-A – that anticipates 'Hey Jude' in its simple grandeur. In this uneasy sleep we are back in real life, or a twisted version of it, and a record peopled with snippets of news stories and circus posters and TV listings ends with the holes in Blackburn's roads transported to London, ghosts in an auditorium. Robert Fripp, tuning into the radio as *Sgt. Pepper* was being played, was as discomfited as Klaus Voormann had been by 'Tomorrow Never Knows': 'It was terrifying,' said the future King Crimson guitarist. 'I had no idea what it was.'[280]

We think of *Sgt. Pepper* as an extravagant record, but it is grounded in community and place. There are references to school, home, buses, traffic wardens, marriage, parents, children and grandchildren, as well as the implied park with its brass band and the circus; even – no wonder the British public took it to their hearts – the Isle of Wight on 'When I'm Sixty-Four', and Blackburn, Lancashire on 'A Day in the Life' (Lennon makes of that copybook journalistic identification a moment of rhythmic delight – this was a gift, his studio count-in for the song a lilting 'sugarplum fairy, sugarplum fairy').

We associate it with the Summer of Love but it is also a record of loss, ageing and diurnal frustration. The front cover is colourful but not garish, lacking the sunny blare of the gatefold: the hand-tinted figures and sky place the Beatles outside time. Stuart Sutcliffe is there (Lennon had arranged with his parents for his photo to be delivered[281]), but he knows no more of *Sgt. Pepper* than do Aubrey Beardsley or Sir Robert Peel, his immediate companions.[282] The Beatles stand waiting like our great-grandparents for a daguerreotype, surrounded by the living and the dead they, like us, would in time be joining.

We consider it the Beatles' tightly choreographed tour de force, but it is also encouraging, welcoming, open. On the night of the orchestral assemblage for 'A Day in the Life' ('such a big orchestra, playing with very little music,' observed Alan Civil[283]), members of the Rolling Stones and the Monkees and The Fool were in attendance. Everything was filmed, the musicians in clown's noses and party hats, balloons on the end of the instruments inflating and deflating as the bassoons blew.

10 April McCartney visits Brian Wilson at the studio in LA

Driving to Dolores' burger joint with assistant Michael Vosse one night in February, Brian Wilson heard 'Strawberry Fields Forever' on the radio. Just like when he heard 'Be My Baby', he had to pull over. Wilson was on Seconal: 'I was real relaxed, and when 'Strawberry Fields' came on the radio I locked right in with it'. Vosse remembers him shaking his head and saying: 'They did it already. Maybe it's too late.'[284]

Sessions for *Smile* continued as late as April, when Paul McCartney visited Wilson in the studio. Dylan and Lennon had talked about collaborating, but never did; McCartney's endeavours were limited to a cameo on 'Vegetables', where he is said to have guested on celery (although great minds have failed to determine this to their satisfaction from the audio). At one point McCartney played an acetate of 'A Day in the Life', before singing 'She's Leaving Home' at the piano. It was a *coup de grâce*, for associates and collaborators were now leaving Wilson, who had taken to convening meetings in his swimming pool, where conversation could not be bugged. Later that week Van Dyke Parks quit the *Smile* project, and at the start of May the grand endeavour, which had started to bring Wilson more pain than pleasure, was shelved.

June to December 1967

1967		Bob Dylan	Beatles	Beach Boys
	Jun			
	Jul		[7] 'All You Need Is Love'	[24] 'Heroes and Villains'
	Aug			
	Sep			[18] SMILEY SMILE
	Oct			[23] 'Wild Honey'
	Nov		[24] 'Hello Goodbye'	
	Dec	[27] JOHN WESLEY HARDING	[8] Magical Mystery Tour (EP)	[18] 'Darlin'' [18] WILD HONEY

NOTE: Magical Mystery Tour was originally issued as a double EP in the UK; the more familiar album that includes the year's three great singles was released in the US. This is the only time the US version of a Beatles record became the canonical one.

Psychedelia broke big in the spring of 1967 when Jefferson Airplane's 'Somebody to Love' made the Top 10. It then peaked in the summer with the Monterey Pop Festival, and the twin anthems 'All You Need Is Love' and 'San Francisco (Be Sure to Wear Flowers in Your Hair)'. A hit for Scott McKenzie around the world, 'Flowers in Your Hair' sounds like the big number you would write for a musical about the Summer of Love, only to be told it was too corny – John Phillips had in fact written it to appease local objections to the Monterey festival. But it has about it the clever simplicity of the Brill Building, and in 1980 it broke my heart to hear it, knowing that I would have fallen hook, line and sinker for something no one believed in any more.

The music of the era was often gentle. But it was also an unforgiving time, as Roger McGuinn foresaw on *Inside Pop* that spring, where he predicted that a lot of heads would roll from the drug revolution. It became a kind of wild steeplechase as bands of young people cantered hopefully into open country, some brought low at once, others injured beyond return, and a few doomed for decades to remain like their own riderless horses at the edges of the culture they had helped to create.*

7 July **'All You Need Is Love'**

Only four days after recording the random loop for the run-out groove of *Sgt. Pepper*, the Beatles were back in the studio recording the title song for *Magical Mystery Tour*. Having set the tone for the Summer of Love, they stayed in paisley and pinks for the rest of the year. In 'All You Need Is Love' the Beatles provided its epigram.

---

* The Beatles, who emerged as relatively sane and resilient from the maelstrom, were largely unscathed. Brian Jones was at Monterey Pop in June but already fading; Syd Barrett was unseated that summer, his work on Pink Floyd's debut LP *The Piper at the Gates of Dawn* undermined by rapidly increasing acid intake.

The song was written to brief, with simplicity in mind, for a global television audience – united for the first time by satellite on *Our World*, broadcast on 25 June.* 'Writing new number with words such as Hello Love You Me Us Them We Together', reported a BBC producer by telegram on 17 May, suggesting that the feeble 'All Together Now', recorded days before, may have been in contention, along with 'Hello, Goodbye'.† The song Lennon came up with for *Our World* is both grand and graceful, the lyric in the verses resolving intention and possibility. The two modes met unhappily during the live transmission at the instrumental break, when it turned out there was something you could play that couldn't be played: Harrison's fingers got stuck in the guitar strings.‡

The world was being reshaped by legislation and protest, and as always the power structure fought back. Just before Monterey Pop, Loving vs Virginia adjudged race-based restrictions on marriage illegal in the United States, and shortly afterwards, Muhammad Ali was sentenced to five years in prison for refusing to fight in Vietnam. At the end of July homosexuality between consenting adults was decriminalized in the UK, although it came too late for Joe Orton, murdered by his lover at the start of August, and for Brian Epstein, who succumbed to a barbiturate overdose a fortnight later.

The two had liaised with McCartney on a potential movie project that spring, although the script Orton wrote for *Up Against It* was returned to its author without comment. McCartney,

---

* 'For the first time,' declared the cover of that week's *Radio Times* (24–30 Jun. 1967), 'TV encircles the earth.'

† The telegram is quoted on p. 221 of Kevin Howlett's *The Beatles: The BBC Archives: 1962 to 1970* (BBC Books, 2013), This process may even have fed into 'I Am the Walrus', whose opening line employs many of the same words.

‡ The song represented the British segment on what was an international broadcast, but began by quoting from 'La Marseillaise'; one can only imagine the reaction in the right-wing press today.

who was a fan and had played Orton 'Penny Lane' before it was released, later said they had rejected it not because it was too far out but because they weren't gay. The script includes drag sequences and kept boys, but also anarchism, assassination and polygamy – even the outline is exhausting, suffering, in exact contrast to *Help!*, from a surfeit of plot.[285]

Epstein's death led the Beatles to abandon a ten-day conference on transcendental meditation in Bangor, North Wales, and to postpone a proposed trip to the Maharishi Mahesh Yogi's ashram in India. They stayed away from Epstein's funeral to ensure the family's privacy; festooned in flowers that summer, they sent a single chrysanthemum bloom, wrapped in newspaper, to be dropped discreetly into the grave.* Epstein's role had dwindled with no tours to arrange, but his death marked the end of the Beatles' irresistible ascent. The enterprising McCartney became his de facto replacement, ensuring an uneasy group dynamic for the rest of their time together.

24 July 'Heroes and Villains', 18 September SMILEY SMILE, 18 December WILD HONEY

The Beach Boys had been due to play at Monterey. That, too, was subject to a last-minute cancellation, either because Brian felt they wouldn't go down with a hip crowd, or because they were nervous about Carl, in dispute over the status of his draft refusal, being dragged offstage by the Feds (although it would have enlivened their creaky stage act). The festival was a coming-out party for the counterculture, but it was also the germ of its commercialization. On page sixteen of the official festival programme was a poster hand-drawn by Lennon and McCartney in coloured pencil, demonstrating why, although Lennon was

---

* Flowers are typically discouraged at Jewish funerals.

a fluent cartoonist, it was prudent for them to have employed professional artists for their LP covers. 'Peace to Monterey from Sgt. Pepper's Lonely Hearts Club Band', it read, although neither they nor Dylan chose to perform or attend.

The Beach Boys' shop of smiles had been boarded up, but Brian Wilson held out hope that the single edit of 'Heroes and Villains', no longer the centrepiece of a more elaborate work, would prosper. He waited and waited until his astrologer Genevelyn deemed the stars propitious, before setting off for KHJ Radio with the group in a cavalcade of Rolls-Royces, pressing in hand – only to be told it wasn't on the playlist. It was one thing after another.[286]

Capitol, with *Smile* shelved, were forced to release *Best of The Beach Boys Vol. 2*. But with the pressure off, the group – now desperately soliciting Wilson's involvement, having for so long been his sometimes reluctant agents – rallied to make a sequence of delightfully offbeat albums, none of them longer than half an hour.[*]

Smiley Smile is bizarre, and not in the way one might expect from a record released in September 1967. Often delivered sotto voce, it contains a mix of feels and songs, some of them carried over from the *Smile* sessions but without that undertaking's oppressive layering. It has a gentle, flickering feel. By the end of the decade it was in therapeutic use at a Texan drug clinic – a touching denouement given the role that drugs had played in the abandonment of *Smile*, but a puzzling one given the unpredictability of songs like 'She's Goin' Bald', where the Beach Boys' voices speed up on a 'sha-na-na' line as if on helium.[†] All is blurred, as if hummed across a piece of perfumed paper. 'Wind Chimes', which jolts into noise on the *Smile Sessions* version, is

---

[*] *Smiley Smile* and *Wild Honey* in 1967, *Friends* in 1968, and *20/20* in 1969.

[†] Where, according to Carl Wilson, it acted 'as a soothing remedy which relaxes them and helps them to recover completely from their trip'. 'Beach Boys Quotes', Carl Wilson, *Surfer Moon*, http://surfermoon.com/essays/quotes.shtml#carl_wilson.

tentative and tender; the irony is that this album, more of a band effort than *Pet Sounds* ever was, is far less commercial.

The group performed live in Hawaii that summer, with Brian briefly on board, but the tapes were deemed unusable. Tracks from a follow-up session in Hollywood which yielded covers of 'The Letter' and 'With a Little Help from My Friends' were abandoned. Their next record, *Wild Honey*, was sung and played harder and lasted all of twenty-four minutes. Carl Wilson's voice cracks all over the title track and a cover of Stevie Wonder's exuberant contemporary hit, 'I Was Made to Love Her'.* The album is left intriguingly loose, with songs that come into the room and leave without saying anything, moments of pastiche and whimsy mixed with snatches of roughly played rock and roll.

^{24 November} 'Hello, Goodbye', ^{8 December} MAGICAL MYSTERY TOUR

The last number one of the year in both the US and the UK was the Beatles' 'Hello, Goodbye'. They filmed a promo in their *Sgt. Pepper* suits, and it reads on paper at least as an elegant farewell in the spirit of Groucho Marx's Captain Spaulding – hello, I must be going.[287] Psychedelia wasn't over, but – following its own logic of indulgence and experiment – it had outgrown the pop-derived discipline of its first flowering.

This is evident in Jefferson Airplane's *After Bathing at Baxter's*, released in November. The group had enjoyed two hits that year in 'Somebody to Love' and 'White Rabbit', but the two singles from *Baxter's* were rebarbative by comparison. The gentle folk-tinged songs that were the light to the shade on *Surrealistic Pillow* were all but gone, the sound heavier and angrier. The Moody Blues' *Days of Future Passed*, released in the same month, was neither heavy

---

* The lead single was repurposed from Wilson and Love's own 'Thinkin' 'Bout You Baby', produced for Sharon Marie four years earlier.

nor angry; instead it was feeble and pretentious, a concept album about the passing of a single day which, for all the squeaking and burbling of a full symphony orchestra, seems to take much longer.

The Beatles' first fall was not far away. Fans heard the songs from *Magical Mystery Tour* before they saw the TV film, and these represent a sort of low-key coda to *Sgt. Pepper*, extending – with the exception of 'I Am the Walrus' – that album's gentler moods. The circus-flavoured title track is 'Mr. Kite'-lite, a rare example of the Beatles repeating themselves. The rushes of panned sound and obbligato brass ensure it remains engaging, but the lyric (they are 'hoping' to take us away) betrays an awareness that the magic might not happen this time.

McCartney's 'Fool on the Hill' extends the reverie of 'Fixing a Hole', foregrounding the parallel key modulation so the chorus sits wistfully in the minor; it drew from my mother a faraway look otherwise reserved for poetry, Mozart arias and acting of the finest distinction. Naturally I played 'Your Mother Should Know' for her; naturally, she smiled. If the Beatles had taken their foot off the gas, they were still able to produce a kind of Sunday morning psychedelia without trying too hard, using the Mellotron to coax every nuance out of 'Flying' (is that Ringo or the Mellotron choir? The latter might have been sampled from the former), and using studio effects to keep 'Blue Jay Way' afloat.

'I Am the Walrus' was Lennon's only serious contribution to the film music, pursuing themes of exclusion and difference in a stream of lyrics both childish and surreal, parodic and defiant. The extravagant George Martin production takes in more cello parts, the Mike Sammes Singers, and a live edit that interpolates a radio performance of *King Lear* with the playground chanting of 'everybody's got one': the voice at 2:26 is not Lennon being Goonish, as on 'Yellow Submarine', but Shakespeare's Earl of Gloucester.

The song, with its distorted vocal, frowning bass part and

playfulness twisted into menace, represents a bridge between that year's sunny psychedelia and the darker moods of 1968. Heard on the EP after the tightly worked 'Your Mother Should Know', it is further proof of the variety achieved by the Beatles in the final flow of group collaboration – work on the two songs proceeded on the same September evenings. Like many of Dylan's untrammelled mid-decade lyrics, which were taken more seriously by critics than by Lennon, the words make sense only with the music: Lennon certainly meant 'I'm crying', talking the following year about universal sorrow that hit 'about once a week', and recalling later how as a child he had seen his own intuition and hallucinatory visions mirrored only in the lives of 'dead people in books'.[288]

There is an Indian summer feel to these songs, intensified by the September light that suffuses the film. The project had grown out of McCartney's experiments with home movies, and benefits from its lack of pretension as much as it suffers from an absence of plot. It is an ode to the British everyday as well as the headier notes of 1967, and an expression of the Beatles' love of comedy. This ranges from music hall – Rubber-Necked Nat Jackley was hired for his daft walks, though a sequence of him chasing women around a pool was discarded – to what we would now call alternative comedy, in the shape of the Bonzo Dog Doo-Dah Band and Ivor Cutler. 'I am concerned for you to enjoy yourselves,' Cutler announces sorrowfully to the coach party, 'within the limits of British decency.'*

On Boxing Day 1967 the *Magical Mystery Tour* TV movie, filmed in colour, was shown in black-and-white on BBC1. A quarter of the population tuned in, and most, according to the BBC's Audience Research Report, found it 'virtually incomprehensible' – the very

---

* The film is worth watching just for Cutler eating a bread roll; he also appears in a romantic dream sequence to an orchestration of 'All My Loving' which makes it sound like Smetana's *Má vlast*.

reason ABC declined to screen Dylan's now-completed edit of *Eat the Document*. The unlikely marriage of art and commerce, innovative ideas and public taste, had passed its zenith. 'I found it unspeakably tiresome,' wrote one member of the BBC's panel; 'maybe I was the fool!' concluded a shipbuilder. Only a schoolboy found it clever, original and funny in parts: 'in colour,' he added touchingly, 'it would be indescribable.'[289] McCartney was hurried into a TV studio to defend it.

For all that the film meanders (and the clue is in the title), it articulates something of the Sixties experience in Britain, wild creativity layered onto decorum and stifled desire. It also presages the work of Monty Python in its juxtaposition of genial eccentricity – vicars playing blind man's buff – with crazed authority, satirized by Victor Spinetti's demented sergeant major ('Why?" asks Ringo. 'Why?'), and undercut by the sound of a detuned and phased military band.* What the middle-aged runners in Everton strips signify is anyone's guess, although McCartney was spotted at the 1968 FA Cup final between Everton and West Bromwich Albion. The sequence for 'I Am the Walrus' sees the group decked out in full flower power frock coats, miming to the song on a disused West Malling airfield, weeds lining the cracks in the runways, the faded grasses of any late summer waving behind them in blissful ignorance of time.

27 December **JOHN WESLEY HARDING**

Dylan sat out psychedelia like a man waiting for the pub to reopen. He made no public appearances, and hunkered down to work with The Band in Woodstock. Here he wrote and made home recordings of a great variety of songs; fourteen were copyrighted for Dwarf Music in October and circulated to interested

---

* The Pythons considered making the film a B-movie to *Monty Python and the Holy Grail* (1975).

parties on an acetate.

The last of the year's psychedelic albums, the Stones' *Their Satanic Majesties Request*, was scrambled for Christmas release, the disembodied faces of the Beatles from the *Sgt. Pepper* sleeve concealed in the lenticular artwork. The lavish sleeve was more complete than the music, a charming and ramshackle collection of songs bearing exotic percussion and the invitation to sing together.

John Wesley Harding was released at the year's midnight, and Dylan wanted no publicity, 'because this was the season of hype'.[290] Certainly there was none in the sepia-rendered Polaroid cover: like a frugal royal he wore the same suede jacket seen on *Blonde on Blonde*, and again on his next LP, *Nashville Skyline*. Dylan had been featured on the *Sgt. Pepper* cover, and the faces of the Beatles, it was rumoured, could be seen in the bark of the tree behind him on his own sleeve, if only one held it upside down. Such were the times.

The album reads as a reaction to his own work as much as anyone else's. Jon Landau characterized it in *Crawdaddy* as a total redefinition, an 'abandonment of myths and melodrama'.[291] The sound is wrapped tight as arms against the frost, and anyone familiar with 'All Along the Watchtower' from Jimi Hendrix's expansive interpretation will find cold comfort until they adjust. Robbie Robertson, who had encouraged Dylan to approach his albums in a more considered way, heard the bare tapes and cautioned against the projected overdubs, advising that it didn't need to be 'hot-rodded'.[292]

Dylan again recorded in Nashville, the sound stripped back to a trio with Kenny Buttrey on drums and Charlie McCoy on bass. The only decoration is Pete Drake's pedal steel, offering blessed relief on the last two songs, its only jaunty notes. The same musicians would collaborate on the buoyant *Nashville Skyline*, where bittersweet ballads vie with jokey hoedowns. But their work this time meets the palate like an exceptionally peaty single malt, more medicinal than enjoyable. Dylan later said that he hadn't wanted to record the album, that he had meant to do an album of cover versions.[293] The prison diary feel belies the companionship Dylan had enjoyed in Woodstock, and which he spurned for the recording. Lennon was barely warmer towards it than Dylan had been to *Sgt. Pepper*: 'It's fine, you know,' he said in 1968, 'I'm just a bit bored with the backing.' But he admitted to not having heard the acetate that everyone was talking about: 'That's something else, you know.'[294]

Half of the songs on the Dwarf Music recording emerged over the next year in cover versions, but none made it onto *John Wesley Harding*; Dylan was prolific in his isolation.* Nor did The Band, and it's a shame: the ragged warmth of their playing and harmony singing, combined with the amiable non sequiturs of the storytelling, make the songs they recorded together delightful; they dart like the light on trout in a brook.†

---

* Peter, Paul and Mary ('Too Much of Nothing'), Manfred Mann ('Quinn the Eskimo' ['The Mighty Quinn'?]), The Brian Auger Trinity ('This Wheel's on Fire', co-written with Rick Danko), The Byrds ('You Ain't Goin' Nowhere' and 'Nothing Was Delivered') and The Band ('I Shall Be Released', 'Tears of Rage', co-written by Richard Manuel, and again 'This Wheel's on Fire').

† The album, which formed the basis of rock's original bootleg, *Great White Wonder*, can now be reconstructed with reasonable certainty from the official *Bootleg Series Volume 11*. For a guide to which takes might have been used on the acetate, refer to soniclovenoize, 'Bob Dylan – Songs For Dwarf Music', *Albums That Never Were* (5 Mar. 2015), http://albumsthatneverwere.blogspot.com/2015/03/bob-dylan-songs-for-dwarf-music.html.

		Bob Dylan	Beatles	Beach Boys
1968	Jan			
	Feb			
	Mar		[15] 'Lady Madonna'	
	Apr			[8] 'Friends'
	May			
	Jun			[24] FRIENDS
	Jul			[8] 'Do It Again'
	Aug		[30] 'Hey Jude'	
	Sep			
	Oct			
	Nov		[22] THE BEATLES (WHITE ALBUM)	
	Dec			[2] 'Bluebirds over the Mountain'

If 1967 was a shared cultural high for fortunate Western youth, 1968 was the morning after, and one which posed hard questions: how might the world in fact be changed? The Beatles had lost their manager, and a little of their post-*Sgt. Pepper* gleam. The Beach Boys soldiered on even as their general faltered, although he was not strapped dead to his horse until the 'Brian's Back' tour in 1976. Dylan largely stayed home. All three artists had in their recasting of pop's potential over the previous three years posed questions of their peers, the musicians who now – as their own output slowed – took up the mantle of change.

But they had also asked questions of society, more or less directly, and therefore of themselves. They now sought answers, the Beatles and Beach Boys embracing transcendental meditation and Dylan burrowing patiently inward: a large Bible, his mother observed, lay open in his study. In January 1968 Brian Wilson told an interviewer that for the first time in millennia 'everybody's got a personal path right to God, and it seems to be working out so great'. Power frequencies, he explained, came courtesy of the Maharishi's mantras.[295] It was, as the interviewer said approvingly, 'every man for himself', but it wasn't working out so great for Wilson, who spent time in a mental institution later that year.[296]

Dylan ventured out in the company of The Band to play at the Woody Guthrie Memorial Concert in January; according to the following month's *Rolling Stone* he was 'seeming to be somewhere else entirely until it was his turn to play'.[297] The event reunited him with early influences and associates Odetta, Tom Paxton and Pete Seeger, whose closing invocation – 'Woody wants to say to you to take this music to the world, because if you do, maybe we won't have any more fascists' – sounds as naive at this distance as a flower in a gun barrel. The brief set at Carnegie Hall failed to revive in Dylan a yearning to perform: his next live appearance, filming *The Johnny Cash Show* at the Ryman Auditorium in Nashville, was over a year away.

15 March **'Lady Madonna'**

In February the Beatles recorded 'Lady Madonna' and 'Hey Bulldog', snapping back into rock and roll mode before leaving for their delayed retreat in Rishikesh, India. 'Lady Madonna' is little more than a doodle played con brio, the harmonies on 'see how they run' the only luxury. But 'Hey Bulldog' is one of

Lennon's best songs, an oblique *cri de cœur* raised from a funky piano riff before unfurling along a rainy chorus. The two modes they would explore for the rest of the Beatles' career were established: McCartney's empathetic and outer-directed, more or less sustained by his facility in different styles; Lennon's increasingly solipsistic and pained, carrying more emotional weight.

In India they reconnected with the Maharishi, the folk singer Donovan, and Mike Love of the Beach Boys. Official pictures show the Beatles and their partners as part of a large group, garlanded with flowers, the tourists almost blanched by the sun. The visit was influential in embedding the hippy trail, a less exclusive grand tour for the new age, in the culture of Western youth. It was also a productive time for the group, who wrote many songs on acoustic guitars. But it was their last great shared adventure. Apple Corps was launched with modest fanfare by Lennon and McCartney in New York in May 1968, but its roots lay in a tax dodge and its purpose was vague: it would be a free service for people who wanted to make films or music, but not a charity – 'a kind of Western communism,' said McCartney.[298] 'We're just blowing up the balloon,' admitted Lennon.[299]

In June 1968 *In His Own Write*, a one-act National Theatre dramatization of Lennon's two books, premiered at the Old Vic. The Beatles still attended en famille, although with Paul absent – and with Yoko Ono, as the gentlemen of the press were quick to note, in Cynthia's place.[300] McCartney was at his fiancée Jane Asher's own premiere but flew to the US the following day, hooking up with Linda Eastman in LA. As both men realigned their private lives with varying degrees of clumsiness, their need for one another diminished: both had fallen in love with older, independent women who were already mothers, and the couples became self-sufficient. In March 1969, Lennon and McCartney married just eight days apart.

Fans could still see the Beach Boys live, the problem being that few wanted to. That April they lost $350,000 on what they had optimistically called the Million Dollar Tour,[301] but which was immediately overshadowed by the assassination of Martin Luther King in Memphis. National Guardsmen closed down their opening show in Nashville, and other cancellations followed. Undeterred, the band set out on the road the following month with a show billed as 'The Most Exciting Event of the Decade!' and featuring the Maharishi Mahesh Yogi. Like a Broadway flop, this closed after five shows, losing the band even more money. 'Maharishi had a soft voice,' recalled Mike Love, 'but he refused to allow anyone to put a microphone on him – he didn't like to be touched.'[302]

The Beach Boys had lost just south of $5 million in today's money; at the 16,000-capacity Singer Bowl in Flushing Meadows, only 800 people showed up. Their summer single was 'Do It Again', and it isn't surprising that the Beach Boys were feeling nostalgic by this point: the song chugs along irresistibly, and with an unintended poignancy which makes it all the more affecting. But it wasn't their year. An appearance at the Fillmore East in October was characterized by the *Village Voice* as 'the weekend the Fillmore tried out as a whore'.[303]

Friends is a fine album, and possibly easier to appreciate now through the lens of indie music than it was at the time. There is an unedited click inside the first second, and plenty of unresolved sounds and buzzes throughout: this is why it is often described as lo-fi, although the recorded sound is rich and full. Wilson's perfectionism had ceded to intimacy and approximation, but the Beach Boys were fine singers, and there were still intriguing corners in the writing. There is great beauty in the title track, in 'Anna Lee, the Healer' (where Mike Love's lyrics reference Rishikesh), and in Dennis Wilson's 'Little Bird'. Brian's 'Busy Doin' Nothin'' is lyrically childlike but musically sophisticated, a bossa nova-infused account of a mind that can take only small steps. 'Do It Again' scraped the Top 20 in the US (and was a number one in the UK), but *Friends* didn't even make the Billboard Top 100.

'Friends' depicts an idyll of loyalty and trust: 'dim dipple ee,' they sing, 'let's be friends'. But making friends could be dangerous in 1968, when even California girls weren't always what they seemed. On his way back into town from an LSD trip in the mountains, Dennis Wilson picked up two young hitch-hikers who told him all about their own guru: 'a guy named Charlie'.[304] Wilson soon found the guru in his driveway; ushered into his own house by Charles Manson, he found that the Family had set up home inside. Manson had ambitions as a songwriter, and the Beach Boys recorded him that summer at Brian's home studio. But the relationship soured as the Family adopted Wilson's clothes, wrecked his Mercedes and spent his money; the collateral benefit of free love led to expensive gonorrhoea treatment for all concerned.[305]

Dennis at length moved out of his own home to avoid having to confront Manson, and by the end of the year the Beach Boys' carefree drummer was living 'in one small room, with one candle'.[306] The association ended with death threats when he changed the title, and some of the lyrics, to Manson's song 'Cease to Exist'. Repurposed as 'Never Learn Not to Love', and prefaced by an ominous backwards recording of a gong, it was the B-side to their last single of the year. The invitation to cease to exist and 'come say you love me' is almost unlistenable in hindsight.*

---

* It was a credulous age. Even as they renounced the Maharishi when launching Apple in May, Lennon and McCartney had eulogized their friend, 'Magic Alex' Mardas, as a beautiful, incredible genius: Mardas it was whose vaunted seventy-two-track console at Apple turned out in January 1969 to be an unusable mess.

When *Friends* only made it to 126 in the US album charts Capitol had a brainwave – *The Best of the Beach Boys Vol. 3*. This was followed a fortnight later by *Stack-o-Tracks*, which featured Beach Boy hits stripped of their vocals; the company stopped short of releasing a Beach Boys record with nothing on it at all.

30 August '**Hey Jude**', 22 November **THE BEATLES**

McCartney's ability to empathize in song reached its high-water mark in that year's second single, 'Hey Jude'. It was a song which – like 'Let It Be' – had its roots in consolation: he felt for Lennon's son Julian, who was struggling with his parents' divorce. The lyrics disguise the immediate inspiration, but that only broadens the canvas: the song is an embrace in musical form for anyone in sorrow or self-doubt.

The group had been working on the songs written in India for months now, and relationships were fraying. 'Hey Jude' was comparatively new, and it shows. The tempo is measured, the playing pushing gently but decisively back into the lyrics: the harmonies are among their best, supporting exquisitely the move to the B ♭ {IV} on the key word 'pain' and the descending motif that follows. The irresistible singalong chorus, now so familiar, works as an emotional release: everyone is smiling as if after tears, a vast brass band joining, McCartney indulging himself at the limits of his register. It's a final moment of pure joy from the group that had given the world so much of it. Lennon was later mean about many McCartney songs (and indeed many of his own), but never about this one.

Events within and without the group were showing that love wasn't enough after all. When they recorded 'Hey Jude' in early September for David Frost's TV show, Ringo Starr looked his jovial self, dressed in a lime-green suit. But he had walked out on the group two weeks earlier, annoyed by McCartney's criticism of his drumming on 'Back in the U.S.S.R.'; McCartney had antagonized Harrison by declining his idea for a guitar part on 'Hey Jude'.

In the world and in the counterculture the mood was combative and streaked with violence. Students and striking workers brought the French state to the brink of collapse in May. Robert Kennedy was assassinated in June, just two months after Martin Luther King. Soviet tanks entered Czechoslovakia in August, ending the Prague Spring. Days later, at the Democratic Convention in Chicago, radical agitation was countered by violent policing. The decade's twin forces of dissent and reaction had reached fever pitch. Police beat protestors, calling them cocksuckers, and were called pigs and whores in return.[307]

It was into this febrile atmosphere that Lennon's song 'Revolution' was released, as the B-side to 'Hey Jude', on the first Monday of the convention. For those who thought the Beatles should not comment on what was happening on the streets, the song was too much. For those doing the protesting, it was not enough. Even Lennon couldn't decide: on the heavier version of the song that accompanied 'Hey Jude' he counts himself out of the violence, but on the (superior) softer take that appeared on the *White Album* he equivocates. When it came to destruction, he sang, you could count him 'out ... in'.

They were no longer in the vanguard. The most vital music of the year came from The Band, on July's *Music from Big Pink*, and from Jimi Hendrix on *Electric Ladyland*, released in October; Van Morrison's *Astral Weeks* was released a week after the *White Album*, and the Rolling Stones picked up steam on *Beggar's Banquet*. There was no defining motif for the rock music of 1968: where 1965 had been the year of folk rock, and 1967 of psychedelia, 1968 had no single colour. Instead the music that the Beatles, Beach Boys and Dylan had pushed to its expressive limits reached a kind of delta, separating into divergent streams that would go mainstream in the 1970s: country rock, psychedelic folk, heavy rock, progressive rock and reggae all had roots in 1968.

One stream looked back to the country music that, unlike folk, had been left largely unexploited in mainstream pop since the Everly Brothers. Dylan's new songs played a role in this, again via the music of the Byrds. Briefly reduced to a trio after firing David Crosby in late 1967, they were now occupied like a host creature by Gram Parsons, a Harvard dropout from a rich and troubled Southern family who found peace only in country music. This led to *Sweetheart of the Rodeo*, from August 1968, which begins with one of Dylan's Dwarf Music songs, 'You Ain't Goin' Nowhere', and ends with another, 'Nothing Was Delivered'. But Parsons' vocals were removed from three songs, and – like Gene Clark, whose gifts had also been underused – he would move through different groups and associations in pursuit of his ideal.

Sweetheart of the Rodeo was a fine record, but Clark released an even better one that autumn in the company of the bluegrass banjo player Doug Dillard. *The Fantastic Expedition of Dillard & Clark* is Gene Clark's masterpiece, his aching songs laden with electric harpsichord and enlivened by Dillard's sparkling banjo. Country rock would break mainstream in the 1970s: a number of songs on *The Fantastic Expedition* were written with Bernie Leadon, who co-founded the Eagles in 1971.

Another emergent stream revisited the well of folk through the lens of psychedelia and hippy culture. It turned out that a blend of fey singing and exotic instrumentation, touched with English wizardry and a hint of Krishna, suited the times: the Incredible String Band took *The Hangman's Beautiful Daughter* to number five in the UK charts in the summer of 1968. A wilfully eccentric record, sounding at times like a troupe of morris dancers battling an unbidden acid trip, it was a major influence on Led Zeppelin.

Fairport Convention were already pivoting from the acid rock of their debut album, released in June 1968. Sandy Denny joined them that summer, and the recordings the group now made were transformed. *What We Did on our Holidays*, recorded in 1968 but released the following January, opens with Denny's airy song 'Fotheringay', her voice a thing of beauty. Dylan's songs loomed large here too: Fairport Convention covered one on *Holidays* and another three on its follow-up, *Unhalfbricking*.

While Fairport Convention moved from acid rock to a lighter, folkier sound, others did the opposite. Cream's 1968 album *Wheels of Fire* is more stolid than the previous year's *Disraeli Gears*, the full-on psychedelia of the latter's cover emblematically exchanged for a black design on silver foil. They were the first supergroup, a category in which the Beatles, Beach Boys and Dylan would have failed at the first audition, had they been interested. The trio epitomized a growing reverence for instrumental brilliance and the seriousness with which a certain strand of blues rock was now taken. The rhythms of soul were fading away, and the ungainly dancing that accompanied pop through its mid-1960s flowering was gradually replaced by the heavy-footed stance of the rock fan, testing only the neck muscles and frowning in appreciation as a song reached its tenth minute: Iron Butterfly's portentous 'In-A-Gadda-Da-Vida' lasted for seventeen.

Led Zeppelin were formed in 1968 and blended psychedelic folk with heavy rock: their music always retained a strand of English pastoral, and Sandy Denny sang on 'The Battle of Evermore' on their fourth album. But they blended it with a form of the blues that was much heavier than that of groups like the Yardbirds from whom they had emerged, enabled partly by the advent of louder amplification. Their cover of the folk song 'Babe I'm Gonna Leave You' on their debut album cycles between delicate fingerpicking and full-on rock.

Finally there is the eternal puzzle of progressive rock, a stream which Yes drummer Bill Bruford says could not have emerged without the Beatles. This was one route out of psychedelic pop, taken with alacrity by Pink Floyd when their chief songwriter Syd Barrett became lost to himself and the group; they fired him in early 1968. Yes formed that year, as did King Crimson (on whose guitarist Robert Fripp *Sgt. Pepper* had made such an impact). Hard to pin down, the genre in its early incarnation seemed to force the volume of blues rock and the wistfulness of psychedelic folk into a fight to the death. 'Epitaph', from *In the Court of the Crimson King*, struts as if scored for the birthday celebrations of an especially humourless dictator, before yielding to the flimsy folk of 'Moonchild'. Both 'Epitaph' and 'Moonchild' contain two other songs; music of this importance could not be contained within single titles.

Even modern jazz took cues from *Sgt. Pepper*: Carla Bley conceived 1971's *Escalator over the Hill – A Chronotransduction* as a response to the Beatles' album, recording it over a three-year period.[308] Again, it's hard to hear what path this inspiration took, unless it's the sense of infinite possibility and liberation from generic restraint that rock musicians also read into *Sgt. Pepper*: at one point in Bley's title track it sounds as if Wagner's Valkryies have taken a heavy landing in a bandstand.

The Beatles would never adopt progressive rock, for all that their experimentation appears to have encouraged it. But the interest in heavier sounds, and the recourse to pastoral and the down-home influence of The Band, are all reflected on the *White Album*. The strength of the album, and its weakness, is that it is equivocal. Except for a handful of songs that find a focused late-Beatle style, it reflects the year's divergent styles without committing to one.

Thus the gentle 'Blackbird', 'I Will', 'Julia' and 'Mother Nature's Son' lean on the fingerpicking folk style they learned from

Donovan in Rishikesh. The heavier 'Birthday', 'Yer Blues' and 'Helter Skelter' gesture unconvincingly at the bigger sound of the louder groups. McCartney dips into a range of pastiche styles, from 'Ob-La-Di, Ob-La-Da' (loosely derived from ska, and a song the rest of the group strongly disliked) to 'Rocky Raccoon' (cod country) and 'Wild Honey Pie' (another soft-shoe shuffle in the vein of 'When I'm Sixty-Four' and 'Your Mother Should Know'). 'Back in the U.S.S.R.' was riffed in Rishikesh in the company of Mike Love; girls from Ukraine, Moscow and Georgia are listed in a bridge that features a Beach Boys-style 'oo-woo-woo' in the backing vocal.*

Within all this can be found a number of songs that sound fully realized and comfortable in their own Beatle skin. These include McCartney's 'Martha My Dear' and Harrison's 'While My Guitar Gently Weeps', but most are by Lennon, including 'Dear Prudence', 'Glass Onion', 'Happiness Is a Warm Gun', 'I'm So Tired', 'Sexy Sadie' and 'Cry Baby Cry'. The White Album is his as much as *Sgt. Pepper* was McCartney's – or would have been, without the guff.

Both found new compositional modes after their informal lessons in fingerpicking with Donovan in India, and these are shown to advantage on side two. 'Blackbird' is the most fully realized of McCartney's acoustic songs on the record. Its elliptical lyric plausibly addresses the hopes and slow realization of the civil rights movement, balancing encouragement with saddened observation.

'I Will' sounds effortless, but it took almost seventy takes for McCartney to achieve the insouciant feel. His perfectionism now grated on the others, although Harrison's 'Not Guilty' was itself abandoned after a hundred takes and four days' work.[309] The cen-

---

* The two now sovereign countries were part of the Soviet Union at the time. The modestly subversive title was a play on the 'I'm Backing Britain' campaign, a source of brief pride and then widespread amusement, also referenced in the film *Carry On up the Khyber* and in the first scene of the first episode of *Dad's Army*, broadcast in July 1968.

tral tune in 'I Will' is as plain-spoken as a hymn, confining itself to the notes in the F major scale save for a single sharpened B at the end of the bridge (over a gospelly {II} chord).

Lennon's 'Julia' begins with words sung tentatively on a single note. The lyric here is borrowed from Kahlil Gibran's 'Sand and Foam', buying time to enter the private world of the song proper. The repeated A in the voice at last breathes out when he feels able to name its subject, his late mother Julia, the name breathed over a whole bar. He calls out her name twice more, the melody only lifting a tone above that opening A the second time, above a magical {vi} A minor chord. He had intended from the start to write about his mother but now calls to 'ocean child', which is one of the meanings in the kanji for 'Yoko'. The ambiguity in the song (and in the psychology) is underpinned by a second magical chord, a G minor {iv} under the lyric 'calls me', which in the second verse becomes 'touch me': past and future, lost mother and new lover, reconciled. There is one more strange and distant chord, the C♯m {vii} under the image of hair as floating sky: as with 'Surf's Up', the construction of this song is brilliant and irreplicable. The imperfect fingerpicking only adds to the intimacy: where the flawless 'I Will' is a love song, almost a greetings card, 'Julia' is in its own words a 'song of love' in all its nakedness and complexity.

They could still be supportive of one another, even amid the bickering: on *Anthology* McCartney can be heard from the control booth encouraging Lennon's attempts to record 'Julia'. But the plain white cover, the photos of individual group members, and the walkouts over that summer by band members and engineering staff, were as far from the collegiate vibe of *Sgt. Pepper* as could be.*

Once 'Helter Skelter' is out of the way, the overgrown end of the *White Album* is a fascinating place to linger. Harrison's tentative

---

* *Let It Be*, the filmed live album project designed to galvanize them as a group at the start of 1969, only drove the wedge in further: Starr briefly left the band in August 1968, as did Harrison in January 1969.

'Long, Long, Long' rattles into the slower version of 'Revolution', before that fades into McCartney's 'Honey Pie' with its snatch of scratchy vinyl from another era; on side four, Lennon's eerie 'Cry Baby Cry' fades via a snatch of a lost song into 'Revolution 9'.* They rejected a lovely take of 'Good Night' with harmonies from the whole band in favour of a blank-faced orchestral accompaniment; for once, they made the wrong choice.

One more flavour of the year, avant-garde experimentation, can be found in songs like 'Why Don't We Do It in the Road?' and 'Everybody's Got Something to Hide Except Me and My Monkey'. It was deliberately crude compared to their experimental music of the previous two years, and in 'Revolution 9' the tape effects and juxtapositions finally escape the bounds of pop music. Where 'Tomorrow Never Knows' had compressed the ideas into music that still communicated something like a song, 'Revolution 9' – which is very beautiful – operates on its own terms. A week after the album was released at the end of November, John Lennon and Yoko Ono released the still more experimental *Unfinished Music No. 1: Two Virgins*, a record on which they appeared naked and which sounds invariably like something stuck in a cat's throat.

Rock and roll, or at least the version of it that had emerged mid-decade, was just one of the musics again. The energy around the turn of the decade reverted to soul music, where albums start to fill out beyond the singles – on Aretha Franklin's Atlantic albums, in Isaac Hayes' towering cumulus productions, on Curtis Mayfield's solo debut, and in Marvin Gaye's *What's Going On*, which summons and aligns the spirit in all of these.

Melodic pop didn't go away, but it lacked the light touch of the best 1960s work. The divergent streams of music that had emerged in 1968 went on to dominate the first half of the 1970s, from the

---

* Lost at least until 2018's Super Deluxe version of the album.

Eagles' country rock to the English folk played by Lindisfarne and Steeleye Span; from the heavy rock of Led Zeppelin and its greasier cousin heavy metal to the progressive rock of groups like Yes and Pink Floyd. Reggae, first mentioned in a song on Toots and the Maytals' 1968 single 'Do the Reggay', went global in the hands of Bob Marley and the Wailers. Our version of the Sixties ended almost as soon as it had begun.

FADE

The enduring quality and unique scope of the best music of 1966 and 1967, combined with the opulence of its fashion and the orgiastic swirls of its poster work, means that the paths of influence in any study of the Sixties will find a centre of gravity there: the advent of experiment, the mutation of form.

Leonard Bernstein addressed this on 1967's *Inside Pop*, highlighting the Beatles' unorthodox three-beat bars in 'Good Day Sunshine', the shift into three-quarter time in 'She Said She Said' and the melodic span of the first phrase in 'Got to Get You Into My Life'. 'That could almost be by Schumann,' enthuses Bernstein, 'it's so expansive and romantic.' In it he sees the pop generation reaching and spreading itself, 'grasping at the unattainable'.

Bernstein wasn't to know this, but they had already attained it. There is no pop music as complex yet fully realized as 'Strawberry Fields Forever' and 'Surf's Up', or their sunnier familiars 'Penny Lane' and 'Good Vibrations', before or after.

The myth of *Sgt. Pepper*, which is also the myth of *Pet Sounds*, and of *Blonde on Blonde*, is that it redefined pop as art and set its practitioners free.[310] Roger Waters of Pink Floyd described Dylan's 'Sad Eyed Lady of the Lowlands' as changing his life: 'When I heard that, I thought, if Bob can do it, I can do it. It's twenty minutes long!' Yet not anyone could do it. Waters' takeout from *Sgt. Pepper* – that it had 'a ton of narrative in it', liberating him and his generation to do whatever they liked – was also mistaken.[311] There wasn't much narrative; the ruse had worked too well.

William Mann, reviewing *Sgt. Pepper* for *The Times*, acknowledged this. But he also foresaw that others might run with the idea of a 'popsong-cycle', or, as he put it, juxtaposing genres and eras with his old mischief, 'a Tin Pan Alley *Dichterliebe*'.[312] This met with unhappy results in the hands of rock groups like The Who on *Tommy*, and unhappier ones in the hands of progressive rock musicians: Mann cannot have anticipated Rick Wakeman's *The Six Wives of Henry VIII*.

Comparisons with older forms drew a blank with the artists, or misrepresented their work. Wilson had said in 1966 that *Pet Sounds* exhibited 'a more conscious, arty production'.[313] But when *New York Times* journalist Richard Goldstein said that the harmonies on *Smiley Smile* reminded him of Fauré's *Requiem*, Brian Wilson recoiled, muttering: 'I never heard of that guy.'[314] John Lennon's response to the idea of 'A Day in the Life' as 'a kind of miniature Waste Land' was: 'Miniature what?'[315*] Writing in the *Village Voice*, Jack Newfield positioned Dylan as the inheritor of an underground American tradition stretching back to Whitman and Poe, but criticized a 'compulsion to rhyme' which diminished his words and music.[316] This misses the point: the rhyme was what kept it in bounds, what made it musical, the debt that kept expression honest.

Something marvellous had happened as Dylan and the Beatles and the Beach Boys absorbed and refracted each other's music, and no one was sure what it was. Writing about 'Strawberry Fields Forever' almost thirty years later, Ian MacDonald described it 'a sort of technologically evolved folk music',[317] albeit one yielding exceptional levels of artistic expression. Bernstein, on *Inside Pop*, also located it in the folk tradition with its simple triads and essentially

---

* Lennon may have followed up the reference, as he did when James Joyce was mentioned in the context of his prose writing; buying *Finnegans Wake,* he told the BBC: 'I dug it and felt as though he's an old friend.' Kevin Howlett, *The Beatles: The BBC Archives: 1962 to 1970* (BBC Books, 2013), p. 251.

limited musical vocabulary, conceding that 'within that restricted language, all these new adventures are simply extraordinary.' For both, it is as if the writers are in a box but reaching outside it.

But our experience of this music is that it comes from *outside* the box of triads and its limited harmonic, rhythmic and melodic grammar. The auditory and emotional impact is different to folk, the expressive intent far removed. The best of it isn't made to broadcast news, it isn't narrative, it isn't locally anchored, except in the loosest sense. 'Highway 61' brings the story of Abraham up against the Cold War; 'Surf's Up' is a shadowy de Chirico with its columnated ruins and dove-nested towers; in 'Strawberry Fields Forever' Lennon's journey is subjective, internal and opaque.* These songs communicate more like visual art, making meaning in the whole eye of the senses.

Dylan in the mid-1960s laughed off interpretations of his songs, perhaps the better to maintain creative momentum: when Joan Baez ventured one, he imagined a future in which all these 'assholes' would be writing about his songs. 'I don't know the fuck where it comes from,' he protested. 'I don't know what the fuck it's about.'[318] Lennon in 1967 insisted his writing was 'for laughs or fun or whatever you call it', and a year later still wore the mask: 'I don't know what we're doing at all,' he said. 'Really, I just like rock and roll.'[319] But prompted with the idea that critics tended to read something into songs that wasn't there, Lennon demurred: 'It is there. It's like abstract art really.'[320]

Perhaps Robert Hunter, who Dylan collaborated with on one of his best late albums, *Together Through Life*, put it best when speaking of his own work with the Grateful Dead: 'It says what it means.'[321] In essence this is what Dylan, the Beatles and Brian

* The broadcaster Steve Race called *Rubber Soul*'s 'Girl' 'a folk song from some undiscovered land, it's so new'. Michael Lydon, 'Lennon and McCartney: Songwriters – A Portrait from 1966' (unpublished, March 1966), via *TeachRock* https://teachrock.org/article/lennon-and-mccartney-songwriters-a-portrait-from-1966/.

Wilson were reaching for in their best mid-1960s work: lyric music in which meaning is immanent rather than extricable.

They were able to do this partly because there was no obvious musical precedent to worry over, and partly because they were by now working outside any existing tradition – but this also meant the art could barely be sustained. There's a clue to this in Bernstein's April 1967 reference to the 'straining tenderness of those high, untrained young voices'.[322] They were still young, around twenty-five at the time, and they *were* untrained. Their inspiration was bound to falter. Dylan soon found that he couldn't produce with the ease of the mid-1960s, saying that one day the lights went out, leading to a kind of amnesia: 'It took me a long time,' he told Jonathan Cott in 1978, 'to get to do consciously what I used to be able unconsciously.'*

The music produced in these years is so alive partly because it is free of intellectual underpinnings. As modern art, music and writing atrophied into theory, and human figures, recognizable structure and narrative forms including melody faded from view – 'art divorced from life,' as James Baldwin put it[323] – pop music offered a world full of these things, seen through new eyes. Van Dyke Parks, Brian Wilson's collaborator on *Smile*, had studied with Aaron Copeland at Carnegie Tech, but dropped out to explore the West Coast scene. 'Going to California meant I escaped John Cage,' he explained. 'I escaped the abstractions, the music you can't remember, the highbrow angst.'[324] From an age in which the application of theory to art led to canvases that were blank,

---

* Jonathan Cott, 'Bob Dylan: The Rolling Stone Interview, Part 2', *Rolling Stone* (16 Nov. 1978),
https://www.rollingstone.com/music/music-news/bob-dylan-the-rolling-stone-interview-part-2-173545/. Dylan went on to say that it happens to everyone, and he's right – even Mozart found he needed 'to make sketches and to revise' when he approached his mid-thirties. Charles Rosen, *The Classical Style* (Viking, 1971), p. 386, via Richard Osborne, *Rossini* (Oxford University Press, 2007), p. 113. Rossini himself lived long enough to emerge from decades of depression and almost complete musical silence with a *Petite Messe Solennelle* grounded in musical craft, reaching back to Bach and forward to Fauré.

and music that was silent, and novels that arrived loose-leaf, it is the untheoretical but memorable and concisely structured pop music that will endure.

Lennon would soon call it all a phase – it was time by October 1968 to be 'more natural, less "newspaper taxis"'[325] – but he couldn't resist referencing the band's songs from 1967: in 'Glass Onion', completed in the month he gave the interview, he name-checks no less than four of them.* One promo filmed for 'Hello, Goodbye' showed the Beatles waving inanely in the collarless jackets they had favoured in 1963: it was jokey, but it was also *about themselves*.† The sleeve for the *White Album* carried its own highbrow humour: each copy was printed with its own number to create, in the words of its designer, the pop artist Richard Hamilton, 'the ironic situation of a numbered edition of something like five million copies'.[326]

Self-awareness, once acquired, cannot be lost. The summer of 1967 marked the end of pop's childhood, and the anxiety of influence, previously kept at bay by the breathless pace of experiment, took hold.

The Beatles had the good fortune, however messy the circumstances at the time, to quit while they were still ahead: their group legacy floats serene. This is partly because they recorded no music as a full group outside the decade they so signally shaped, and because the last recording they all worked on together was called 'The End'. Concluding the 'long medley' on side two of *Abbey Road*, it hinges on McCartney's lyric about the love you make

---

* 'Strawberry Fields Forever', 'I Am the Walrus', 'The Fool on the Hill' and 'Fixing a Hole'. It also mentions 'Lady Madonna', which had already referenced 'I Am the Walrus', which quoted from 'Lucy in the Sky with Diamonds'.'

† Their initial pitch for the *Abbey Road* sleeve two years later was the remake of the *Please Please Me* cover that was eventually used on the *Blue Album* in 1973. They weren't alone: Frank Zappa parodied the cover on *We're Only in It for the Money*, replacing blue skies with a thunderstorm; the image was relegated to the interior – and the album delayed until 1968 – by corporate nerves.

being equal to the love you take; in the Beatles' case they made a great deal more than they could ever take.

Abbey Road is not as good as its reputation suggests, and *Let It Be* – recorded eight months earlier but released eight months later – a little better. But the second side of *Abbey Road*, which contains not a second of slack and is beautifully recorded on EMI's new eight-track tape machines, represents a coda of unearthly grace. It has a floating, almost sedative quality. Where *Let It Be* pushes and pulls (notably on 'I've Got a Feeling', where Lennon effectively starts singing a different song halfway through), *Abbey Road* achieves resolution by design.

As ever with the Beatles, seeming effortlessness was the result of hard graft. 'Because' features an electric harpsichord played by George Martin in exact synchronization with Lennon's guitar, and vocals for the song were recorded three times each by Lennon, McCartney and Harrison. They had first recorded eleven years earlier, singing 'In Spite of All the Danger' and 'That'll Be the Day' in a studio constructed in a living room, with a tin bath for a reverb chamber; this was the last time the three of them sang together.

They kept working, and to start with made remarkable solo albums, including Lennon's *Plastic Ono Band*, McCartney's *Ram* and Harrison's *All Things Must Pass* – all of them recorded by mid-1971. But as solo artists labouring through the 1970s and 1980s, like the Beach Boys and even Dylan, they suffered lapses of taste and judgement and almost total loss of inspiration. A nadir of sorts was reached in 1987 when a chance meeting at a Malibu medical facility led to Dylan contributing vocals to an unreleased Brian Wilson song called, with bitter irony, 'The Spirit of Rock and Roll'. It sounds utterly washed up, although both men would in time reclaim their past, via re-releases and reconstructions, and – to differing extents – the muse.

John Lennon never became friends with Bob Dylan after moving to New York, as he had imagined he might. Instead it was George Harrison who collaborated with Dylan at intervals, notably in the novelty group the Traveling Wilburys around the turn of the 1990s. Time was unkind to the Beatles, who lost Lennon and Harrison, and the Beach Boys, who lost Dennis and Carl Wilson. McCartney and Wilson both struggled with their once pristine voices as they aged, whereas Dylan, who for so long had sounded like a young man who yearned to be old, grew into his and learned to work the cracks like Rembrandt did the umbers, siennas and earths in his late paintings.

Brian Wilson's most recent work with the Beach Boys, *That's Why God Made the Radio*, often awkwardly humorous and sentimental, but in its final suite of songs touchingly elegiac, came out in 2012. McCartney, for so long used to making hit records, continued to collaborate with successful producers – something Dylan wisely came to eschew. At one point during sessions for his 2018 album *Egypt Station* McCartney was nonplussed by progress on a co-write: 'This doesn't amount to anything,' he complained, adding ruefully, 'Y'know – I wrote "'Eleanor Rigby".'[327] 2020's lockdown album, *McCartney III*, was self-produced and the better for it.

Dylan, indefatigable, released a seventy-minute album of new songs in June 2020. The cover art to *Rough and Rowdy Ways* reaches back to the 1950s or earlier, but the music achieves in 'Murder Most Foul' a reckoning of sorts with the 1960s and all that followed. 'Play me a song,' sings Dylan, addressing the disc jockey Wolfman Jack, before listing the influencers and the influenced, as if the floodgates of remembrance have opened: from Little Richard to Carl Wilson, Elvis to Etta James. Look up Wolfman Jack, or maybe don't: he sounds like no one so much as Donald Trump. Dylan sings the imperative 'play' sixty times, a Benedicite for comedians, gangsters, singers and genres: classical, gospel, folk and blues, handholds in the darkness, some kind of home.

○

That's what this music has been to me. My life, driven like a tuning fork into the September of 1965, has vibrated to that era ever since.

In 2016 the V & A summarized the second half of the 1960s in an exhibition, *You Say You Want a Revolution?* I was surprised and moved to see two of the Beatles' *Sgt. Pepper* suits, together with the beautiful olive and rose frock coat Lennon wore to film 'All You Need Is Love'. But I was equally struck by the corridors that traced the protest, energy and constructive rage of the anti-war and Black Panther movements.

The counterculture was assimilated on the one hand – psychedelic design poured into everyday life in simplified forms, cheerfully influencing design into the 1970s – and fractured on the other by its embrace of Maoism. But grassroots initiatives for environmental protection and social justice endured, and at intervals were revived. Black Lives Matter and Extinction Rebellion manifested at the turn of the 2020s on the streets and on social media, drawing on the graphic styles of Emory Douglas and the Atelier Populaire, and reliving some of that era's challenges. Black Lives Matter found its central theme embraced by brands in the wake of George Floyd's murder by police, but its radical solutions (diverting funding from the police to community and welfare groups) were quickly questioned: as with Martin Luther King's later sermons and the Poor People's Campaign, trying to fix the problems at source was going too far.

The exhibition at length opened out in a recreation of Woodstock, complete with Astroturf where people might recline and reflect, Hendrix playing out the decade at dawn in split-screen stars and spangles. In a sense the culture has been beached on that Astroturf all this time, unable to reconcile its artistic energy and radical politics with the commercialization of its music and the long march of neoliberalism.

At first I was annoyed at the V&A by the slow pace of the crowds, coachloads of retirees alternating a visit to a National Trust property, as I imagined, with a trip into town. People dither and stumble with headsets on, we all lose our visual bearings. But people also dither with age. And as I adjusted to the pace and watched the faces of people in their sixties and seventies staring with a kind of wonder through the glass, occasionally smiling as if to someone they had forgotten, I realized that they were the ones who had lived it.

Author's note

This book was largely written during the pandemic of 2020–21, so any time I might have spent in reference libraries was instead spent at home, online. This is not necessarily a bad thing. There are plenty of compelling primary sources online – such as footage from press conferences, studio outtakes, and images taken from contemporary magazines – much of it uploaded by fans, for fans. But fitting this shape-shifting maze of unofficial and sometimes temporary content back into the box of a conventional reference system was not always easy. Nor was the process of tracing (often widely shared) quotes back to their original source. Sarah Terry did some great sleuthing at the copy-edit stage, and we have done our best to ensure that the book is factually correct, that original sources are correctly identified, and that links are current. I hope you enjoy following some of the same paths I did.

Acknowledgements

My first thanks are due to Neil Griffiths, who asked me to write this book and helped shaped its theme, and to Marcus Wright, who has introduced me to so much of its music. The germ of the book came from shared conversation between the three of us, in bars on London's South Bank.

Neil trusted me to write it in the first place, helped guide it on its way over numerous drafts, and teased out its potential over a series of long walks: the chapter on 1968 in particular benefited from those exchanges. The books I relied upon for detail on Dylan were all gifts from him over the years.

Marcus was there when I bought my first Beatles album, and lent me my first book about the group, which I'm ashamed to say I returned in tatters. He gave me a great deal of seminal music and music writing along the way, sharing a love of the Beach Boys which was not always fashionable.

That first book was *The Beatles: An Illustrated Record*, long out of print, but full of language I still recall; perhaps it's best that I don't have it and couldn't reread it, as cadences from the best criticism have a tendency to lodge inside me and I was loath to reproduce them. I didn't touch *Revolution in the Head* until the book was almost done.

I'm extremely grateful to Damian Lanigan and James Tookey at Weatherglass for their thoughtful readings, suggestions and support; and to Sarah Terry, whose copy-edit was both sensitive to the style of the book and unfailingly attentive to its detail.

I want to thank Simon Bray and the Sea Rockets for the music we've shared, recorded and performed in recent years – with a note to my old friend and bandmate Richard Chamberlain, who I hope would have enjoyed this book.

The dedication is to my children Zaki and Marina, and my wife Lea, who have had the not unalloyed pleasure of watching someone write a book but have remained encouraging and supportive at all times. I love watching, playing and listening to music with you.

Finally, my thanks are due to my parents Tom and Pauline, who let me discover pop music and football for myself but introduced me to everything else I enjoy; to Marcus's mother Doris, who encouraged my passions and lit up in a smile when the Beatles were playing; and to my sister Tamsin, who shared those days and many since.

Of all this the love was made.

Merton Abbey Mills, 2021

Appendix 1:
musical notation in Western pop

Letters

The '50s progression' can be heard in countless songs. Sometimes it's called the 'Stand by Me' progression, as that song is so well known (although it came out in 1961). It song was recorded by Ben E. King in the key of A. Try and imagine that song in your head: the chord sequence is A – F♯m – D – E.

Numerals

The reason that musicians and writers use Roman numerals is that not all songs are in the key of A (and not everyone wants to sing 'Stand by Me' in A anyway.) Representing this chord sequence or turnaround as I – vi – IV – V means that it can be replicated in any key, using the home chord (the key in which the song is going to be played) as the I. So in this case, I = A, vi = F♯m (the lower-case numerals representing a minor chord), IV = D and V = E. If we were to play the song in C, the same numerals would work even though the letter chords change: I = C, vi = Am, IV = F, V = G.

I'm most comfortable with letter chords because I play guitar, and guitarists (and many pop musicians on other instruments) typically use the 'letter' chord abbreviations. But the Roman numerals used in this book are a way to convey the nature of the chord changes without getting into the detail of the key in which the songs are played or written.

Names

There are also names for the chords, which identify how they relate to each other. This takes us closer to musical theory, and farther from the scope of this book. However, the terms are sometimes useful to mark where a chord choice is unexpected. In the case of the 50s progression, the root chord is the I 'tonic' and the last chord in the sequence that brings us home to the tonic the V 'dominant'. Using letters, numerals and names, the 50s turnaround from 'Stand by Me' can be represented in four different ways:

A	I	tonic
F♯m	vi	submediant
D	IV	subdominant
E	V	dominant

Many great songs live within the bounds of this deck of chords; plenty of blues and folk (including 'Blowin' in the Wind') get away with three chords, I – IV – V, not even using the minor vi chord.

The music in our book gets interesting when it shuffles them and introduces new ones where you don't expect them. In 'I Want to Hold Your Hand', for example, the verse starts with three chords from our 50s turnaround, but in a different order, starting I – V – vi before introducing a surprising III chord. As discussed in the 1964 chapter, this is the chord heard on 'under-*stand*' and then on I want to hold your *hand*', and although we may have heard the song countless times, we have heard the 50s turnaround even more often. So 'I Want to Hold Your Hand' still sounds fresh.

Appendix 2: Timelines

TIMELINE 1: KEY RELEASES, 1964–67*

		Bob Dylan	Beatles	Beach Boys
1964	Jan	THE TIMES THEY ARE A-CHANGIN'		
	Feb			'Fun, Fun, Fun'
	Mar		'Can't Buy Me Love'	
	Apr			
	May			'I Get Around'
	Jun			
	Jul		A HARD DAY'S NIGHT	ALL SUMMER LONG
	Aug	ANOTHER SIDE OF BOB DYLAN		'When I Grow Up (To Be a Man)'
	Sep			
	Oct			
	Nov		'I Feel Fine'	THE BEACH BOYS' CHRISTMAS ALBUM
	Dec		BEATLES FOR SALE	
1965	Jan			
	Feb			

	Mar	'Subterranean Homesick Blues' BRINGING IT ALL BACK HOME		THE BEACH BOYS TODAY!
	Apr		'Ticket to Ride'	'Help Me, Rhonda'
	May			
	Jun			
	Jul	'Like a Rolling Stone'		SUMMER DAYS (AND SUMMER NIGHTS!!) 'California Girls'
	Aug	HIGHWAY 61 REVIS-ITED	HELP!	
	Sep			
	Oct			
	Nov			BEACH BOYS' PARTY!
	Dec		'Day Trip-per'/'We Can Work It Out' RUBBER SOUL	
1966	Jan			
	Feb			
	Mar	'Rainy Day Women #12 & 35'		'Sloop John B'
	Apr			
	May		'Paperback Writer'	PET SOUNDS
	June	BLONDE ON BLONDE		

	Jul			
	Aug		REVOLVER	
	Sep			
	Oct			'Good Vibrations'
	Nov			
	Dec			
1967	Jan			
	Feb		'Penny Lane'/'Strawberry Fields Forever'	
	Mar			
	Apr			
	May		SGT. PEPPER'S LONELY HEARTS CLUB BAND	
	Jun			
	Jul		'All You Need Is Love'	Heroes and Villains'
	Aug			
	Sep			SMILEY SMILE
	Oct			
	Nov		'Hello Goodbye'	
	Dec	JOHN WESLEY HARDING	Magical Mystery Tour (EP)	WILD HONEY

TIMELINE 2: ALBUM SESSION TIMELINE,
January 1964–May 1967

		Bob Dylan	Beatles	Beach Boys
1964	Jan	THE TIMES THEY ARE A-CHANGIN'		
	Feb		Sessions for A HARD DAY'S NIGHT (scheduled around filming)	Sessions for ALL SUMMER LONG
	Mar			
	Apr			
	May			
	Jun	Session for ANOTHER SIDE, 9th		Sessions for BEACH BOYS CHRISTMAS
	Jul		A HARD DAY'S NIGHT	ALL SUMMER LONG
	Aug	ANOTHER SIDE OF BOB DYLAN	Sessions for BAEATLES FOR SALE	Sessions for TODAY!
	Sep			
	Oct			
	Nov			THE BEACH BOYS' CHRISTMAS ALBUM
	Dec		BEATLES FOR SALE	Sessions for TODAY!
1965	Jan	Sessions for BACK HOME, 13th-15th		
	Feb		Sessions for HELP! (scheduled around filming)	Sessions for SUMMER DAYS

	Mar	BRINGING IT ALL BACK HOME		THE BEACH BOYS TODAY!
	Apr		Sessions for HELP! (scheduled around filming)	Sessions for SUMMER DAYS
	May			
	Jun	Sessions for HIGHWAY 61		
	Jul			SUMMER DAYS (AND SUMMER NIGHTS!!)
	Aug	HIGHWAY 61 REVISITED	HELP!	Sessions for BEACH BOYS' PARTY
	Sep			
	Oct		Sessions for RUBBER SOUL	
	Nov			BEACH BOYS' PARTY
	Dec		RUBBER SOUL	
1966	Jan			Sessions for PET SOUNDS
	Feb	Sessions for BLONDE ON BLONDE		
	Mar			
	Apr		Sessions for REVOLVER	
	May			PET SOUNDS
	Jun	BLONDE ON BLONDE		
	Jul			Sessions for SMILE (completed 2004)
	Aug		REVOLVER	
	Sep			
	Oct			
	Nov			
	Dec		Sessions for SGT. PEPPER	

1967	Jan			
	Feb		*Sessions for SGT.*	
	Mar		*PEPPER*	*Sessions for SMILE (completed 2004)*
	Apr			
	May		SGT. PEPPER'S LONELY HEARTS CLUB BAND	

NOTE: Studio albums only; session dates simplified for legibility.

ENDNOTES

THE SINGULARITY

1 'Q&A with Bill Flanagan', *bobdylan.com* (22 Mar. 2017), http://www.bob-dylan.com/news/qa-with-bill-flanagan/.

2 Candacy Taylor, 'The Roots of Route 66', *The Atlantic* (3 Nov. 2016), https://www.theatlantic.com/politics/archive/2016/11/the-roots-of-route-66/506255/; Hadley Meares, 'Hawthorne's Deceptively Sunny History', *Curbed LA* (30 Jan. 2018), https://la.curbed.com/2018/1/30/16933546/hawthorne-history-south-bay-racism.

3 'European Traders', *Liverpool Museums*, https://www.liverpoolmuseums.org.uk/history-of-slavery/europe.

4 Geoff Wonfor and Bob Smeaton (dirs), 'Episode One', *The Beatles Anthology* (EMI Records/Apple Corps, 1995). The documentary was released by EMI Records in eight volumes on VHS and Laserdisc the following year, and rereleased on DVD in 2003, along with a bonus disc of special features.

5 T. P. Ratcliff (ed.), *News Chronicle Song Book: Community Songs, Negro Spirituals, Plantation Songs, Children's Songs, Sea Shanties, Hymns & Carols* (News Chronicle Publications Department, 1931).

6 Mike Love with James S. Hirsch, *Good Vibrations: My Life as a Beach Boy* (Faber & Faber Ltd, 2016), p. 7 [Kindle edition].

7 Mark Lewisohn, *The Beatles – All These Years: Volume One: Tune In* (Little, Brown and Company, 2013), p. 19 [Kindle edition].

8 Michael Gray, *The Bob Dylan Encyclopedia* (Continuum, 2006), p. 728.

9 Otto Fuchs, *Bill Haley: The Father of Rock 'n' Roll* (Wagner Verlag, 2011), p. 93.

10 Laurie Stras, 'Sing a Song of Difference: Connie Boswell and a Discourse of Disability in Jazz', in *Popular Music*, 28/3 (2009), p. 301.

11 Erin White, 'Queer, Black & Blue: Sister Rosetta Tharpe Is Muva of Them All', Afropunk (7 Mar. 2019), https://afropunk.com/2019/03/rosetta-tharpe/.

12 'Rock and Roll; Renegades; Interview with Sam Phillips [Part 3 of 6],' *GBH Archives,* http://openvault.wgbh.org/catalog/V_73CF632E91E04313B17779D-8D90A9610.

13 Dave Little, 'Big Boy's "That's All Right"', *Scotty Moore the Official Website* (16 Jan. 2005), http://www.scottymoore.net/thatsallright.html.

14 Larry Lehmer, *The Day the Music Died: The Last Tour of Buddy Holly, the Big Bopper and Ritchie Valens* (Music Sales Group, 2003), p. 7.

15 'Q&A with Bill Flanagan', *bobdylan.com.*

16 'Bob Dylan Exhibit', *Hibbing Public Library* (May 2013), http://www.ci.hibbing.mn.us/home/showdocument?id=18.

17 Charles White, *The Life and Times of Little Richard: The Quasar of Rock* (Harmony Books, 1984), p. 84.

18 Interview with American Forces Network radio, 24 January 1964, via *The Beatles Bible,* https://www.beatlesbible.com/1964/01/24/radio-american-forces-network/.

19 'Beatles Interview: Carnegie Hall 2/12/1964', available at *The Beatles Ultimate Experience,* available at http://www.beatlesinterviews.org/db1964.0212.beatles. html.

20 Interview for Swedish radio by Klas Burling (28 May 1966), https://www.interferenza.net/bcs/interw/66-apr29.htm.

21 'Bob Dylan Talking by Joseph Haas', *Chicago Daily News* (27 Nov. 1965), available at https://www.interferenza.net/bcs/interw/65-nov26.htm.

22 'Simpering, dripping treacle': Greil Marcus, 'How Amy Winehouse made "To Know Him Is to Love Him" her own', *The Guardian* (29 Aug. 2014), https://www.theguardian.com/books/2014/aug/29/amy-winehouse-made-to-know-him-her-own.

23 Lewisohn, *The Beatles – All These Years: Volume One*, p. 201 [Kindle edition]

24 Shaun Ponsonby, 'Why Do Fools Fall in Love – Frankie Lymon & the most important song in pop history', *Planet Slop* (10 February 2017), https://planet-slop.co.uk/articles/why-do-fools-fall-in-love/.

25 Love with Hirsch, *Good Vibrations*, p. 28.

26 Lewisohn, *The Beatles – All These Years: Volume One*, p. 348.

27 Harrison's quote is from Ron Howard (dir.), *The Beatles: Eight Days a Week – The Touring Years* (Apple Corps, Imagine Entertainment, White Horse

Pictures, 2016). The remaining information is taken from Lewisohn, *The Beatles – All These Years: Volume One*, p. 54, and he references it back to Wonfor and Smeaton's *Beatles Anthology*.

28 Lewisohn, *The Beatles – All These Years: Volume One*, p. 384.

29 The Beatles, *The Beatles Anthology* (Chronicle Books, 2000), p. 56.

30 Howard Sounes, *Down the Highway: The Life of Bob Dylan* (Grove Press, 2001), p. 68.

1961-62: RECORDING ARTISTS

31 'Live: Palais Ballroom, Aldershot', *The Beatles Bible*, https://www.beatlesbible.com/1961/12/09/live-palais-ballroom-aldershot/.

32 Robert Shelton, '20-Year-Old Singer Is Bright New Face at Gerde's Club', *New York Times* (29 Sep. 1961), https://archive.nytimes.com/www.nytimes.com/books/97/05/04/reviews/dylan-gerde.html.

33 Fred Goodman, T*he Mansion on the Hill: Dylan, Young, Geffen, Springsteen, and the Head-on Collision of Rock and Commerce* (Vintage Books, 1998), p. 88. Grossman anticipates the management style of Peter Grant, manager of Led Zeppelin, who split the money five ways between himself and the band and protected their creative space by any means necessary.

34 Martin Scorsese (dir.), *No Direction Home* (Paramount Pictures, 2005).

35 Chris Hodenfield, 'George Martin Recalls the Boys in the Band', *Rolling Stone* (15 Jul. 1976), https://www.rollingstone.com/music/music-features/george-martin-recalls-the-boys-in-the-band-115547/.

1963: MILLION SELLERS

36 'Sunday-Night Play: The Madhouse on Castle Street', *Radio Times* (10 Jan. 1963), via https://genome.ch.bbc.co.uk/029af0a39485464592688785823-3a906.

37 For a detailed musical appreciation, see: Greg Panfile, 'Mind of Brian 2: The Lonely Sea', *Surfer Moon*, https://www.surfermoon.com/essays/mob2.html.

38 Guilbert Gates, 'Listen to Bob Dylan's Many Influences', *New York Times* (15 Oct. 2016), https://www.nytimes.com/interactive/2016/10/14/arts/music/

bob-dylan-influences-playlist-spotify.html.

39 'Q&A with Bill Flanagan', *bobdylan.com* (22 Mar. 2017), http://www.bob-dylan.com/news/qa-with-bill-flanagan/.

40 Malcolm MacDonald, *Brahms (Master Musicians Series)* (Oxford University Press, 2002), p. 384.

41 Sound Check, 'The Black Man Behind Bob Dylan', *Afropunk* (19 Feb. 2015), https://afropunk.com/2015/02/feature-the-black-man-behind-bob-dylan/.

42 Martin Scorsese (dir.), *No Direction Home* (Paramount Pictures, 2005). Clancy characterizes him as part Charlie Chaplin, part Dylan Thomas, part Woody Guthrie, 'constantly moving'.

43 'Mick Jagger inducts The Beatles – Rock and Roll Hall of Fame Inductions 1988', *Rock Hall*, https://www.rockhall.com/inductees/beatles.

44 Jonathan Cott, 'John Lennon: The Last Interview', *Rolling Stone* (23 Dec. 2010), https://www.rollingstone.com/music/music-news/john-lennon-the-last-interview-179443/. 'To put Yoko or Sean or the cat or anybody in mind other than meself – me and my ups and downs and my little tiddly problems – is a strain.'

45 Chris Maume, 'Mandy Rice-Davies: Showgirl who became famous for her part in the Profumo affair and went on to enjoy a successful business career', *The Independent* (19 Dec. 2014), https://www.independent.co.uk/news/obitu-aries/mandy-rice-davies-showgirl-who-became-famous-her-part-profumo-af-fair-and-went-enjoy-successful-business-career-9937022.html.

46 Personal correspondence with Peter Viney and Ken Wilson, via social media.

47 'Brian Wilson on Phil Spector and Be My Baby', *YouTube* (uploaded 15 Jun. 2013), https://www.youtube.com/watch?v=KiScLYNAoSc. As well as writing songs about cars, Wilson often had transformative musical experiences in them, from hearing the Four Freshmen to encountering 'Be My Baby' and, later, 'Strawberry Fields Forever'.

48 'Joe Meek's Bold Techniques, 2nd Edition by Barry Cleveland – Book Promo', *YouTube* (uploaded 8 May 2015), https://www.youtube.com/watch?v=_QepdppzYQg.

49 Ibid. Young players including Ritchie Blackmore, Steve Howe and Jimmy Page climbed the stairs to Meeksville Sound Ltd.

50 Olivia Harrison, *George Harrison: Living in the Material World* (Abrams, 2011), p. 68.

51 Craig McGregor, 'So in the End, the Beatles Have Proved False Prophets', *New York Times* (14 June 1970), https://www.nytimes.com/1970/06/14/archives/music-so-in-the-end-the-beatles-have-proved-false-prophets.html.

52 Hunter Davies (ed.), *The John Lennon Letters* (Weidenfeld & Nicolson, 2012), p. 194. The underlining is Lennon's.

53 Clinton Heylin, *Behind the Shades: The 20th Anniversary Edition* (Faber & Faber, 2011), p. 137. In Scorsese's *No Direction Home*, his contemporary in the Village, the folk singer Dave van Ronk, remembered Dylan as being less politically engaged or certain than his peers.

54 'Bob Dylan and the NECLC', https://www.corliss-lamont.org/dylan.htm.

55 '1963, London Prince of Wales', *The Royal Variety Charity*, https://www.royalvarietycharity.org/royal-variety-performance/archive/detail/1963.

56 Jack Whatley, 'Remembering the Beatles' 1963 Royal Variety Performance', *Far Out Magazine*, https://faroutmagazine.co.uk/the-beatles-1963-royal-variety-performance/.

1964: LISTENING IN

57 Daniel Mendelsohn, 'Rebel Rebel, Arthur Rimbaud's brief career', *New Yorker* (22 Aug. 2011), https://www.newyorker.com/magazine/2011/08/29/rebel-rebel.

58 William Mann, 'What Songs the Beatles Sang', *The Times* (27 Dec. 1963), *The Beatles Bible*, https://www.beatlesbible.com/1963/12/27/the-times-what-songs-the-beatles-sang-by-william-mann/.

59 Anthony Scaduto, 'Bob Dylan: An Intimate Biography, Part Two', *Rolling Stone* (16 Mar. 1972), https://www.rollingstone.com/music/music-news/bob-dylan-an-intimate-biography-part-two-237760/.

60 Ibid.

61 'Radio: American Forces Network', *The Beatles Bible*, https://www.beatlesbible.com/1964/01/24/radio-american-forces-network/.

62 'Beatles say – Dylan shows the way', *Melody Maker* (9 Jan. 1965), via https://amoralto.tumblr.com/post/60467020158/melody-maker-beatles-saydylan-shows-the-way.

63 '0911 The Freewheelin' Bob Dylan – Bob Dylan (1963)', *Songs We Were*

Singing: 4004 Songs for Fans of The Beatles, https://dannyfriar.wordpress.com/tag/the-freewheelin-bob-dylan/.

64 'Beatles say – Dylan shows the way', *Melody Maker*.

65 Jordan Runtagh, 'Rock Legend Ronnie Spector Recalls Her Close Friendship (and Almost Romance!) with John Lennon', *People* (30 Nov. 2018), https://people.com/music/ronnie-spector-john-lennon-friendship/.

66 Olivia Harrison, *George Harrison: Living in the Material World* (Abrams, 2011), p. 55.

67 Jonathan Cott, 'John Lennon: The Rolling Stone Interview', *Rolling Stone* (23 Nov. 1968), https://www.rollingstone.com/music/music-news/john-lennon-the-rolling-stone-interview-186264/.

68 Bob Dylan, *Chronicles: Volume One* (Simon & Schuster, 2004), p. 288.

69 Mike Love with James S. Hirsch, *Good Vibrations: My Life as a Beach Boy* (Faber & Faber Ltd, 2016), p. 407 [Kindle edition].

70 Malcolm Leo (dir.), *The Beach Boys: An American Band* (High Ridge Productions, 1985).

71 Matthew Longfellow, Martin R. Smith (dirs), 'The Beach Boys: Pet Sounds', *Classic Albums* (Eagle Rock Film Productions, 2010).

72 Capitol record memo (23 Dec. 1963), *Mitch McGeary's Songs, Stories and Pictures of the Beatles website,* via http://www.rarebeatles.com/photopg2/comstk.htm.

73 Al Aronowitz, 'The Beatles: Music's Gold Bugs', *Saturday Evening Post* (Mar. 1964), via 'Beatlemania in 1964: "This has gotten entirely out of control"', *The Guardian* (29 Jan. 2014), https://www.theguardian.com/music/2014/jan/29/the-beatles.

74 William Mann understood this: William Mann, 'What Songs The Beatles Sang', *The Times* (27 Dec. 1963), via *The Beatles Bible*, https://www.beatlesbible.com/1963/12/27/the-times-what-songs-the-beatles-sang-by-william-mann/. Also see Tillekens for a fascinating, and exhaustive, account: Ger Tillekens, 'Words and chords: The semantic shifts of the Beatles' chords', *Soundscapes* (Jun. 2000), http://www.icce.rug.nl/~soundscapes/VOLUME03/Words_and_chords.shtml. Or just listen to the start of 'It Won't Be Long'.

75 Jason I. Brown, 'Mathematics, Physics and A Hard Day's Night', CMS Notes 36/6 (2004), 4–8, available at https://www.mscs.dal.ca/~brown/noct04-harddayjib.pdf.

76 Arthur Conan Doyle, 'A Scandal in Bohemia', *The Adventures of Sherlock Holmes* (George Newnes, 1892).

77 'The "A Hard Day's Night" opening chord', *The Beatles Bible*, https://www.beatlesbible.com/features/hard-days-night-chord/. A transcription of the whole chat can be found at https://forums.stevehoffman.tv/threads/george-harrison-yahoo-chat-transcript-02-15-2001.11962/.

78 Robert Erickson, *Sound Structure in Music* (University of California Press, 1975), p. 18.

79 *South Bank Show*, 'John Lennon's Jukebox' (televised by ITV 14 March 2004, uploaded 26 March 2013), https://www.youtube.com/watch?v=rONf-4gytiZQ.

80 'Beatles say – Dylan shows the way', *Melody Maker*.

81 The Beatles, *The Beatles Anthology* (Chronicle Books, 2000), p. 120.

82 'The Supremes - Eight Days A Week', *YouTube* (televised by Shindig 24 February 1965, uploaded 22 February 2015), https://www.youtube.com/watch?v=oBZ6SuFODYg.

83 '1964', *BeachBoysGigs*, https://www.beachboysgigs.com/1964-2/.

84 Nat Hentoff, 'Bob Dylan, the Wanderer', *New Yorker* (16 Oct. 1964), https://www.newyorker.com/magazine/1964/10/24/the-crackin-shakin-breakin-sounds.

85 Ron Howard (dir.), *The Beatles: Eight Days a Week – The Touring Years* (White Horse Pictures, Apple Corps Limited, StudioCanal and Polygram Entertainment, 2016).

86 Hentoff, 'Bob Dylan, the Wanderer'.

87 Ron Rosenbaum, 'Bob Dylan: A candid conversation with the visionary whose songs changed the times', *Playboy* (March 1978), via https://www.interferenza.net/bcs/interw/play78.htm.

88 'Collapse of the Sellers Hotel', *Minnesota Historical Society*, https://www.mnhs.org/school/online/communities/milestones/MOVnws1T.php.

89 Michael Billig, *Rock 'n' Roll Jews* (Five Leaves Publications, 2000), p. 131, via My Jewish Learning [website], https://www.myjewishlearning.com/article/bob-dylan/.

90 Benjamin Kerstein, 'Bob Dylan Is America's Greatest Jewish Artist', *The Algemeiner* (29 Jul. 2020), https://www.algemeiner.com/2020/07/29/bob-

dylan-is-americas-greatest-jewish-artist/. The singer's friend Louie Kemp drew a more straightforward parallel between instinctive Jewish support for the underdog and Dylan's impulse to write songs that mattered – 'born, at least in part, from his roots as a Jew'. Nadine Epstein, 'My Adventures with Bob Dylan: An Interview with Louie Kemp', *Moment* (24 May 2019), https://momentmag.com/my-adventures-with-bob-dylan-an-interview-with-louie-kemp/.

91 Irwin Silber, 'An Open Letter to Bob Dylan', *Sing Out!* (Nov. 1964), via http://www.edlis.org/twice/threads/open_letter_to_bob_dylan.html.

92 David Horowitz, 'Bob Dylan: genius or commodity?' *Peace News* (11 Nov. 1964)'.

93 Mikal Gilmore, 'Bob Dylan Unleashed', *Rolling Stone* (27 Sep. 2012), https://www.rollingstone.com/music/music-news/bob-dylan-unleashed-189723/.

94 Douglas R. Gilbert and Dave Marsh, *Forever Young: Photographs of Bob Dylan* (Da Capo, 2005).

95 Ibid., p. 148.

96 'Johnny Cash - Live At Newport Folk Festival 1964', *YouTube* (recorded 26 July 1964, uploaded 29 March 2014), https://www.youtube.com/watch?v=KhTDSBNAsEQ.

97 Saving Country Music, 'On this day in 1964, Johnny Cash took a full page Billboard ad to call out country radio for not having guts to play "Ballad of Ira Hayes"' [Twitter post], 9.21 p.m., 22 Aug. 2017, https://twitter.com/KyleCoroneos/status/900090635105030145.

98 Antonio d'Ambrosio, *A Heartbeat and a Guitar: Johnny Cash and the Making of Bitter Tears* (Nation Books, 2009), p. 169. Also Gilbert and Marsh, *Forever Young*, p. 153.

99 'Bob Dylan turns The Beatles on to cannabis', *The Beatles Bible*, https://www.beatlesbible.com/1964/08/28/bob-dylan-turns-the-beatles-on-to-cannabis/.

100 Philippe Margotoin and Jean-Michel Guesdon, *All the Songs: The Story Behind Every Beatles Release* (Black Dog & Leventhal, 2015), p. 152.

101 Gilbert and Marsh, *Forever Young*, p. 83.

102 Barry Miles, *Paul McCartney: Many Years from Now* (Secker & Warburg, 1997), p. 189.

103 Peter Brown and Steve Gaines, *The Love You Make: An Insider's Story of the Beatles* (Penguin, 2002), p. 144.

104 Al Aronowitz, 'Let's 'ave a larf', *The Blacklisted Journalist* (1995), http://www.johnlennon.it/al-aronowitz-eng.htm.

105 Michael Gray, *The Bob Dylan Encyclopedia* (Continuum, 2006), p. 405.

106 'John Lennon attends a Foyle's literary luncheon', *The Beatles Bible*, https://www.beatlesbible.com/1964/04/23/john-lennon-attends-foyles-literary-luncheon/.

107 Jann S. Wenner, 'Lennon Remembers, Part Two', *Rolling Stone* (4 Feb. 1971), https://www.rollingstone.com/music/music-news/lennon-remembers-part-two-187100/.

108 Steve Binder (dir.), *T.A.M.I. Show* (American International Pictures, 1964). Even then, the Beach Boys were only featured for the movie's initial theatrical run at Christmas; their songs were pulled from subsequent releases because of a copyright dispute.

109 David E. James, *Rock 'n' Film: Cinema's Dance with Popular Music* (Oxford University Press, 2016), p. 194.

110 Peter Gerstenzang, '14 Things You Didn't Know About Epic Rock Doc *The T.A.M.I. Show*', *Esquire* (26 Aug. 2014), https://www.esquire.com/entertainment/music/a29785/tami-show-facts/.

111 Frank Mastropolo, 'The T.A.M.I. Show: Soul Superstars Shatter Race Barriers 50 Years Ago', *The Boombox* (29 Oct. 2014), https://theboombox.com/james-brown-diana-ross-chuck-berry-smokey-robinson-tami-show/.

112 *South Bank Show*, 'John Lennon's Jukebox'. Fontella Bass's career stalled as she fought for a songwriting credit of any sort on 'Rescue Me'.

113 Tom Nolan, 'Beach Boys: A California Saga', *Rolling Stone* (28 Oct. 1971), https://www.rollingstone.com/music/music-news/beach-boys-a-california-saga-244579/.

114 Mark Linett, liner notes for 'The Beach Boys Today!' (Capitol Records, 1990), Album Liner Notes, http://albumlinernotes.com/Today_Summer_Days.html.

115 Nolan, 'Beach Boys: A California Saga'.

1965: CONVERGENCE

116 D. A. Pennebaker (dir.), *Dont Look Back* (Leacock-Pennebaker, Inc. 1967). 'What is this, Mercyside?' asks Dylan, finally rattled, as the scene concludes.

117 David Sheff, 'Interview with John Lennon and Yoko Ono', *Playboy* (January 1981), via *The Beatles Ultimate Experience*, http://www.beatlesinterviews.org/dbjypb.int4.html.

118 Evan Schlansky, 'The 30 Greatest Bob Dylan Songs: #11, "Subterranean Homesick Blues"', *American Songwriter*, twelve years ago), https://americansongwriter.com/the-30-greatest-bob-dylan-songs-11-subterranean-homesick-blues/. The Velvet Underground in turn took up the baton from 'Norwegian Wood', with John Cale identifying the influence of acid: 'what you remember in a flashback is a sound, how your senses were bombarded.' Phil Alexander et al., 'The 101 Greatest Beatles Songs', *Mojo* (July 2006), p. 90.

119 John Einarson, *Mr. Tambourine Man: The Life and Legacy of the Byrds' Gene Clark* (Backbeat Books, 2005), p. 38.

120 Ron Wynn, 'How Miles Davis helped the Byrds, and why guitarist Roger McGuinn likes the Internet', *Nashville Scene* (27 May 2010), https://www.nashvillescene.com/music/article/13034143/how-miles-davis-helped-the-byrds-and-why-guitarist-roger-mcguinn-likes-the-internet.

121 Craig Slowinski, 'The Beach Boys – The Beach Boys Today!: Dance, Dance, Dance', p. 17.

122 Idem, 'The Beach Boys – The Beach Boys Today!: *Summer Days* session outtakes: Help Me, Rhonda (Version Two) (The "Murry Wilson" Session)', pp. 54, 59.

123 Pennebaker, *Dont Look Back*.

124 Einarson, *Mr. Tambourine Man*, p. 55.

125 Jonathan Bellman (ed.), *The Exotic in Western Music* (Northeastern University Press, 1998), p. 294.

126 Here as elsewhere, *The Beatles Bible* website has been invaluable for detail and dates: https://www.beatlesbible.com/history/2/.

127 The Beatles, *The Beatles Anthology* (Chronicle Books, 2000), pp. 177–8.

128 'The person who introduced Brian Wilson to LSD' [forum post], *Black Cat Bone*, http://bcb-board.co.uk/phpBB2/viewtopic.php?t=110823.

129 Peter Ames Carlin, *Catch a Wave: The Rise, Fall and Redemption of the Beach Boys' Brian Wilson* (Rodale, 2006), pp. 174–5.

130 Derek Taylor, 'The Byrds: Strictly for The Byrds!', *Melody Maker* (17 Jul. 1965), via 'Behind Byrdmania – an archive piece from 1965', *The Guardian* (15 Jul. 2015), https://amp.theguardian.com/music/2015/jul/15/behind-byrdma-nia-an-archive-piece-from-1965.

131 Ibid.

132 Robert Shelton, *No Direction Home: The Life and Music of Bob Dylan*, Da Capo Press (2003), p. 294.

133 'MBE Reaction (1965 ITV Interview)', *YouTube* (recorded 12 June 1965, uploaded 23 June 2015), https://www.youtube.com/watch?v=DireiL4BNc0.

134 *The Beatles Explosion* (Jersey Productions/Legend Films, 2007), *YouTube* (uploaded 25 November 2015), https://www.youtube.com/watch?v=m5VOai-qmCXo. The short excerpt containing the quote is available at 'Beatles MBE Interview #1', YouTube (uploaded 12 January 2008), https://www.youtube.com/watch?v=B7YIaCaikAs.

135 Martin Scorsese (dir.), *No Direction Home* (Paramount Pictures, 2005).

136 Maureen Cleave, 'How Does a Beatle Live? John Lennon Lives Like This', *Evening Standard* (4 Mar. 1966).

137 Mikal Gilmore, 'Bob Dylan Unleashed', *Rolling Stone* (27 Sep. 2012), https://www.rollingstone.com/music/music-news/bob-dylan-unleashed-189723.

138 Geoff Boucher, '"California Girls" The Beach Boys | 1965' (*Los Angeles Times*, 12 Aug. 2007), https://www.latimes.com/archives/la-xpm-2007-aug-12-ca-socalsong12-story.html.

139 Ibid.

140 [no author], *1000 Days That Shook the World: The Psychedelic Beatles – April 1, 1965 to December 26, 1967* (Mojo, 2002), p. 4.

141 Nat Hentoff, 'Bob Dylan: a candid conversation with the iconoclastic idol of the folk-rock set', *Playboy* (March 1966), via https://www.interferenza.net/bcs/interw/66-jan.htm.

142 Michael Gray, *The Bob Dylan Encyclopedia* (Continuum, 2006), p. 713.

143 Rob Hughes, 'The sensational story of Mike Bloomfield: from prodigy to tragedy,' *Classic Rock* (7 Oct. 2018), https://www.loudersound.com/features/mike-bloomfield-tombstone-blues.

144 Gray, *Bob Dylan Encyclopedia*, p. 357. 'Nobody ever counted off for Dylan [in the studio], he always did what the fuck he wanted to,' says Bob Johnston in Scorsese's *No Direction Home*. 'I took all the clocks down, nobody had a fucking clock in there, it's just like play some music, what about this thing, what about this?'

145 Murray Lerner (dir.), *Festival!* (Patchke Productions, 1967).

146 Amy Goodman, 'We Shall Overcome: An Hour with Legendary Folk Singer & Activist Pete Seeger', *Democracy Now!* (4 Jul. 2007), https://www. democracynow.org/2007/7/4/we_shall_overcome_an_hour_with.

147 Scorsese, *No Direction Home*.

148 Robert Shelton, 'Folk Singer Offers Works in "New Mood" at Forest Hills, *New York Times* (30 Aug. 1965), https://archive.nytimes.com/www.nytimes. com/books/97/05/04/reviews/dylan-unruly.html.

149 Jeff Slate, 'Bob Dylan's Fans Called Him a Traitor. 51 Years Later, He Returns to the Scene of the Crime', *Esquire* (8 Jul. 2016), https://www.esquire. com/entertainment/music/a46535/bob-dylan-at-forest-hills/.

150 Scorsese, *No Direction Home*.

151 Kevin Avery, *Everything Is an Afterthought: The Life and Writings of Paul Nelson* (Fantagraphics Books, 2011).

152 Montreal Gazette, 'Robbie Robertson of The Band on playing with Bob Dylan', *YouTube* (recorded 18 November 2016, uploaded 28 February 2018), https://www.youtube.com/watch?v=wXtow6a4E-k.

153 Scorsese, *No Direction Home*.

154 Montreal Gazette, 'Robbie Robertson of The Band on playing with Bob Dylan'.

155 Scorsese, *No Direction Home*.

156 Goodman, 'We Shall Overcome'.

157 Ibid. Seeger cited Dylan, Woody Guthrie, Buffy Sainte-Marie, Joni Mitchell and Malvina Reynolds as the greatest songwriters of the twentieth century, 'even though Irving Berlin made the most money'.

158 'Live: Teatro Adriano, Rome, Italy', *The Beatles Bible*, https://www.beatlesbible.com/1965/06/27/live-teatro-adriano-rome-italy/. 'Ungracious little shits' would have been a more stylish phrasing.

159 'A History of the PA System', *Insure4Music*, https://www.insure4music.

co.uk/blog/2017/09/27/a-brief-history-of-the-pa-system/.

160 The video can be viewed here: Fraser Lowry, '10 Things We Learned Watching The New Version of The Beatles At Shea Stadium', *Classic Rock* [n.d.], https://www.loudersound.com/features/10-things-we-learned-watching-the-new-version-of-the-beatles-at-shea-stadium.

161 Chuck Stenberg (prod.),'The Beatles in Portland the Complete Story – 10th Anniversary Edition', *YouTube* (recorded 2005, uploaded 28 March 2016), https://www.youtube.com/watch?v=AIO5gbCHSJ4.

162 Keith Badman, *The Beach Boys: The Definitive Diary of America's Greatest Band on Stage and in the Studio* (Backbeat Books, 2004), p. 98.

163 Allen Ginsberg, 'Portland Coliseum', *Collected Poems 1947–1997* (Penguin Modern Classics, 2013).

164 Jann S. Wenner, 'Lennon Remembers, Part One', *Rolling Stone* (4 Feb. 1971), https://www.rollingstone.com/music/music-news/lennon-remembers-part-one-186693/.

165 David Fricke, 'Roger McGuinn', *Rolling Stone* (23 Aug. 1990), https://www.rollingstone.com/music/music-news/roger-mcguinn-230892/. | https://www.beatlesbible.com/1965/08/24/lsd-los-angeles-byrds-peter-fonda/

166 Hunter Davies (ed.), *The John Lennon Letters* (Weidenfeld & Nicolson, 2012), p. 89.

167 The Beatles, *The Beatles Anthology*, p.191. The Beatles cartoon debuted on ABC the following month, with thirty-nine episodes running over two years. The Monkees' TV show, in its own way a cartoon of the Beatles, launched a year later.

168 Chuck Crisafulli and Piers Beagley, 'Elvis Meets the Beatles', *Elvis Information Network* (April 2010), http://www.elvisinfonet.com/spotlight_elvis_meets_the_beatles.html.

169 Einarson, *Mr. Tambourine Man*, p. 74.

170 Jay Spangler, 'Beatles Press Conference: Los Angeles 8/29/1965', *The Beatles Ultimate Experience*, http://www.beatlesinterviews.org/db1965.0829.beatles.html.

171 Mark Dillon, *Fifty Sides of the Beach Boys: The Songs that Tell Their Story* (ECW Press, 2012), p. 73.

172 Steve Turner, *Beatles '66: The Revolutionary Year* (HarperCollins, 2016), pp. 433–6 [Kindle edition].

173 Holden McNeely, 'Making Masterpieces: The Beach Boys and the Beatles Inspired Each Other', *CultureSonar* (26 Aug. 2017), https://www.culturesonar.com/beach-boys-and-beatles-inspiration/. It sounds more like a vocal part than the organ Wilson identified, presumably via the US album sleeve credit to 'Organ' Evans on Hammond; the UK release makes no mention of this.

174 'WNEW-FM 102.7 New York – John Lennon Interview – September 28 1974 (1/3)', *YouTube* (recorded 28 September 1974, uploaded 18 Aug 2018), https://www.youtube.com/watch?v=P58WfP4F8ew.

175 Steve Turner, *The Complete Beatles Songs* (Carlton Books, 2015), p. 128.

176 Michael Lydon, 'Lennon and McCartney: Songwriters – A Portrait from 1966' (unpublished, Mar. 1966), via *TeachRock*, https://teachrock.org/article/lennon-and-mccartney-songwriters-a-portrait-from-1966/.

177 For a note on the humour in tracks on *Rubber Soul*, see Ian MacDonald, *Revolution in the Head: The Beatles' Records and the Sixties* (4th Estate, 1994), p. 130.

178 Joshua Wolf Shenk, 'The Power of Two', *The Atlantic* (Jul./Aug. 2014), https://www.theatlantic.com/magazine/archive/2014/07/the-power-of-two/372289/. They held it together until the *White Album*, worked together for another year, and – after a period in the early 1970s when they sniped at each other on their own solo records – gradually rebuilt their friendship. Lennon in 1974 was upbeat about a possible reunion, ruling out only the prospect of touring again, and two years later he and McCartney briefly considered taking up *Saturday Night Live*'s offer of $3,000 for a Beatle reunion. (McCartney has confirmed that they were watching the following week's show together at Lennon's apartment in New York, a cab ride away. 'How did 'Saturday Night Live' nearly reunite The Beatles? Paul McCartney confirms the rumours', Far Out, https://faroutmagazine.co.uk/the-beatles-reunion-snl-saturday-night-live-paul-mccartney/).

179 Lee Tusman (ed.), *Really Free Culture: Anarchist Communities, Radical Movements and Public Practices* (n.d., PediaPress), pp. 96–98. Available for download at http://pediapress.com/books/show/really-free-culture-anarchist-communities/.

180 ''Lydia Smith, '11 June 1965: Allen Ginsberg and the beat poets create a cultural storm at the Hall', *Royal Albert Hall*, https://www.royalalberthall.com/about-the-hall/news/2016/january/11-june-1965-allen-ginsberg-and-the-beat-poets-create-a-cultural-storm-at-the-hall/. The Liverpool poet Spike Hawkins

called it 'a launchpad for the Sixties' ('The International Poetry Incarnation: The Beat goes on', *The Independent* (30 Apr. 2013), https://www.independent.co.uk/arts-entertainment/books/features/the-international-poetry-incarnation-the-beat-goes-on-314324.html.)

181 Aaron Millar, 'Golden daze: 50 years on from the Summer of Love', *The Guardian* (21 May 2017), https://www.theguardian.com/culture/2017/may/21/golden-daze-50-years-on-from-summer-of-love-san-francisco-festivals.

182 As quoted in the *Daily Mail* at the time. 'International Poetry Incarnation, 11 June 1965', Royal Albert Hall, https://memories.royalalberthall.com/content/international-poetry-incarnation-0.

1966: EXCHANGE

183 'History of lysergic acid diethylamide', *Wikipedia*, https://en.wikipedia.org/wiki/History_of_lysergic_acid_diethylamide.

184 Sean Moores, '"Ballad of the Green Berets" singer's biographer talks about Barry Sadler's meteoric rise, murder charge, violent death', *Stars and Stripes* (27 Apr. 2017), https://www.stripes.com/lifestyle/ballad-of-the-green-berets-singer-s-biographer-talks-about-barry-sadler-s-meteoric-rise-murder-charge-violent-death-1.465731.

185 See 'The miniskirt myth', *V & A Museum*, https://www.vam.ac.uk/articles/the-miniskirt-myth and 'About Paco Rabanne', *Paco Rabanne*, https://www.pacorabanne.com/ww/es/storypacorabanne#:~:text=His%20manifesto,at%20once%20sculptural%20and%20seductive.

186 Tom Goodwyn, 'Brian Wilson says "Pet Sounds" isn't as good as The Beatles' "Rubber Soul"', *NME* (27 May 2011), https://www.nme.com/news/music/the-beach-boys-35-1286165.

187 Neal Umphred, 'What Is a "Record Album" and When Did the Term Originate?', *Medium* (30 Aug. 2019), https://medium.com/tell-it-like-it-was/what-is-a-record-album-and-when-did-the-term-originate-ff099c3bc048.

188 Zac Johnson, review of *Rubber Soul* (US), *Allmusic*, https://www.allmusic.com/album/release/rubber-soul-us-mr0001519594.

189 Brian Wilson, 'Pet Sounds Box Intro', The Beach Boys, *The Pet Sounds Sessions* (1997), via http://albumlinernotes.com/Pet_Sounds_Box_Intro.html.

190 Matthew Longfellow and Martin R. Smith (dirs), 'The Beach Boys: Pet

Sounds', *Classic Albums* (Eagle Rock Film Productions, 2010).

191   The Beatles, *The Beatles Anthology* (Chronicle Books, 2000), p. 193. 'Plastic soul, man, plastic soul' is a phrase muttered by Paul McCartney at the end of the first take of 'I'm Down'.

192   Ibid. The snare/tom combination was one of Blaine's signature Beach Boys moves, spreading the sound across the tonal spectrum.

193   Nick Kent, 'The Last Beach Movie: A Story of Brian Wilson', *New Musical Express* (21 Jun. 1975). Asher's complaints ranged from Brian's bad taste in movies to his general 'untogetherness'.

194   Longfellow and Smith, 'The Beach Boys: Pet Sounds'.

195   Ibid.

196   Ibid.

197   Ibid.

198   Tom Nolan, 'Beach Boys: A California Saga', *Rolling Stone* (28 Oct. 1971), https://www.rollingstone.com/music/music-news/beach-boys-a-california-saga-244579/.

199   Ibid. He could, for example, have followed the example of Kanye West, who, when working in 2010, booked all three session rooms at Avex in Honolulu, twenty-four hours a day, so he could work on different songs in each between power naps. Roger Cormier, '15 Albums that Cost a Fortune to Make', *Mental Floss* (8 Jul. 2014), https://www.mentalfloss.com/article/57656/15-albums-cost-fortune-make.

200   Nolan, 'Beach Boys'.

201   Longfellow and Smith, 'The Beach Boys: Pet Sounds'.

202   Ren Grevatt, 'Beach Boys Blast', *Melody Maker* (19 Mar. 1966), via John Mulvey (ed.), *The History of Rock 1966* (Time Inc. (UK) Ltd., 2015), p. 129.

203   'Bruce Johnston brings Pet Sounds to Lennon & McCartney in London', *YouTube* (uploaded 1 February 2012), https://www.youtube.com/watch?v=1B-18FBcqsZ4.

204   Steve Turner, *Beatles '66: The Revolutionary Year* (HarperCollins, 2016), p. 180 [Kindle edition]. The source for the 'whispered conversation', and not necessarily the most reliable one, was 'industry legend' Kim Fowley.

205   'Bruce Johnston brings Pet Sounds to Lennon & McCartney in London'.

206   David Leaf, 'Pet Sounds – Perspective', *The Pet Sounds Sessions* [booklet],

1997. Liner notes reproduced at http://albumlinernotes.com/Pet_Sounds_-_ Perspective.html.

207 Holden McNeely, 'Making Masterpieces: The Beach Boys and the Beatles Inspired Each Other', *CultureSonar* (26 Aug. 2017), https://www.culturesonar. com/beach-boys-and-beatles-inspiration/.

208 Turner, *Beatles '66*, p. 175. Brian Jones and Keith Richards were also there.

209 Cott, 'John Lennon: The Rolling Stone Interview'.

210 Clinton Heylin, *Bob Dylan: Behind the Shades Revisited* (Harper Entertainment, 2003), p. 189.

211 Jordan Runtagh, 'Remembering Bob Dylan and John Lennon's Drugged-Out Limo Ride', *Rolling Stone* (27 May 2016), https://www.rollingstone.com/ music/music-news/remembering-bob-dylan-and-john-lennons-drugged-out-li-mo-ride-155141/.

212 Tudor Jones, *Bob Dylan and the British Sixties: A Cultural History* (Routledge, 2018), p. 107.

213 Robbie Robertson, *Testimony: A Memoir* (Crown, 2016).

214 Chris Barker, 'Interview: The recording history of Abbey Road', *MusicRadar* (7 Mar. 2012), https://www.musicradar.com/news/tech/inter-view-the-recording-history-of-abbey-road-533359.

215 Geoff Emerick and Howard Massey, *Here, There and Everywhere: My Life Recording the Music of the Beatles* (Gotham Books, 2006). The relevant excerpt is available at https://www.penguin.com/ajax/books/excerpt/9781101218242.

216 Mark Lewisohn, *The Complete Beatles Recording Sessions* (Sterling; reprint edition, 2013), p. 72.

217 Ibid, p. 74.

218 Richard Buskin, 'Bob Dylan "Sad Eyed Lady Of The Lowlands" | Classic Tracks', *Sound On Sound* (May 2010), https://www.soundonsound.com/peo-ple/bob-dylan-sad-eyed-lady-lowlands-classic-tracks.

219 Sean Wilentz, *Bob Dylan in America* (Vintage, 2011) p. 120.

220 Rob Bowman, 'Playing with Bob Dylan', *The History of The Band*, http://theband.hiof.no/history/part_4.html. Taken from the article 'Life Is A Carnival', *Goldmine*, 17/287 (1991).

221 See Philippe Margotin and Jean-Michel Guesdon, *Bob Dylan: All the Songs* (Black Dog & Leventhal, 2015), p. 237, and Steve Turner, *The Complete Beatles*

Songs (Carlton Books, 2015), p. 132.

222 Martin Scorsese (dir.), *No Direction Home* (Paramount Pictures, 2005).

223 Richard Toledo, 'Bob Dylan – Ballad of a thin man "No direction home"', *YouTube* (uploaded 9 October 2014), https://www.youtube.com/watch?v=-AN-2rfP6Wcc. While the YouTube clip is attributed to *No Direction Home*, I have been unable to locate the footage within the film.

224 Swingin' Pig, 'Bob Dylan – Ballad Of A Thin Man (LIVE HD FOOTAGE & RESTORED AUDIO) [May 1966], *YouTube* (uploaded 13 February 2019), https://www.youtube.com/watch?v=63ucJmVonAc&list=RD63ucJm-VonAc&start_radio=1.

225 Scorsese, *No Direction Home*.

226 Ron Rosenbaum, 'Bob Dylan: A candid conversation with the visionary whose songs changed the times', *Playboy* (March 1978), via https://www.interferenza.net/bcs/interw/play78.htm.

227 Margotin and Guesdon, *Bob Dylan*, p. 240.

228 Douglas Brinkley, 'Bob Dylan Has a Lot on His Mind', *New York Times* (12 Jun. 2020), https://www.nytimes.com/2020/06/12/arts/music/bob-dylan-rough-and-rowdy-ways.html.

229 Bob Dylan, 'Bob Dylan Nobel Lecture', *The Nobel Prize* (2017), https://www.nobelprize.org/prizes/literature/2016/dylan/lecture/.

230 Turner, *Beatles '66*, p. 174 [Kindle edition].

231 Maureen Cleave, 'How a Beatle Lives, No. 4: Paul all alone: running hard to catch up with the music', *Evening Standard* (25 Mar. 1966). The article can be viewed at https://truthaboutthebeatlesgirls.tumblr.com/post/64047580055/the-following-is-the-original-article-as-written.

232 Hunter Davies (ed.), *The Beatles Lyrics* (Weidenfeld & Nicolson, 2014), p. 146. 'The last bloke I went to was great,' McCartney conceded. 'I'm sure he could teach me a lot.'

233 Cleave, 'How a Beatle Lives, No. 4'.

234 Ian MacDonald, *Revolution in the Head: The Beatles' Records and the Sixties* (4th Estate, 1994), p. 167.

235 Davies, *The Beatles Lyrics*, p. 146.

236 MacDonald, *Revolution in the Head*, p. 230.

237 Robin Stummer, 'How I drew a pop art masterpiece for the Beatles – a

snip at just £50', *The Guardian* (24 Jul. 2016) https://www.theguardian.com/music/2016/jul/23/beatles-revolver-cover-klaus-voormann.

238 Lewisohn, *Complete Beatles Recording Sessions*, p. 72.

239 'Illustrated Psychedelia: Klaus Voormann & The Beatles' Revolver', *Illustration Chronicles*, https://illustrationchronicles.com/Illustrated-Psychedelia-Klaus-Voormann-The-Beatles-Revolver.

240 'seven levels': ibid., p. 158; 'ode to pot': Davies, *The Beatles Lyrics*, p. 176.

241 Mikal Gilmore, 'Beatles' Acid Test: How LSD Opened the Door to "Revolver", *Rolling Stone* (25 Aug. 2016), https://www.rollingstone.com/music/music-news/beatles-acid-test-how-lsd-opened-the-door-to-revolver-251417/.

242 Maureen Cleave, 'How Does a Beatle Live? John Lennon Lives Like This', *Evening Standard* (4 Mar. 1966).

243 John C Stoskopf, 'Beatles Press Conference Chicago [11 August 1966]', *Daily Motion*, https://www.dailymotion.com/video/x4p2sfk. The transcript can be found at 'Travel: London to Chicago', *The Beatles Bible*, https://www.beatlesbible.com/1966/08/11/travel-london-to-chicago/2/.

244 Maureen Cleave, 'George Harrison: How a Beatle Lives Part 3: George Harrison – avocado with everything...' *Evening Standard* (18 Mar. 1966).

245 Jordan Runtagh, 'When John Lennon's "More Popular Than Jesus" Controversy Turned Ugly', *Rolling Stone* (29 Jul. 2016), https://www.rollingstone.com/feature/when-john-lennons-more-popular-than-jesus-controversy-turned-ugly-106430/.

246 Maureen Cleave, 'How a Beatle Lives, No. 4: Paul all alone: running hard to catch up with the music, *Evening Standard* (25 Mar. 1966).

247 Robert Rodriguez, *Revolver: How the Beatles Re-Imagined Rock 'n' Roll*, p. 246 [Scrib'd edition].

248 'Live: Busch Stadium, St Louis', *The Beatles Bible*, https://www.beatlesbible.com/1966/08/21/live-busch-stadium-st-louis/.

249 Jordan Runtagh, 'Remembering Beatles' Final Concert', *Rolling Stone* (29 Aug. 2016), https://www.rollingstone.com/music/music-features/remembering-beatles-final-concert-247497/.

250 Runtagh, 'Remembering Beatles' Final Concert'.

251 'Beatles Los Angeles Press Conference 1966' [video], *YouTube* (uploaded 31 July 2011), https://www.youtube.com/watch?v=O8MgItRRaTo.

252   Ben Corbett, 'Understanding the Impact of Bob Dylan's Motorcycle Accident', *LiveAbout* (updated 15 April 2018), https://www.liveabout.com/bob-dylans-motorcycle-accident-1322021.

1966-67: MUTATION

253   Michael Hill, '50 years later, Bob Dylan's motorcycle crash remains mysterious', *Seattle Times* (27 Jul. 2016), https://www.seattletimes.com/nation-world/50-years-later-dylans-motorcycle-crash-remains-mysterious/.

254   David Felton, 'The Beach Boys: The Healing of Brother Brian', *Rolling Stone* (4 Nov. 1976), https://www.rollingstone.com/music/music-news/the-beach-boys-the-healing-of-brother-brian-190679/.

255   Derek Taylor, 'A Hard Day's Surfin' Safari: When Brian Met Macca', *World Countdown News* (1967), https://www.rocksbackpages.com/Library/Article/a-hard-days-surfin-safari-when-brian-met-macca-. A dub is a dubplate or acetate.

256   Simon Cosyns, 'I Knew It Would Be Special', *The Sun* (1 Jul. 2016), https://www.thesun.co.uk/tvandshowbiz/1371699/beach-boys-legend-brian-wilson-on-beautiful-choir-that-came-together-for-pet-sounds/.

257   Taylor, 'A Hard Day's Surfin' Safari'.

258   Domenic Priore, *Smile: The Story of Brian Wilson's Lost Masterpiece* (Sanctuary Publishing Ltd, 2005), Kindle location 1396.

259   Tony Peters, '#118 – MARK LINETT – BEACH BOYS SMILE PART ONE', *Icon Fetch* (11 Oct. 2011), https://iconfetch.com/shows/mark-linett-beach-boys-smile-interview.

260   Jules Siegel, 'Goodbye Surfing, Hello God!', *Cheetah Magazine* (1967), via *Atavist Magazine* (2011), https://magazine.atavist.com/goodbye-surfing-hello-god.

261   Liner notes to *The Smile Sessions* (2013).

262   Ryan Dombal, '5-10-15-20: Van Dyke Parks', *Pitchfork* (22 Apr. 2011), https://pitchfork.com/news/42269-5-10-15-20-van-dyke-parks/.

263   Van Dyke Parks, '"Smile": Van Dyke Parks, reply by Scott Staton', *New York Review* (12 Jan. 2006), https://www.nybooks.com/articles/2006/01/12/smile/.

264 Tom Nolan, 'Beach Boys: A California Saga', *Rolling Stone* (28 Oct. 1971), https://www.rollingstone.com/music/music-news/beach-boys-a-california-saga-244579/.

265 Priore, *Smile*, Kindle location 1858.

266 Steven Gaines, *Heroes and Villains: The True Story of the Beach Boys* (Da Capo Press, 1986), p. 160.

267 Leonard Bernstein, 'Berlioz Takes a Trip', CBS Television (25 May 1969), https://leonardbernstein.com/lectures/television-scripts/young-peoples-concerts/berlioz-takes-a-trip.

268 Tony Peters, 'Smile Sessions – Mark Linett Interview (Transcript)', *Icon Fetch*, (21 Oct. 2011), https://iconfetch.com/blog/smile-sessions-mark-linett-interview-transscript.

269 'Beatles Press Conference: Tokyo, Japan 6/30/1966', The Beatles *Ultimate Experience*, http://www.beatlesinterviews.org/db1966.0630.beatles.html.

270 Jonathan Cott, 'John Lennon: The Rolling Stone Interview', *Rolling Stone* (23 Nov. 1968), https://www.rollingstone.com/music/music-news/john-lennon-the-rolling-stone-interview-186264/.

271 'Strawberry Fields Forever History', *Beatles Music History!*, http://www.beatlesebooks.com/strawberry-fields-forever.

272 Ian MacDonald, *Revolution in the Head: The Beatles' Records and the Sixties* (4th Estate, 1994), p. 179.

273 Siegel, 'Goodbye Surfing, Hello God!'.

274 Mark Lewisohn, *The Complete Beatles Recording Sessions* (Sterling; reprint edition, 2013), p. 92.

275 Detail of studio visits ibid., pp. 99, 104.

276 Neal Umphred, 'the byrds' mind gardens and outrageous fortunes' [sic], *Rather Rare Records*, (17 Sep. 2014), https://www.ratherrarerecords.com/mind-gardens/.

277 Joe Orton, *The Orton Diaries: Including the Correspondence of Edna Welthorpe and Others* (Harper & Row, 1988), p. 74.

278 Victoria Broackes and Geoffrey Marsh (eds), *You Say You Want a Revolution? Records and Rebels 1966–1970* (V & A Publishing, 2016), p. 205.

279 Route TV, 'Bob Dylan San Francisco Press Conference 1965', *YouTube* (recorded 3 December 1965, uploaded 20 September 2016), https://www.youtube.

com/watch?v=wPIS257tvoA.

280 Brice Ezell, '10 Albums That Might Not Exist Without Sgt. Pepper's', *Consequence of Sound* (1 Jun. 2017). https://consequenceofsound. net/2017/06/10-albums-that-might-not-exist-without-sgt-peppers/.

281 cccchrischrischris, 'Exclusive: Nigel Hartnup, the man who *really* took the photo', *Sgt Pepper Photos* (12 Jul. 2017), https://sgtpepperphotos.wordpress. com/2017/07/12/the-man-who-really-took-the-photo/.

282 A beautiful interactive guide to the cover and its characters can be found at https://sgtpepper.udiscovermusic.com.

283 Lewisohn, *Complete Beatles Recording Sessions*, p. 96.

284 David Leaf (dir.), *Beautiful Dreamer: Brian Wilson and the Story of SMiLE*, available at John1948OneC2, 'Beautiful Dreamer – Brian Wilson and the Story of "SMiLE"', *YouTube* (uploaded 8 January 2013), https://www.youtube.com/ watch?v=0SriaRRcA6w&t=2s.

285 Teddy Jamieson, '"I didn't realise it at the time, but I was having a wonderful sixties." Kenneth Cranham on Joe Orton, Helen Mirren, George Best and how to turn deterioration into an asset', *The Herald* (1 Feb. 2020), https:// www.heraldscotland.com/arts_ents/18202789.didnt-realise-time-wonderful-sixties-kenneth-cranham-joe-orton-helen-mirren-george-best-turn-deterioration-asset/. Did their manager have a say in turning down the movie, and would it have been a necessarily cautious one?

286 Terry Melcher was the source for this, in 1971: Nolan, 'A California Saga'. For an exhaustive rebuttal, if you enjoy a great deal of spare time, read the thread at http://smileysmile.net/board/index.php?topic=13985.10;wap2.

287 Groucho Marx, 'Hello, I Must Be Going', *Animal Crackers* (Paramount, 1930).

288 Kevin Howlett, *The Beatles: The BBC Archives: 1962 to 1970* (BBC Books, 2013), p. 253.

289 BBC Audience Research Department, 9 February 1968, facsimile insert ibid. The capitalized Ship-Builder and Schoolboy [sic] sound like characters in Lewis Carroll.

290 Barney Hoskyns, *Across the Great Divide: The Band and America* (Pimlico, 2003), p. 174.

291 Jon Landau, 'John Wesley Harding', *Crawdaddy* 15 (15 May 1968).

292 Philippe Margotin and Jean-Michel Guesdon, *Bob Dylan: All the Songs* (Black Dog & Leventhal, 2015), p. 280.

1968: FLUX

293 'I didn't want to record this last album. I was going to do a whole album of other people's songs, but I couldn't find enough.' *Sing Out!* (Oct.–Nov. 1968), via Mikal Gilmore, 'Bob Dylan's Lost Years', *Rolling Stone* (12 Sep. 2013), https://www.rollingstone.com/music/music-news/bob-dylans-lost-years-66637/.

294 Cott, 'John Lennon: The Rolling Stone Interview', *Rolling Stone* (23 Dec., 2010) https://www.rollingstone.com/feature/john-lennon-the-last-interview-179443/

295 'Brian Wilson Interview with Jamake Highwater (1968-01-11)', *YouTube* (recorded 11 January 1968, uploaded 28 Oct 2019), https://www.youtube.com/watch?v=a3OQ4w77l0g.

296 Peter Ames Carlin, *Catch a Wave: The Rise, Fall and Redemption of the Beach Boys' Brian Wilson*, (Harmony/Rodale, 2007), p. 141.

297 Sue C. Clark, 'Bob Dylan Turns Up for Woody Guthrie Memorial', *Rolling Stone* (24 Feb. 1968), https://www.rollingstone.com/music/music-news/bob-dylan-turns-up-for-woody-guthrie-memorial-197917/.

298 Peter Ames Carlin, *Paul McCartney: A Life* (JR Books Ltd., 2009), p. 171.

299 Ignazio2693, 'Paul McCartney & John Lennon 1968 Full Interview', *YouTube* (uploaded 27 September 2009), https://www.youtube.com/watch?v=Qp0i90n0BP8.

300 'In His Own Write', *Theatricalia* [website], https://theatricalia.com/play/4pm/in-his-own-write/production/a73.

301 Keith Badman, *The Beach Boys: The Definitive Diary of America's Greatest Band on Stage and in the Studio* (Backbeat Books, 2004), p. 218.

302 Mike Love with James S. Hirsch, *Good Vibrations: My Life as a Beach Boy* (Faber & Faber Ltd, 2016), pp. 198–9 [Kindle edition].

303 Love with Hirsch, *Good Vibrations*, p. 196.

304 'Dennis Wilson: I Live With 17 Girls', *Record Mirror* (21 Dec. 1968), via Uncanny, http://www.smileysmile.net/uncanny/index.php/dennis-wilson-i-live-with-17-girls.

305 Badman, *The Beach Boys*, pp. 216–24.

306 'Dennis Wilson', *Record Mirror.*

FADE

307 '1968 Democratic National Convention', *Wikipedia*, https://en.wikipedia.org/wiki/1968_Democratic_National_Convention#Protests_and_police_response. Inside the convention hall, Senator Abraham Ribicoff rose to nominate George McGovern for president: with McGovern in charge, he said, there would be no 'Gestapo tactics' on the streets of Chicago. On the floor the city's mayor Richard J. Daley batted away a white balloon: 'Fuck you, you Jew son of a bitch,' he shouted. 'You lousy motherfucker, go home!' 'How hard it is,' said Ribicoff, pausing for dramatic effect. 'How hard it is,' he added, looking straight at Daley. 'How hard it is to accept the truth.' 'Mc Govern Nominating Speech', C-Span (26 Aug. 1968), https://www.c-span.org/video/?3422-1/mc-govern-nominating-speech.

308 John Lewis, 'Carla Bley hears Sgt Pepper', *The Guardian* (17 Jun. 2011), https://www.theguardian.com/music/2011/jun/17/carla-bley-sgt-pepper.

309 Mark Lewisohn, *The Complete Beatles Recording Sessions* (Sterling; reprint edition, 2013), pp. 147–8.

310 It's a view summarized by David Wild in *The Beach Boys – Pet Sounds, Classic Albums*, who states that the Beach Boys, Beatles and Bob Dylan 'all stopped trying to make pop music in the traditional sense and tried to make art, and that's why popular music became art'. Matthew Longfellow and Martin R. Smith (dirs), *Classic Albums – The Beach Boys: Pet Sounds* (Eagle Rock Film Productions, 2010).

311 'Roger Waters on Howard Stern – January 18, 2012', *Soundcloud*, https://soundcloud.com/rogerwaters/roger-waters-on-howard-stern.

312 William Mann, 'The Beatles revive hopes of progress in pop music with their gay new LP', *The Times* (29 May 1967), https://www.thetimes.co.uk/article/the-beatles-revive-hopes-of-progress-in-pop-music-with-their-gay-new-lp-976n9jwfdqh. The article is also available without a paywall at 'Procol mentions in *The Times*', https://procolharum.com/99/ph_times_670529.htm.

313 Ren Grevatt, 'Beach Boys Blast', *Melody Maker* (19 Mar. 1966), via John Mulvey (ed.), *The History of Rock 1966* (Time Inc. (UK) Ltd., 2015), p. 129.

314 Richard Goldstein, 'I got high with the Beach Boys: "If I survive this I

promise never to do drugs again"', *Salon* (26 Apr. 2015), https://www.salon.com/2015/04/26/i_got_high_with_the_beach_boys_if_i_survive_this_i_promise_never_to_do_drugs_again/.

315 Jonathan Cott, 'John Lennon: The Rolling Stone Interview', *Rolling Stone* (23 Nov. 1968), https://www.rollingstone.com/music/music-news/john-lennon-the-rolling-stone-interview-186264/.

316 Jack Newfield, 'Bob Dylan: Brecht of the Juke Box, Poet of the Electric Guitar', *Village Voice* (26 Jan. 1967), https://www.villagevoice.com/2020/05/19/bob-dylan-brecht-of-the-juke-box-poet-of-the-electric-guitar/.

317 Ian MacDonald, *Revolution in the Head: The Beatles' Records and the Sixties* (4th Estate, 1994), p. 175.

318 Martin Scorsese (dir.), *No Direction Home* (Paramount Pictures, 2005).

319 The first quote is taken from Hunter Davies' *The Beatles Lyrics* (Weidenfeld & Nicolson, 2014), p. 109; the second is from Cott, 'John Lennon: The Rolling Stone Interview'.

320 Cott, 'John Lennon: The Rolling Stone Interview'.

321 Jennifer Finney Boylan, 'The Genius Behind the Grateful Dead', *New York Times* (16 Oct. 2019), https://www.nytimes.com/2019/10/16/opinion/grateful-dead-robert-hunter.html.

322 David Oppenheim (dir.), *Inside Pop: The Rock Revolution*, CBS (broadcast 25 April 1967).

323 Houman Barekat, 'James Baldwin: Living in Fire by Bill V Mullen review – a smart, concise introduction', *The Guardian* (14 Nov. 2019), https://www.theguardian.com/books/2019/nov/14/james-baldwin-living-in-fire-bill-v-mullen-review.

324 Danny Eccleston, 'The Seldom Seen Kid', *Mojo* (Sep. 2012).

325 Cott, 'John Lennon: The Rolling Stone Interview'.

326 Neal Umphred, 'Just What Is It That Makes the White Album so Different, so Appealing?' *Medium* (16 Jan. 2019), https://medium.com/tell-it-like-it-was/just-what-is-it-that-makes-the-white-album-so-different-so-appealing-f212fe7a6005.

327 Stephen Thomas Erlewine, 'Paul McCartney, Egypt Station', Pitchfork (11 Sep. 2018), https://pitchfork.com/reviews/albums/paul-mccartney-egypt-station/.

WHAT THEY HEARD

LUKE MEDDINGS

First published in 2021
by Weatherglass Books

001

Cover design by Luke Bird
Text design and typesetting by James Tookey
Proofreading by Gary Kaill
Printed in the U.K. by TJ Books Limited, Padstow

A CIP record for this book is published by the British Library

ISBN: 978-1-8380181-4-6

www.weatherglassbooks.com

Weatherglass
Books